GW00771707

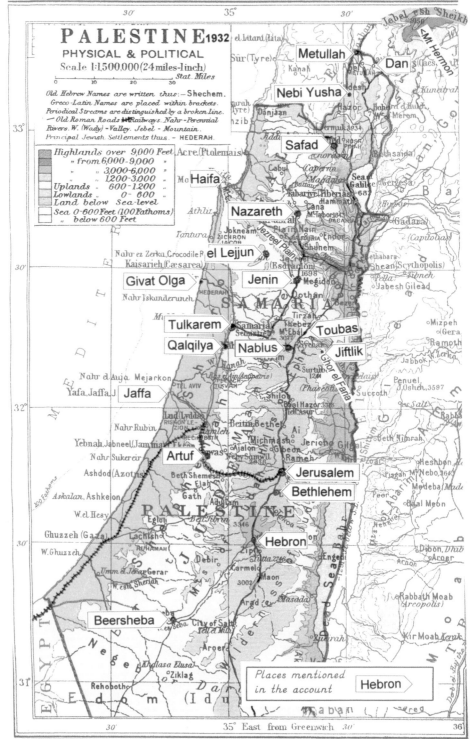

Map taken from the *Phillips New School Atlas - 1932*

PALESTINE 1932
PHYSICAL & POLITICAL
Scale 1:1,500,000 (24 miles=1 inch)
Stat. Miles

0   10   20   30

Old Hebrew Names are written thus:—Shechem.
Greco-Latin Names are placed within brackets.
Periodical Streams are distinguished by a broken Line.
━━ Old Roman Roads ╫╫╫ Railways. Nahr=Perennial
Rivers. W. (Wady)=Valley. Jebel=Mountain.
Principal Jewish Settlements thus.- HEDERAH.

Highlands over 9,000 Feet
  "   from 6,000-9,000 "
  "   "   3,000-6,000 "
  "   "   1,200-3,000 "
Uplands   600-1,200 "
Lowlands   0- 600 "
Land below Sea-level
Sea 0-600 Feet (100 Fathoms)
  "   below 600 Feet

Places mentioned
in the account   Hebron

Projection: Conical with two standard parallels

George Philip & Son Ltd The London Geographical Institute

Palestine Betrayed

A British Palestine Policeman's Memoirs

(1936 – 1948)

Robin H. Martin

Additional Accounts:
Fred Canter, Jack K. Ammonds, Ron Bourne and Martin Duchesne

Editor: Anne Blackman

Published in 2007
by Seglawi Press

Copyright © Robin Martin and Anne Blackman 2007

Reg 279693

All rights reserved. Except for brief quotations in a review, this book,
or any part thereof, may not be reproduced, stored in or introduced
into a retrieval system, or transmitted, in any form or by any means,
electronic, mechanical, photocopying, recording or otherwise, without
prior permission of the authors and editor.

Published by
Seglawi Press, PO Box 6777, Ringwood, BH24 9DG UK

Printed by
Creeds the Printers, Bridport, Dorset

ISBN No. 978 – 0 – 9556211 – 0 – 9

Contents

FOREWORD

Hound Street
Sherborne

Sometimes I have watched people, perhaps on a beach or in a field, walking slowly with their eyes down and a long pole at hand. Friends tell me it is a metal detector and they are looking for hidden treasure. How exciting! But I have never seen anyone find anything yet. As a writer, I do something similar, for ever nosing around bookshops, stalls and sales hoping to find some literary rarity-with similar results. Until last year. It was January when I was handed a manuscript which had been hidden away in an attic for some years. Within five minutes I knew I had found a treasure beyond anything those detectors would unearth, even on a good day.

The treasure was the story of an Englishman, now 92 years old, who had been in the Palestinian Police during the second half of the British Mandate, until it was passed to the United Nations in 1947. The wonderful thing was the immediacy of the style and the awful thing was the tale it told. For too long the story has been lost in the mists of time, but here the truth of those fateful years was re-discovered and told with the sharpness of a participant whose life was at risk, yet who viewed the calamities with compassion.

It was a relief to meet Mr. Robin Martin in his Hampshire home and receive his agreement for the publication of these memoirs. It was equally good that his daughter, Anne, was willing to type the whole manuscript and do further research, discover suitable maps and photographs so that this publication could be brought to light. And light is a good word. The period is shrouded in darkness. It was the time that the British Government, given the leasehold, managed to give away the freehold and so enable Palestine to be turned into Israel. It was the time when Britain, exhausted by the Second World War, gave in to the terrorism of the highly organized Jewish militias. It was not a period to be proud of and a veil has been drawn over it but here Mr. Martin's vivid personal account reveals all and explains the unresolved bitterness sixty years on.

The manuscript discovered that January day was both a literary gem and a political time bomb. And that time bomb makes the old story of how it all happened the more important to hear and understand. It deserves a huge readership.

Tim Biles, 28.3.2007

Author's Notes

One evening in August 1944, I sat in the courtyard of Qalqilya Police Station, with a drink to hand, and wrote an account of that day's patrol. This subsequently led to an account of how I came to be there in Palestine, as I had the idea that, one day, I would write a book about my work as a British Palestine Policeman and the incidents that I came across everyday. However I did not know then how badly things would turn out for Palestine and the Palestine Arabs. As the War ended events in the country became very savage and confused due to continuous illegal and terrorist Jewish activity, and the vociferous, general anti-British stance of a significant element of the Jewish population. In spite of the politicians' best endeavours to satisfy the demands of the majority of those concerned, no satisfactory solution could be agreed to, and consequently, Ernest Bevin, on behalf of the British Government, decided to give up the Mandate to Govern Palestine, and the British personnel were withdrawn. On the 15th May 1948 we "threw our hand in" and left the other parties to it. For a long time I was sick at heart because of the disastrous situation the Arabs found themselves in and did no further work on the book, but in 1983 I eventually decided to write up my notes and memories – in an account for friends and family to read. Only very recently, in 2006, the manuscript came to be read by Canon Tim Biles He knows the Holy Land well and he felt the account should have a wider readership. So, at the great age of 92, I have finally gone into print! It is only as a result of the encouragement, support and help of several people that this account is now in the public domain and thanks are due to many people: Roger An Grows and Maggie Nightingale, and Canon and Mrs Biles for their encouragement in this endeavour – Canon Biles, having successfully published many books himself, showing us the way; Rosemary Brinton and Ken and Barbara Roberts for their help with proof-reading; Carole Smith for her expert help with editing and proof correction; Marilyn Harrison and Kathy Halson, compositors at Creeds the Printers, for patiently reworking the proofs while preparing the book for printing, and her colleagues for the print work; fellow ex-Palestine Policemen, Fred Canter, Jack Ammonds, Ron Bourne and Martin Duchesne, for agreeing to have the accounts of their different but complementary experiences included in this book; and finally Sharon Wallace for allowing Jack Ammond's letter to be reproduced.

The original account has expanded quite a lot in response to my daughter's numerous questions and requests for clarification. Here we must acknowledge how useful the Internet has been, particularly sites like the United Nations Website, en.wikipedia.org/ and http://wwwPalestineRemembered.com. PalestineBeforeNakba at http://www.PalestineRemembered.com was an excellent reference for the sketch maps. There is a useful summary of all the British Government's correspondence, reports and committees on Palestine from 1916 – 1947 in *Zionism and Britain* on The Jewish Agency for Israel website. (The spellings of Arabic and Hebrew words and place names vary in the English script. In general those we adopted were those in common use pre-1948.) I have included as many names of my old Palestine Police Comrades as I can remember, as I frequently read in the Palestine Police Old Comrades Association Magazines letters from sons and daughters and other relations asking for information about their loved ones who served in the PP.

As we have read through the pages of this final account, it has struck me again, as it often has during my life, how lucky I have been to have my Palestine memories to look back on, to have met so many interesting people and situations, and to have survived to tell the tale. Sadly, I have also been reminded again of the tragedy of the Palestine Arabs in the loss of their homes and lands, and the apparent hopelessness of their cause, mainly due to a lack of understanding of their situation and lack of effective political influence, and help for their cause, in America. Insert any of the Arab village names mentioned in this account in the Yahoo Image Search Engine and you will be shocked by the heart-breaking images of destroyed homes, communities and farmland that come up and the devastating effect of the huge fences that surround and divide the people from their land.

I would like to dedicate these memoirs to the people I have shared the experiences with: my old British comrades; the Arab policemen who taught me so much; my Jewish friends and those Jews who seek justice for their Arab neighbours; but particularly to the Palestine Arab People – wishing them peace and unity, and success in their quest for justice.

June 2007

Mounted patrol leaving the rear of Qalqilya Police Station.

Day Patrol – Qalqilya, August '44 (from my notebook)

The sun was just rising over the Nablus Hills, after beautiful roseate hues had heralded the dawn. The horses had been watered & fed, and brushed well down, and now, as they stood lined up, waiting to move, they made a pretty picture – four greys, a chestnut and a bay. Two Arab constables, wearing the traditional Arab headdress of kafiah and agal, also added to the scene. The British personnel, all looking very fit and sunburned, were no weak specimens either, and I, from previous experience, knew they could all be trusted to make a good job of any incident which might occur during the patrol.

Of the duration [of the patrol] I could not say, as anything might occur from a running fight with a few absconded offenders to a gang of cattle thieves to be tracked down, a case of theft or maybe just a petty assault to be dealt with.

The little Arab horses were impatient to be away and on being given the order to move off in half sections [in twos], stepped off friskily out of the Station yard.

Once clear of the village of Qalqilya, a scout was sent ahead and a connecting file [one] detailed to keep contact with the scout and the remainder of the party [four riders].

The inhabitants of the first village were well astir by the time we arrived there, and the Muhktar came out to greet us, welcoming the party in the usual terms, "Allah was sahlam" (God's peace on you – you are as welcome as one of us).

I knew this man well and had a good opinion of him and while chatting with him asked what were the local Arabs' feelings regarding the recent outrage, namely the attempt to assassinate the H Com Sir Harold MacMichael. His reply was – the Arabs were very sorry that this should have happened, as he was a good friend of the Arabs. They were however sincerely glad that H.E. had escaped with only superficial wounds.

When asked if the Arabs were contemplating fighting for their rights again, as they had done in the years 1936-39, the Muhktar told me that they were content, at this period, to wait and see what the Govt. would do for them after the War. All had their doubts that the British Govt would come up to expectations for it appeared that the lot of the Arab was to be let down, again and again, and that the policy always seemed to be just that little bit evasive and indefinite. At the present time they had no plans to form a National Guard, as had been hinted and rumoured in official quarters.

We were served a refreshing cup of Turkish coffee and ate a few luscious figs, fresh from the trees and still cold with the night's dew on them, and then took our leave of the Muhktar, who was going to be busy that day. He had the tax collectors as guests & they were bent on getting in the taxes. This is always a long job for, generally speaking, when the Arab villager reports to pay his dues, he regards it as his right to sit and listen and never offer his money until he is asked for it. He always tries to bargain with the tax collector in the same way he does with his business associates when negotiating a deal. Eventually he throws the money at the tax collector and demands a receipt in a downright sort of fashion!

The patrol continued on past a sheikh's tomb and along the foothills to the next village five miles away. The going was good and justified a trot to cut down time a bit, & the horses were obviously glad to be out of a walk as the flies were worrying them terribly. The poor beasts were continually kicking at their bellies, stamping with their forefeet and shaking their heads in an endeavour to dislodge the flies, which were biting most unmercifully into their skins.

On arrival at the second village I made a careful mental note of the members present, for this place was renowned for its cattle thieves, and local dealers were known to call frequently to see if there were any cheap cattle for sale. The only man I had found at this place who was really worth his salt was the Muhktar, quite a young man who had been sent to school by his father and who had definite, progressive ideas. He was, however, not above a little dealing in contraband if it was likely to yield a fair profit. The remainder of the male population, with the exception of a few youths, were not so progressive and were eaten up with obsessions to continue ancient feuds, of which there were plenty. They had no good reason for this, for their feuds had only petty origins, not one murder amongst them. It was simply a case of feud for feud's sake, owing to the prompting of the malicious minded old men and lack of education. One of these old men, about seventy years old, was known to have paid £P300 to various people to keep the trouble going, as he liked to appear a venerable old gentleman and to intervene between the opposite parties, suggesting ways in which peace could be made. He would, when approached, sit with much dignity & pomp to act as a judge. If peace was concluded he would, forthwith, seek some means whereby he could throw a match and set the whole affair aflame once more. Once, when asked why he would not make the pilgrimage to Mecca, he replied that he was far too young yet and must work some more years in mediating for the feuds; then when he was no longer able to continue he would go to Mecca, & become a Haj and thereafter would live a decent life. When asked to contribute towards building a school in the village, he pooh-poohed the idea, and would not subscribe a bean.

To return to the business of the day, I made a few enquiries as to the whereabouts of this and that person[1] so I could keep a further check on them should occasion demand.

Then a conversation about the progress of the war took place and comparisons between the conditions of the Arabs in this war and the last 1914-18 War were made.

This war was, as far as the Arabs were concerned, a "Cakewalk". No one was starving and thousands had made much money, many making real fortunes. In the last war the Arabs had been driven off to fight for the Turks, whom they greatly disliked, but feared and respected. Those remaining had practically been on the point of starvation & many had succumbed. It was said that the soldiers in the Turkish Army had often been reduced to collecting the grain from the Army horses' dung and washing it to grind and bake bread with it. (I have heard this from many sources and am sure the story must have a truthful foundation.) The senior officers in the Turkish Army were wont to sell the soldiers' rations and clothing to the highest bidder and many were the soldiers who had marched hundreds of miles in their bare feet.

Incidentally, graft in these parts is regarded as a profession, and a clever grafter, one who can make himself a pile, is seldom referred to as a crook but is spoken of "Sharta" – a clever man – usually in terms which denote the utterer's admiration.

Having decided I had spent long enough at the village, we took our leave and headed for the next inhabited place.

After covering a mile or so the patrol was well in the hills and the going was increasingly rough, so the horses were allowed to pick their way very carefully, receiving only occasional aid from the riders. The animals are bred to this sort of country & are very surefooted, and some are exceedingly clever in covering rough & stony tracks. Just prior to reaching my next village a very steep valley had to be crossed. The way became a series of steep rocks, alternating with flat-ledges – like huge natural steps. Here I dismounted the men and ordered the horses to be led. It is, in my opinion, grossly unfair to expect horses to carry a rider over such tracks. Doing so can be the cause of many saddle and girth galls, which takes time to treat regularly and properly.

On the arrival at the village I called the Muhktar and he reported all the regulars. He was illiterate and so, unable to sign the Patrol Register, affixed his thumbprint on the book in the appropriate place. I declined his invitation to a drink of tea for the horses were nearing the time for their water and

---

[1]after checking my notebook, in which were notes from the Absconded Offenders and Wanted Persons' Register,

the water at this village is filthy[1]. I was also weary of picking up fleas, and the fleas in this village are the best specimens I had come across. They are usually the size of a bull ant and are so lazy that once they crawl on one they haven't the ability to fall off onto someone else, but just take little hops of two or three inches. So if you do not catch the flea it remains on your person. I did not tarry at this village as no useful information ever came from here. I was once on the trail of a wanted man with £P500 on his head, and had been close-trailing him for three days. The inhabitants here denied they had ever seen him, though I learnt later that he had been in the village the night before and had received £P15 from the people to help him on his way. He was one Hamad Zawata, wanted for the murder of two B/Cs in Nablus Town.

I left the loudly protesting Muhktar (who wanted us to stay for a chat) & headed on to my next calling point which was only a couple of miles further on down on the plain. Here the horses were watered and patrol personnel rested. The village runner, who acts as a general factotum, makes excellent coffee, and soon had the pot on the fire.

A few months before, an aeroplane had made a forced landing nearby and the pilot[2] made his way into the village. He was received by the Muhktar, who directed him to the Police Station, sending an escort with him. The Muhktar also detailed some of his men to go and guard the plane until the arrival of the police. When the RAF took over the plane, it was found that nothing had been stolen and the plane's guns and ammunition were all present & up to scale. The usual report was sent in and in due course the Muhktar received an appreciation from H.E. the High Commissioner, congratulating him on his action and expressing thanks on behalf of H.M. Government. The Muhktar was very pleased and proud about this. It is worth noting that usually firearms and ammunition go missing at the slightest opportunity.

Having rested up both the horses & men, I continued on to the next stop but this time working round in a homeward direction. We moved down a spur and onto more level ground and after covering ten miles without incident arrived at our next halt. Here we were invited to lunch, and as the time was getting on, & the Station still a good way off, I gladly accepted the invitation.

---

[1] As many of the streams in the hills dry up in the long, hot, dry summers, water was very precious and had to be collected and stored in tanks during the winter rains. Water from off the roofs and gullies was channelled into the tanks and covered with cement slabs. Each family had a tank and great care had to be exercised when the tanks were being filled to ensure that the quality of the water, which had to be kept for a year, was good.

[2] The pilot was a Pole who had been rather too adventurous when practising, and had tried to dive under some aerial cables. He clipped the wing and had to eject. As the village escort knew the pilot was not English, he wanted to be sure that he was of bona fide nationality when he brought him in.

The horses were watered & fed and & unsaddled to allow them the maximum rest possible. In the meantime the personnel were made comfortable with mattresses on the floor on which to recline.

The usual conversation ensued, everyone being unanimous in their hope for an early end to the War. Politics and religion were debated, the latter always a dangerous subject & even more so when Moslems were involved. They quoted to me a certain man, living in their village, who had changed from being a Christian to becoming a Mohammedan, and in their simple way bragged to me at having taken a Christian from the fold & converting him. I invariably pull the villagers' legs with regard to their views, for I am convinced that the special benefits of Islam make the religion attractive. In this instance I suggested that the convert most likely wanted to marry a second wife or get an early divorce from his present one. It is very easy for a Moslem to obtain a divorce: all he has to do, in the presence of a religious sheihk, is say to his wife, three times, "I divorce thee," and from that time on he is free from any obligation to her.

After a while a very nice meal was produced, consisting of chicken and rice with various salads, olives, pickled pepper pods and newly baked bread.

Much has been written of the way in which these meals are eaten, so I will not dwell on the subject. I will just comment, in passing, that the only way to really enjoy such a meal as this is to forget all western etiquette and tear the chickens apart with the hands & to continue to use the hand wherever practical. It is a simple matter to wash the grease off after the meal is finished. After a taste had been acquired for the various spices & flavourings used, the meals prepared by the Arabs can be very agreeable.

The meal finished, conversation was continued, touching many and various subjects, for after a good meal everyone is in a good mood and there is much laughing & joking. As a friend, Abu Ahmed in Lejjun, once said to me after a feast, "I have a very friendly feeling."

Having stayed what I decided was the requisite length of time so as not to appear rude to the host, we took our leave of all, while they answered, "God be with you." A steady ride with an occasional trot brought us back to the Station. I considered it unwise to stay out the night as the recent Jewish attacks on Government buildings had put me well on the alert and the Station strength was rather depleted with six men away on patrol & two men on leave.

On arrival back at the station, our horses were given a good roll in the sand bath & then watered. It is surprising how much a horse will drink on its return to the Station, though there is of course a very good reason. The water in the trough is always cool and clear, so unlike the water that has to be relied on in the villages.

And so concludes just another of the hundreds of patrols I have completed.

The S.S. Rajputana (P&O Line).

Aboard the Rajputana.

Chapter 1

Outward Bound and in at the Deep End

When I was a young man, in the 1930s, world travel was not as easy an affair as it is today. Most travel took place by sea, and it took days or weeks to complete a journey. Aviation was still in its infancy and I remember watching the lumbering old biplanes of the Hannibal class clawing their way through the air, at a top speed of about 60 mph over the Kentish landscape, en route to Paris from Croydon. These were planes of the Imperial Airways, which was then one of the leading airlines of the world. In those days no workingclass holidaymakers went abroad for their annual holidays; from the channel ports, however, one could take a day trip to France or Belgium. If one wished to travel the World there were two options – those who were wealthy enough could be completely independent and do as they wished, or those less fortunate could obtain employment which necessitated travel, taking them away from home for several years at a stretch, and this was a big step to take.

I was of the second group. I very much wanted to travel and see something of the World, but I could not afford to do so independently. I therefore looked around to see what employment was available abroad. One article I read, about a manager on a tea plantation in India, sounded appealing, so I wrote to Percy Coutts Ltd., an agency which specialised in putting applicants in touch with various overseas employers, such as rubber and tea planters and so on; but before I received a reply, I saw an advertisement in *The Daily Telegraph* inviting young men to join the Palestine Police Force.

My letter of application resulted in an interview, which took place at the Crown Agents at Millbank. Among questions about my educational attainment and my working experiences, it was put to me that, in all probability, my superior officer would be an Englishman like myself, but in some places the senior officer would be likely to be an Arab or a Jew. "How would you feel in this situation?" I was asked. I replied that I would have no objection to serving under an Arab or Jew, as I would assume that he would be the proper person to have that authority.

Following a medical, conducted by Alfred Horn, later Sir Alfred, I was accepted as fit to serve. My family and friends were very concerned when I received my letter of appointment – indicating that I should shortly be going abroad – because it was a big step for a member of my family to take, and they knew that there was some danger involved. From leaving school at 16, I had worked as Clerk to the Guardians of Coxheath Public Assistance Institution [formerly the Poor Law Institution or Workhouse] and subsequently as the Master's Senior Clerk at Pembury Hospital. I was lucky to get these posts,

Feeling like a million dollars!
Fellow recruits: From left to right: – Robin Martin (the author),
Geoffrey Binstead, Len Board, Dixie Pike and Tom Hookey.

Marseilles Taxi.

as work was very hard to come by when I left school – in July 1930 – at the height of the depression, when, unlike in previous years, no employers came to Maidstone Junior Technical School offering jobs to school leavers. My father suggested to me that, if I were to stay at Pembury Hospital, I should be able to look forward to a good career in hospital administration. However, I had something of the wanderlust, and so had determined that going to Palestine was the course I wished to take.

Sea Voyage

On that reputedly unlucky day, Friday 13th March 1936, I set out on a journey that was to have a great bearing on the rest of my life and found myself, with 19 other young men (see p.226), on the SS *Rajputana*, bound for Port Said, en route to Palestine. This was the start of a journey that led me to see – and experience things, both good and bad, that I had never dreamed of as a young boy growing up in a Kentish village. I wondered, as the ship left the quay, if ill luck might befall me, but on reflection I must conclude that it was fortune that favoured me, for I have many happy memories to look back on – the bad times one tends to forget.

The voyage was quite an adventure in itself, but at the start there was something of a surprise. Having said our farewells at Woolwich Docks, we sailed for the open sea and headed for the English Channel and I assumed that, when we dropped a pilot at Dover that night, the twinkling lights along the South Coast were the last I should see of England for three years. I was therefore quite amazed to awake next morning and find we were alongside in Southampton! We sailed again that night and three days later reached Gibraltar. From Gibraltar we sailed to the famous French port of Marseilles, which was reached on the seventh day of the voyage. Here more passengers joined our ship, having come overland by train – the shorter route.

The weather was very pleasant, for even in March the temperature on the French coast was warm compared with England. The port of Marseilles was quite unlike any other city-port I had so far seen. The facilities appeared much more extensive than was the case in British ports and, because the Mediterranean is virtually tide-less, ships were constantly docking, loading and/or unloading and departing, and the port never slept. Down on the docks I saw a ship going out with a load of very wild looking men and was told it was a prison ship with a cargo of prisoners bound for Devil's Island, the French Penal Colony off the coast of French Guiana. A taxi took us for a run around, and then up to the top of the hills. This gave us a wonderful view that took in the city, with its very narrow congested streets and the whole of the port area beyond.

The rest of the journey through the Mediterranean was a most pleasant experience. I remember Aubrey Nye, a fellow recruit, sitting on the ship's railings and exclaiming, "I feel like a million dollars!" At times the sea was unbelievably calm and had the appearance of a huge sheet of glass, disturbed only by the ripples from the wake of the ship. The colour was a beautiful ultramarine, and I loved leaning on the ship's rail, watching the fish and the dolphins leap in the bow wave, and also the flying fish as they leaped out of the water, alongside, and skimmed the sea's surface with the tip of their tails. However, on 23rd March, the lovely blue turned to a sandy grey, possibly due to the sediments from the Nile. We were nearing Port Said and that evening we disembarked, waving farewell to the *SS Rajputana*. I never saw her again for she was sunk during the 1939-45 War.

To Jerusalem by Train

At Port Said, our party was met by a very smart corporal, Joseph Creedon, ex-Guards. He had come to escort us to Jerusalem and it was obvious that he was in charge from the start. He gave our orders in crisp military fashion and left us in no doubt that we were not on a Cook's Tour. After our very pleasant and relaxing sea voyage, it was obviously his task to set the tone, put us in our place and prepare us for the very serious work ahead. One of the party lagged a bit as we left the ship, and the corporal, in no uncertain manner, shouted to him, "Get a move on you idle fellow." I think the "idle fellow" didn't know quite what had hit him. While we waited for the evening train in the bar at Port Said, the corporal gave us what he called "good advice", as well as a few amusing yarns of his experiences.

To get to Palestine we had to go by train from Port Said to Kantara West on the Suez Canal, cross over the canal to Kantara East, and board the Jerusalem train, which ran across the Sinai Desert to El Arish, before entering Palestine. While at Kantara I saw two Italian troopships going south, fully laden with soldiers, for the Italo/Abyssinia war was still on – though by then the Italians had almost completed their conquest of the country. These soldiers crowding on the decks of their transports were an unkempt, scruffy-looking lot, but I suppose all troops on board troopships appear untidy, except when they are paraded for any reason. That night I was very struck by the sunset. The sky at the horizon was bright orange which then merged with the deep blue overhead. I had seen colours like this on picture postcards but I never believed that such sunsets actually happened until I saw this one.

The Egyptian money-changers were much in evidence on both sides of the canal, walking around with huge wads of notes, monotonously crying out "Change your money. Change your money." I estimated that they must have made a good living, continually charging a little commission on each transaction. While at Kantara I was able to observe the Bedouin at close quarters for the first time and was struck by the air of authority that some of the men had, and, most striking of all, their quiet dignity. They were a ferocious looking lot, with daggers in their belts and a defiant air, as, with their dark, piercing eyes they surveyed their fellow passengers and passers-by. Noticing my interest, Corporal Creedon remarked, as he indicated one rather tall and impressive Bedu, "See that chap there, he'd cut your throat for a tanner." He may have been right, for some years later a young Arab policeman, Cons. Ismail Muswadi – in Qualquilya – told me that he had spent a night with some Bedouin in the Sinai, and he hadn't slept a wink lest they kill him for his money. However, I think the corporal was simply trying to impress me.

About 11 pm our train prepared to leave Kantara to cross the Sinai Desert, and that was a journey I shall never forget. With such a clanking of iron and hissing of steam as one only dreams of, we shunted backwards and forwards, linking up carriages and trucks, until the train was complete, and then we eventually pulled out of the station! The journey was far from comfortable, but my companions and I made the best of it, and all tried to get some sleep in the small hours. I made for the luggage rack in search of a little comfort, but it was a forlorn quest as the sand of the desert continually blew through the ventilators. I was forced to abandon my bed and return to the hard seat below. The night air of the desert was very cold, so I huddled up in my overcoat and tried to doze away the hours of darkness.

At last came a glorious dawn. The sun rose like a ball of fire and with it the world seemed to spring to life. I found we were approaching the more inhabited areas of the Negev desert. From the train I could see Arabs driving scores of donkeys. I never imagined there could be so many of the small beasts in the world. Wherever I looked, herds of donkeys were being driven along in a hurry. None was just walking, or taking it easy, all were at the trot or canter, and the boys or men driving them were shouting and waving their sticks about. Obviously, all were on their way to work. Without these little donkeys many Arabs would starve, for they really are beasts of burden and uncomplainingly they stagger on under heavy loads, and heavy blows. They are marvellous little animals, carrying anything up to two hundredweight while the larger breeds are often weighted with three hundred pounds and more.

Soon we came to really well-cultivated land, and shortly after, had our first glimpse of the famous Palestine orange groves, producing the highly prized Jaffa oranges, long cultivated by the Arabs. It is said that Richard the Lionheart spent the winter of 1191 in an orange grove at Jaffa, when on a Crusade. Oranges had been a major export from Palestine to Britain since at least Victorian times. We continued on towards Jerusalem, through large grain-growing tracts of land. At Artuf Station we entered the Judean Hills and started the long climb up to the Holy City, which stands about 2,200 ft above sea level. As we neared it we could see that the steep hillsides were terraced all the way up, to heights of between 600 and 1,000 feet in some places. The crops planted included grapes, tomatoes and melons. A captain in the Army later told me that these terraces compared with the finest he had seen in Italy.

At last we reached Jerusalem Station and there to meet us were two police tenders, one for us and one for our luggage. Ours was covered with wire mesh and I was told that this was a protection against bombs which might be thrown at us. Disturbances in Palestine had been reported in the British press but they had not appeared to be too enduring. It was only now that I, and several of my companions, began to fully appreciate just what dangers we might expect to face in the future. Peter Jelasics, a handsome man of Balkan origin, and a fellow squad member, said to me, "What the hell have we let ourselves in for?"

After a ride at breakneck speed through the city of Jerusalem, we arrived at Mount Scopus Camp, the Police Training School for British recruits and Depot,[1] and were soon enjoying a breakfast of ham and eggs. This was a very special breakfast for new recruits – to keep up our spirits, and to give a good impression of the Force prior to being sworn in! (Lunch afterwards was less impressive and Tom Hookey, a farmer's son from the Isle of Wight, remarked that it was a "bloody awful lunch. On our farm we wouldn't give the dogs stuff like that! I'm going to resign." He was so unhappy that he walked around with a miserable face, almost a scowl, for several days. However he perked up considerably when we made a journey out to Affuleh and smelt the ripening corn. "Wheat!" he shouted, with a big smile on his face. He was still there in Palestine when we left in 1948!)

Now came the most important item of our first day. About 11am on 25th March 1936, four months before my 22nd birthday, the members of our squad were sworn in. We were enlisted as British Constables of the Palestine Police Force and vested with the "powers, immunities and privileges" of police officers from that date. Just what the privileges and immunities were was a very debatable question, and I have heard some highly unprintable opinions on the subject. I was, however, soon to find that it involved my working often more than 16 hours a day and not having a day off duty for months. The Police Ordinance clearly stressed that leave was a privilege and not a right. No overtime payments were ever made, nor expected. Conditions of pay were good, however, as although our pay was equivalent to that of a constable's in England, lodging and meals were all found, so there were no living expenses.

---

[1] The Training School for Palestinians, Arabs and Jews was in the Headquarters – just inside the Old City.

The Feast of Nebi Musa

Our arrival at the Depot coincided with the preparations for the Christian Easter Feasts, the Moslem Feast of Nebi Musa [the Prophet Moses] and the Jewish Feast of the Passover, all being celebrated within a fortnight or so.

It was alleged that the Tomb of Moses had been discovered near Jericho, 45 kms distant, and it was deemed proper for the Moslems to gather in Jerusalem and from there proceed to the site of the tomb. I was taught, in political instruction sessions, that the feast of Nebi Musa had been instigated by the Turks – who governed Palestine until the end of the First World War – so that there would be a large-scale pilgrimage of Moslems into the Holy City to counterbalance the influx of the thousands of Christians and Jews who came to the City at Eastertide and Passover. The main idea was that, in the event of any one section of the populace attempting an uprising, the other religious communities would be useful in helping the authorities quell the revolt.

After devotions at the site of the tomb, the pilgrims of Nebi Musa would return to the Mosque at Jerusalem, and then on to their homes and villages. However, it often occurred that the Moslems had many confrontations amongst their various contingents from the outlying towns. For example, there was great rivalry between the Hebronites (distinguishable by their yellow turbans) and the Nabulsis, and I well remember hearing some of the Nablus crowd in 1936, calling out to the Hebronites, asking if they were now the sons of sheep since they had not tasted blood that year. This referred to the fact that in the Nablus area some travellers had been robbed and killed, just prior to the outbreak of the 1936 Disturbances – as they came to be known.

Normally new recruits would spend 3 months in the Police Training School before passing out and being posted, but after 2 days in training, in anticipation of these feasts, our party of new recruits was sent to Police Headquarters in Jerusalem – housed in the old Russian Compound – to reinforce the police strength of the city.

The first few days were spent in watching the arrival of the various contingents of Moslems and generally patrolling the thoroughfares. At times parties of recruits were sent out, with trained policemen as guides, in order to become acquainted with the streets of Jerusalem, particularly those of the Old City, so that if at any time we were posted there, we could find our way about. This was necessary because the Old City of Jerusalem is a complete maze and none of us had any useful knowledge of Arabic or Hebrew at that time.

Soon the day of the great processions arrived and the whole available strength of the police was assembled at Headquarters and assigned to its many duties. As the parties of pilgrims arranged themselves, police parties were drafted in at varying intervals, to be able to counteract any trouble that might arise. Four foot and four mounted policemen were posted together and then began the tedious job of slowly proceeding through the streets of the Old City to the Mosque of Omar. This was indeed a slow process, for at every few yards the procession, which was only of men, would halt and begin to sing and dance. Young men with long, curved-blade swords would be carried on the shoulders of others, and, slashing and stabbing imaginary opponents, would advance and retreat towards one another. This stuck me as almost barbaric at the time. As the pilgrims proceeded they sang about the, "Sword of religion and Haj Amin Husseine," the Grand Mufti, intoned as a repetitive chant, something like, "*Saif ed din / wa Haj Amin.*" The followers would repeat the chanting in unison. In other parties there were various forms of personal expression. Some danced round singing and clapping, while others joined hands and formed circles, dancing small, intricate steps. All the women had gathered on roof tops and high ground overlooking the route of the procession, giving vent to their feelings by making a strange, shrill, trilling sound, waggling their tongues between their teeth (known as ululating, I believe) and shrieking with delight. After a few hours, some of the men had shouted themselves hoarse and others were frothing at the mouth, as a result of the frenzies which they had worked themselves up into. It took five hours for the procession to cover half a mile and after a while I found it very tedious, but I much admired the strength of the men who held their companions aloft for all that time.

After the procession, all the pilgrims congregated in the Mosque area where they stayed the night, resting and praying. The following morning a second procession took place, progressing from the Mosque to the Jericho Road outside Jerusalem. Here buses, trucks and taxis were waiting to convey the pilgrims down to the place known as Nebi Musa, near the Dead Sea, more than 1,000 feet below sea level. There, at the place of the prophet Musa, was much praying, feasting and not a little horseplay, when pilgrims raced against each other on their beautiful little steeds, across the flat land surrounding the area.

Having completed the ceremonies there, the pilgrims returned to Jerusalem and we had another hard and monotonous day escorting the slowly moving parties from the outskirts of the city, back to the Mosque, and finally out once more to the places where each contingent embarked on buses for their homes.

After all had gone I heard one senior officer of the Government remark, "Thank God that is all over for another year!" His words echoed, I'm sure, the thoughts of many, but personally I was very glad to have been able to witness the spectacle. This was not the end of the seasonal celebrations, however, for we had the ceremony of the Holy Fire, the Washing of the Feet

Hebronites – showing a distinctive orange turban.

Nebi Musa procession.
Note the spectators on the roof and the swordsman, encircled.

The Church of the Holy Sepulchre after the scaffolding had been removed.
Watercolour by the author.

and the Passover to contend with.

The Washing of The Feet

I was on duty at the next ceremony, the Christian ceremony of The Washing of the Feet. This was a celebration of the time when Our Lord Jesus Christ washed the feet of his disciples before The Last Supper. A large platform had been erected near the entrance to The Church of the Holy Sepulchre, and here the Patriarch, representing Jesus, washed the feet of the 12 of his priests who were seated on the platform. This was a very quiet and dignified service in spite of the fact that a very large crowd had assembled to witness it. A priest stood on a nearby balcony and, throughout the ceremony, chanted in Greek the passages from the scriptures that described the event.

The Ceremony of the Holy Fire

My next duty at a religious ceremony was the Ceremony of the Holy Fire in the Church of the Holy Sepulchre. This ceremony symbolises the bright light of the tomb at the time of the resurrection of Jesus Christ. Thousands of people wished to attend but space is limited and Christians of all denominations struggled and fought for admission to the church, and many were the fights which occurred inside the church itself, between various religious sects. In retrospect I was, again, very privileged to have been posted in the church to witness these events.

During the ceremony each different sect was given, or rather confined to, its own special area inside the church. Sections of police were drafted in between the various sects in an endeavour to prevent trouble. A party of youths just behind me started to get a little excited, and in the heat of the moment pushed me in the back just as a British Inspector of Police walked past. The officer noticed this and he turned and struck one of the offending youths saying, "Take that you bloody bastard, I'll teach you to push my policemen!" Being new to the job, and wishing to preserve the sanctity of the church, I had not intended to make an issue of the pushing, and was somewhat shocked by the Inspector's behaviour. I must admit, however, that I was also a trifle amused that such things should occur.

The interior of the Church of The Holy Sepulchre is not unlike a theatre, for it has boxes around the walls. These were mainly filled with women and children. The ground floor, or main body of the church, was mainly filled with men but there were a few women. The Holy Sepulchre is almost in the centre of the building. I was told a priest stood inside the Sepulchre, waiting for the sun to reach a certain height when a shaft of light would appear through an aperture in the roof.[1] All the people inside the church had unlit

---

[1] D. V. Duff, (1953, *Bailing With A Teaspoon*) revealed that a priest, concealed in a small staircase – leading to the top of the tomb – carried "highly flammable articles" which, at the appropriate time, produced fire that gushed out of holes in the side of the tomb.

candles with the object of lighting them from the "Holy Fire" which was to issue from the tomb. As the sun reached the required height, the priest inside the tomb produced the Holy Fire which was then passed to the waiting crowds. At this point of the proceedings a scramble now began, and I can't think what to liken it to. A rugby scrum compared to this is a tame affair! In less time than it takes to tell, the crowd were all fighting tooth and nail to get at the fire and light their candles. Some policemen holding back the crowds became covered in candle-grease. Then, as the fire was passed up to the boxes which contained the women and the children, the whole assembly became a mass of screaming fanatics. I saw women smearing candle-grease on the foreheads of tiny infants, muttering prayers to the Almighty as they did so. Up aloft in the gallery sat many tourists and local notables who had paid for seats to witness the show, and really, for anyone who is not devout, it is worth paying to see such a spectacle!

After a brief procession of priests and choirboys around the interior of the church, the service was concluded and the crowds quickly disappeared. We had been on duty, then, for about eight hours and were now, at last, able to report to our assembly points, just outside the church, for a cup of tea and a sandwich provided by the catering staff. I considered this was richly deserved, though a square meal would have been better.

At this time I did not attend the Stations of the Cross, but in subsequent years I was occasionally posted to accompany parties of pilgrims and tourists while they made their devotions down the Via Dolorosa and up the Street of the Cross, to ensure they were not interfered with.

The Wailing Wall

I was not involved in the Jewish Passover procession, where hundreds of Jews made their way to the Wailing Wall and congregated in what was the narrow passage beside it. The wall is the remaining part of Solomon's Temple and the Jews were in the habit of going to the wall to bewail their former greatness. Now, when the Jews have established themselves very forcibly in the modern state of Israel and become a formidable military presence in the Middle East, and extremely arrogant to boot, I doubt that they would wish to bewail their former greatness, for I do believe, from all the history that I have read, that the Jews have greater influence in the World than they ever had before.

The start of the Arab Revolt and General Strike 1936

The feasts, which had been spread over the fortnight, had then ended, so with the rest of my squad I was sent back to the Police Training School to complete my normal police training. However, events overtook us all, for in the middle of April, after two days of drill, some law lectures and one Arabic

The Wailing Wall.

Old Jewish Quarter.

Fawzi edDin el Kawkaji:
Rebel commander-in-chief.

1936 Destruction of rolling stock – a common occurrence.

The Rebel Commander – Fawzi edDin el Kawkaji and his aids. (Purchased photograph).

lesson, riots broke out in Jaffa. Taking our blankets, and Greener riot guns[1] with us, we were dispatched to Jaffa to reinforce the police, and give a hand in the restoration of law and order.

The Arabs had run amok in the Manshieh district, the area joining the ancient Arab port of Jaffa to the modern Jewish town of Tel Aviv. Much damage was done to property there and many Jews had been killed, including several women and children. By the time of our arrival the actual rioting had been quelled, but many fires were still burning where Jewish houses had been fired. Armed with the riot gun, under the supervision of B/Sgt. (British Sergeant) Charlie Dent – our squad instructor – I was posted at a crossroads, to prevent any Arabs from moving into the Jewish area. (Sgt. Dent was a grand man, very fair but always trying to get the best out of everybody.) While at this spot, I could see down the road a large gathering of Arabs being harangued by one of the leading agitators. However, the crowd dispersed and moved off without further incident. For a young man, inexperienced as I was at that time, it was a worrying situation, and I wondered just what would have happened if the mob had decided to riot and sweep up the street. Obviously we could have defended ourselves for a while, but soon Sgt. Dent and I would have been overrun. Luckily it didn't happen.

The Arab leaders had formed a body to direct their action – I think it was called The Arab Supreme Council – and this Council decided to call a general strike among the Arab workers throughout the country, in protest at the continuing Jewish immigration into Palestine. Business among the Arabs then came practically to a standstill, and at the same time armed bands were formed in the rural areas, to bring transport and bus services to a halt. To counteract this, the Government then organised the vital transport into convoys, which were escorted by troops and police. (There were two battalions of infantry permanently stationed in the country as the Palestine Garrison and they had been there, on and off, since the end of the First World War, but it was never enough.[2] By 1936 they had been reinforced so that there was virtually a whole division, some 20,000 strong, stationed in the country, including the posting of some Territorials called up from the UK.) As a result of Government effort and protection to keep the transport moving, the Arab rebels started attacking both the army and the police. Then began six months of guerrilla warfare – between roving Arab bands and the Government forces, including the Royal Air Force, which was often called in for air support.

---

[1] Greener riot gun – a heavy duty shot gun with a stronger breech, as the cartridges are stronger than the ones used for small game.
[2] Douglas V. Duff (1953 *Bailing with a Teaspoon*) reports that there was no garrison in Palestine at the time of the 1929 Riots and not more than 90 British Police officers and other ranks in the whole country.

One, Fwazi ed Din Kauwakji, who had served with distinction in the Turkish Army before 1917, was called in by the Palestinians to assume overall command of the Arab rebel forces. And right well he did it. Several of our aeroplanes were shot down by rifle fire and the rebels put up some very good fights against the British ground troops. There were a number of casualties among the forces and a lot of Arabs were killed. During this period several British constables were killed in action against the rebels and some by cowardly terrorist attacks. John Wren, who was a member of my squad, was killed near Nablus. Another, Fletcher ("Fletch" of Maidstone), whom I met when he was stationed at Affuleh and knew quite well, died in an ambush near Rosh Pina in the North of Palestine, when a party of five constables was killed. As a result of these disturbances, the training we should have received in general police duties was cut. The personnel on the Depot strength were utilised for various security duties, such as escorting convoys from one town to another, or in large-scale organised searches of the Arab population in the towns and villages.

Broken glass and nails were strewn on many roads in the towns and, under the Emergency Regulations, an order was made compelling persons, so ordered by the police, to stop and pick up these items. Many police were needed, of course, for the implementation of the law. The local notables felt great blows to their dignity when ordered in the streets to pick up glass and nails, and some asked if they might be allowed to hire boys to complete the degrading task for them. The boys, on the other hand, seemed to enjoy clearing the road, and, with pride, would walk up to the policemen to show just how hard they had been working at their tasks.

Meeting Musa in Shoufat Village

One night, the Police Depot at Mount Scopus was sniped upon from the hills to the north. I was in a party sent out to attack and drive them off. It was a mild attack and the snipers withdrew in haste as we neared them, but in the early hours next morning a large party of us was sent out to the nearby village of Shoufat to follow up the search. (It was a typical little Arab village of domed-roof houses – so designed to enable rainwater, flowing off the roofs, to be collected in a big tank, or well, dug nearby.)

The whole village was searched and only one round of ammunition was found. Not exactly a good haul! I approached a house just at dawn and knocked on the door, which was opened by a middle-aged Arab in the usual native garb. Imagine my surprise then when he spoke to me in English with a strong American drawl and asked, "What's all the bother about?" I told him that I had orders to search his house for firearms – the entire village was being searched because the police camp had been fired on the previous night. "Come in," he said, "You are welcome. Have a cup of cawfee". The thorough

Musa at the house he was building at Shoufat village,
near Mt. Scopus Police Training School.

The Governor's Trotting Escort, led by Bill "Burglar" Williams.
Used for official visits and such occasions as the
King George VI Coronation parade.

search I made, while he was busy preparing coffee, proved fruitless, and I was glad to sit down to a very welcome drink, for the morning air was rather crisp, and I had had nothing to drink since the previous evening. Over coffee Musa and I sat chatting and my host told me of his years in America: and what a fine country he thought it was for the opportunities that it afforded. He said he was thinking of returning. He was disappointed with his homecoming to Palestine, as there was always some sort of trouble going on, especially over the question of Jewish settlement. I met Musa several times later in Jerusalem, usually when he came to the Mosque to pray on Fridays. We struck up a friendship which lasted several years. I often visited him at Shoufat village where he built a very fine house. He cut the stone ashlars himself for he was an excellent mason.

The search of the village was concluded and the officer-in-charge called together all the men of the village and warned them that any future cases of shooting at the police camp would entail severe administrative action against the whole village. The poor old chap in whose house the round of ammunition was found was arrested and taken away for prosecution. The British constable who had found the ammunition later told me that he felt so sorry for the poor old man that he wished he had not reported his find!

Over the next few days, some hours were snatched to study the laws of Palestine – then based on the Ottoman Penal Code – but the training I received at this period was scant, to say the least of it. About twice each week a party of us, under an NCO, would be detailed for convoy duty. This meant reporting for duty at 2 00 pm and then travelling north, up through the Arab towns of Nablus and Jenin, to Affuleh, a Jewish settlement in the Jezreel Valley, about 100 miles away. A number of Jewish farming settlements were established in this fertile valley which leads to the coastal plane and Haifa. It is surrounded by hills, from which the Arabs used to launch their attacks. We toured the valley, visiting the outlying settlements, and then returned to Affuleh at around midnight. Here we awaited the milk lorries' arrival and formed into convoy to escort them back, through the night, to Jerusalem, arriving in time for breakfast.

On to Tulkarem

One afternoon a few weeks later, and still having had practically no training, we were ordered to pack up our kit. We left the depot at 40 minutes' notice. I drew my rifle and ammunition, with which I had been previously issued, but I was unable to load the rifle, as I had only been trained to use the Greener riot gun. Inspector Glaysher, who was seeing us off – a real gentleman and very kind to the recruits – gave me hurried instructions, saying, "You had better understand this, you may need it on the way." At 20 minutes to three o'clock that afternoon, I left the depot with my comrades,[1] heading for Tulkarem on a hired Arab truck, as all the police transport was in use and none could be spared for us – and so ended the first chapter of my Palestine experiences.

---

[1] Including Ron Armstrong, Sam Culverhouse and Owen "The Colonel" – so-called because of his deep voice.

Chapter 2
The Arab Revolt 1936
Fears of Rebellion in Tulkarem

Tulkarem Station was the Headquarters of the Tulkarem Division of the Nablus District. The reason for this hasty move was because the Arab policemen in Tulkarem had attempted to mutiny. It seems that there had been a degree of disaffection among the police in Tulkarem for some little time, and, this day, an excuse had presented itself for some of the Arabs in the force to rebel. A young British constable who was in the recruit stage had, while battering down a locked door with a rifle butt, shot and killed an Arab constable who was standing behind him. It should never have happened of course, and had the constable been properly trained he would never have battered the rifle on the door with a round of ammunition in the breech.

Snatching at this opportunity, some of the Arab policemen then planned to attack the Britishers in revenge. Luckily, the British Corporal[1] overheard them. He locked the would-be rebels in the room they were in, while he informed the Assistant Superintendent-in-Charge. Our party arrived to reinforce the police strength there. We were given a brief address by the ASP, who explained what had happened, and described it as a "particularly nasty incident". That night I was posted as guard on the roof of the police station, which was then an old Turkish building. During the night three bombs exploded near the building walls, but none of these did any damage.

Tulkarem means the "Hill of Mercy and Contentment". In my day it wasn't a big town. I imagine about 10,000-15,000 Arabs were living there, the farmers' lands being spread out on the plain around the hill on which the town was built. Wheat and maize and various vegetables were grown. The merchants working in the town appeared to be quite busy and successful and it seemed to be rather a prosperous little place.

The start of my Wanderings – Nazareth, Affuleh, Jerusalem

I found that I had now started my wanderings, for after only two days in Tulkarem I was transferred, with four other men,[2] to Nazareth. My stay in Nazareth was also brief but most pleasant, for that town, which is situated high on a range of hills, is very healthy and had a neat appearance, with trees giving shade along the streets. From what I remember of the town there were some well-built stone houses with red tiled roofs. Throughout Palestine there were many excellent examples of fine stone masonry, as a number of Arabs were highly skilled craftsmen. The countryside around appeared too

---

[1] Corporal was a rank in the Force below the rank of sergeant.
[2] including Ron Armstrong and Tom Hookey.

Wadi Haramia [Valley of Thieves] Road check.

Rebel action. (Purchased photograph).

Nazareth from an old postcard.

hilly for agricultural crops, but perhaps there was good grazing for sheep; and tourists and pilgrims would have been an important source of income.

I believe the Hill of Temptation,[1] where Jesus is believed to have been tempted by the devil, is nearby. From there you can look down and feel you can see all the world. To the south is Jenin, Nablus and the Nablus hills; to the west is Haifa and the Mediterranean sea; and across to the east you can see Beisan and Transjordan.

I spent one week in Nazareth where a young Arab constable and I were employed on night traffic checks at a road junction, just south of the town. One night I was pleasantly surprised to hear the voices of two young German girls singing a folk song in harmony as they came up the slope. In the cool night air the song sounded very sweet to me. It is one of my most cherished memories, and has always remained with me. As the singers neared us they interrupted their happy sound, and bid us, "Good evening". They chatted to the Arab constable in what appeared to me to be quite fluent Arabic, and then speaking to me in English, I discovered that they were employed at the Galilee Hotel in the town. I often wondered what might have happened to those two pretty young frauleins, for three years later we were at war with Germany.

While I was in Nazareth I took the opportunity of visiting some of the religious and historical sites, including Mary's Well, and also The Grotto – under the Church of the Sisters of Nazareth. Mary's Well is just an ordinary stone-lined depression in the yard, about 3 ft in diameter. The surrounding ground level may have been built up over the years, as several very ancient steps lead down to the water level. It gave me a feeling of elation to imagine Our Lady Mary, Mother of Jesus, going down those steps with her pitcher to get water almost 2,000 years ago. The Grotto is believed to be the excavated site of the original house where the Holy Family lived. A sweet-faced nun, who acted as my guide, told me that The Sisters of Nazareth had supervised and taken part in the actual excavations, and they were quite sure it was authentic. It was claimed that a bell of a Crusader's church, which had been built on what was believed to be the site of Joseph's house, had been found during the excavations that were begun in the 1880s. My mother would have loved to have seen all these historic religious sites, and I planned to bring her out to Palestine to visit them, but unfortunately it was never to be.

On to Affuleh

After this pleasant week in Nazareth I was sent down to Affuleh, the small Jewish town on the edge of the Jezreel Plain. This was in sharp contrast to the Arab towns and was rather like a Wild West cowboy town. It would

---

[1] There is also a Mount of Temptation near Jericho

have made an ideal setting for a Western film. A few horses were tied up to some wooden rails outside buildings of breezeblock and concrete. We were housed in a police billet, over some shops. This is where I first met Constable Fletcher, from Maidstone. As mentioned previously, a year later he, and several other policemen, were killed by a big gang on the Rosh Pina Road. Police duties at this time of unrest were mostly confined to night car patrols, visiting the outlying settlements to ensure that all was well, and lying in ambush along the tracks – hoping we might surprise roving, armed Arab bands. On several occasions we went into action against attackers who disappeared into the night.

One night, as we approached a settlement named Beit Alpha [First House], we found that the attackers had positioned themselves on the hill overlooking the settlement. A squad of the Transjordan Frontier Force – a military force with police powers, also under the control of the Palestine Government – had come up from the Jordan Valley and joined forces with us to drive the attackers off the hill. The TJFF had some machine guns with them and some thousands of rounds of ammunition must have been fired that night before the attackers withdrew. The advantage was nearly always with the attackers, for the hillsides abounded with rocks, which afforded excellent cover. No casualties occurred among the police or the TJFF, or among the Jewish settlers.

Another engagement was more in our favour. We arrived to join battle before dark and killed two of an armed gang. This little affray was short and sharp, and after they had lost two of their party the rest of the Arabs made off, covering the ground at such a fast pace we had no chance of catching up with them. They were truly fit and hardy. After the engagements were over and we were back in our billets, the conversations were quite amusing. Everyone would be claiming possibles and probables – it was a wonder there were any Arabs left to carry on the battle!

Back to Jerusalem

I stayed in Affuleh only one month and was then transferred back to Jerusalem. Ron Armstrong and I had a lift on a convoy, escorted by troops of the Cameron Highlanders, to the City and on arrival I was posted to – MeaShearim Police Station, one of the five stations for the City of Jerusalem. (The others being The Old City, Central, The German Colony and Mustashfa.) This was an entirely different sort of life from that which I had been living for the previous few weeks. Much of the duty, then, was guarding government buildings, or static duty at some strategic point, which could become very boring, especially in the heat of the day in Palestine's long, dry summer and very hot on the feet! At other times we undertook anti-intimidation patrols, to protect people who did not wish to observe the General Strike.

1936 An Arab Inspector interrogating fellaheen [villagers/farmers].

British troops on patrol.

At one time the Arab rebel committee issued an order to the Arab population outlawing the wearing of the *tarboush* [the Arab red fez] of the townsman and compelling the wearing of the traditional *hatta* and *agal* [head-cloth and cord] of the rural *fellaheen* [farmers]. It was felt that if everyone wore the *hatta* and *agal* it would make identification much more difficult and easier for any of the rebels coming in from the country to pass among the crowds unobserved. Gangs of youths then took it upon themselves to enforce this edict and they would tear a fez from the head of anyone wearing one and destroy it underfoot or by burning. The poor offender had to walk bareheaded to the nearest store and buy a headdress. To walk bareheaded in public is very undignified for an elderly Arab gentleman, and many were deeply hurt when this happened to them.

One afternoon when an Arab constable and I were patrolling around the Old City Wall in a hired taxi, we were signalled to stop by an Aircraftsman of the R.A.F. As I stepped from the car I saw another R.A.F man lying injured on the roadside. I quickly discovered that an Arab had shot both these men in the back as they were returning from the Garden of Gethsemane. Their assailant had made off along the Kedron Valley – a deep cutting outside the east wall of the old city, leading to rough country. We rushed both these unfortunate men to the Government Hospital, where one of them died. The other, I am happy to say, was only slightly wounded and recovered fully after a few weeks. Both the poor fellows were unarmed at the time and unable to defend themselves.

At night, patrols were carried out to ensure that the curfew which had been imposed was being properly observed. Around the Jewish quarters of Mustashfa and Rehovia the inhabitants regularly broke the curfew, and large crowds would often be found in the streets and market areas. This was of course understandable as it was very hot inside the houses. However, at the approach of the police patrols, people would fly in all directions like rabbits startled by a dog. Late one night I was on patrol and met a handsome Jew coming along the road, breaking the curfew. I stopped him and asked if he had a curfew pass. He said he had not. I then asked if he could identify himself and he produced an identity certificate showing that he was a medical doctor. He had his tie in his hand and his shirt open to the waist. I asked him, "Have you been out on business?" and he replied, "Yes, very private business, hers and mine." I thought then of the old saw, "All the world loves a lover," and I escorted him home and wished him well.

Some nights, Arabs would creep up near the Jewish area at the back of MeaShearim, and open fire on the houses. The Jews would return the fire and we would join in, in an effort to repel attackers. The land adjoining the residential area was extremely rocky and favoured the attacking Arabs, for it was a simple matter for them to get down behind and between the huge boulders. They would hold their positions until they had used most of their ammunition, then quietly withdraw and slip away into the night.

We were often posted on duty at Damascus Gate, with orders to search everyone going though the gate, for bombs, firearms and ammunition. It was a very good place to get to know some of the Arabs who lived and worked in the vicinity and, of course, we also encountered all the people who entered the Old City of Jerusalem from the villages of the Nablus Road, on their way to the Mosque of Omar. On Fridays, I often met my friend Musa from Shoufat here, as he made his way to the Mosque to pray, and we would greet each other with a warm handshake.

The High Commissioner's Milk Run

One job that fell to the night duty car patrol was to go to the Arab village of Tor, on the top of the Mount of Olives, collect the High Commissioner's milkman and convey him to Government House. This task was one I thoroughly enjoyed, for Tor Village stands high and overlooks the Jordan valley. We would wait for the eastern sky to light up with the rising sun. All would be quiet as steadily the sky became brighter – then the rim of the sun appeared and daybreak was upon us. The sun rocketed into the sky and all at once the cocks began to crow, the donkeys and mules bray and the dogs bark. The doors opened and men and women emerged. The distant mountains of Moab, far to the east in Transjordan, were lit up by the sunlight, which also reflected off the Dead Sea – about 20 miles away and nearly 4,000 feet below. The whole world seemed to spring to life and I thought of the words in the Bible, "God saw it and it was good!" I always felt this was a moment worth waiting for.

By now the General Strike and the Arab Troubles had been going on for some three months or more, and at times, while on patrol, it was necessary to keep wide-awake for bomb-throwers or gunmen. One afternoon, in the Mamillah Road, as we were patrolling, a bomb exploded outside the shop of a Jew. We ran up to the shop while about ten others appeared from all directions and started to give us a description of the man who had thrown the bomb. However, although we gave chase along a couple of lanes, we saw no one. The miscreant had disappeared. The poor old Jewish shopkeeper was very badly shaken.

At other times I saw both Jews and Arabs shot and killed, and also a party of Arabs badly injured by a bomb, for Jews had begun to take reprisal measures. However, on many days in Jerusalem, nothing very exciting happened. Out in the hills of Samaria and Galilee it was a very different matter, for a state of war existed between Fawzi ed Din Kauwakji's Arab Rebel Army and the Government Forces, and considerable casualties were suffered on both sides.[1]

[1] For a more detailed report of the "Disturbances" in 1936 see *Report by His Majesty's Government in the United Kingdom and Ireland to the Council of the League of Nations on the Administration of Palestine and Trans-Jordan for the Year 1936. www.domino.un.org/UNISPAL.NSF*

Jerusalem: Static duty at Damascus Gate
[Bab el Amound – Gate of the Pillars].

Jerusalem Souk: A proud Arab
cloth merchant.
Effendi [man of some standing]
in the foreground.

Jerusalem: Search in progress outside Old City on the Hebron Road.

End of The General Strike

Then His Majesty's Government in Britain promised a Royal Commission to enquire into the causes of this unrest and look into the Arabs' grievances.

After six months, the General Strike was called off. The rebel army faded away, Fawzi, the Commander, went back to Syria and Iraq, taking with him many rebel soldiers.

I was escorting Mr Howard Beard – Assistant Superintendent – through the Old City of Jerusalem on the day that the Arab shops were being opened for the first time since the strike was called. Where, only the day previously, footsteps had echoed through the deserted *souk*, the place was now like a beehive. All was a-hustle and a-bustle. The shopkeepers laughed and joked as they took out their goods from the interiors of the shops to air and dust them, and gave their shops a good spring clean. A few months' peace followed, the tourist trade began to operate and we met many Americans and Europeans in the streets once more. Tourists used to buy a lot of Arab clothing, perhaps to use for fancy dress, and they also patronised the gold and silver smiths of the Old City. The visitors often asked, "Do you speak English?" We were reminded that they would not know who we were, and so we were not to be offended and reply inappropriately. The odd wag would say, "No, I don't, but that chap over there does!"

The Peel Commission – November 1936

The Royal Commission, under Lord Peel, arrived and commenced the inquiry into the causes of the disturbances, and to make recommendations. After a few hearings the Arabs became disenchanted with the Royal Commission and refused to give any further evidence. They felt that the scales were loaded against them at the outset, in favour of Jewish immigration. The Jews, as always, were in the limelight, pressing their claims for their return to their former homeland. There were many influential and wealthy Jews in the British establishment, including Freemasonry, and support also came from a substantial number of Jewish Members of the British Parliament, while the Arabs had no Members of Parliament, no influential members in British public and financial life, and no Arab-owned newspapers in Britain to explain and publicise their concerns.

Back to Training School

During this period of comparative tranquillity, we returned to normal duties, spending one week on day-duty and one week on nights. We were then sent back to the Training School at Mount Scopus, to pick up from where we had left off when we were hurriedly sent away to Tulkarem. Parades, inspections, lectures and refresher courses at the Training School were now our lot. Depot Inspector Bill Black, "Kawaja Aswad" [Mr Black] as we called him, said to us, "You young chaps have not had a fair start. I'll give you some drill training and start nice and easy." We were able to follow the first few commands which were fairly self-evident, but, perhaps because we were doing so well, when he gave the command, "On the left, form squad!" total confusion resulted. A lot of us didn't know what we had to do, and old Bill Black took his hat off and tore his hair. He went to find Charlie Dent and said to him, "*You* take this bloody lot and see what you can do with them!" Bill Black was a dear old fellow, but he didn't have much brain! When it was my time to give drill instructions, I found it much more effective to explain first what had to be done, before giving orders! I quite enjoyed the month we spent at Training School and got a good report at the end of that time, when I was placed second in the squad of 20.

Trips to the Dead Sea

During this, comparatively, more peaceful time, in the early part of the year, some of my fellow constables and I made a couple of trips down to the Dead Sea. After coming off night duty we would take the 40 km, hour or so, taxi ride down to Jericho, and have a splash in the salt waters near a little café. The warm water was reputed to be 42% mineral, and it was so dense you could virtually sit in it, with your knees sticking out. When we came out and stood around for 10 minutes or so, we would be covered in a thin white crust of salt, which could be washed off with a sweet water shower. Some people appeared to think the mud was beneficial, as they would plaster themselves with it and leave it to dry before washing it off. There were also some saltpans, where the crystallised minerals were gathered and bagged up and taken to Jerusalem by the Palestine Potash Company. It was not a pleasant place to visit in the summer months, the temperature being like an inferno.

Jerusalem "Fire Brigade"

There was no Fire Brigade in Jerusalem at this time, and whenever fires occurred the police dealt with the conflagration as best they could, using a municipal watercart. On one occasion a fire had started in a timber yard near Meashearim Police Station and police arrived from all directions, followed by the watercart, and hoses were connected. Then the fun started! A crowd of tourists arrived and wanted to see what was happening. They lined a wall overlooking the timber yard and every so often the police would give them a good squirt with the hosepipe. There were plenty of shrieks from the women as the water doused them, but they seemed to have taken it all in good part, for we had no disciplinary charges to answer.

Local Leave in The Lebanon

Early in 1937 I thought it would be interesting to visit Mount Hermon in The Lebanon, and Goring, a fellow constable in MeaShearim Station, agreed to

Floating in the Dead Sea.

Café at the Dead Sea.
From left to right: Smith, Arthur "Monty" Montgomery,
Theunisun, Robin Martin.

come with me. We set off by taxi on the 175 km journey from Jerusalem to Haifa, and then hired a second taxi from Haifa to Beirut, a distance of about 60 km. Having spent the night in Beirut, we set off again by taxi to the hotel and winter resort at Arze up in the mountains, a particularly popular resort with skiers. However, the last 2 km of the road to the hotel were steep and icy, with snow piled on either side, and the taxi was unable to go any further, so we hired a couple of mules from a little village for the last leg of the journey. Unfortunately, when we got to our destination, we found the hotel was full – a big party having just arrived and taken all the accommodation. We made our way back down the mountain and decided to holiday on the coast. We first visited the little town of Tripoli, fairly close to the Turkish frontier, and had a pleasant and restful stay there.

After a couple of days in Tripoli we went down to Beirut where we stayed a week touring the city and the country around. Beirut itself was a very elegant, well-planned city of wide tree-lined avenues and squares.

The Rebels' Recall to Arms – The Peel Commission Reports

Peace was not to last for many months. The Arab political leaders, feeling they could not trust the British Government to fully appreciate their concerns, decided once more to use force in an endeavour to achieve a solution to the "Palestine Problem" which would be favourable to them. They greatly feared that they would be homeless if Jewish immigration into Palestine continued. They were also cognisant of the fact that Jews were smuggling large quantities of arms into the country and they drew the obvious conclusions. So now, a few politically-minded anti-Zionist Arabs were sent out into the country to rouse the *fellaheen* so that they would once again rebel against the Zionist policies. As usual, when such conditions arise in any country, self-seeking individuals seize the opportunity to get to the top. Many bad characters and former gang leaders managed to assert themselves and take advantage of the situation. Formerly disbanded armed gangs began to re-form, and though small at the outset they were soon very active in perpetrating acts of violence and terrorism on Jews, Government officials and members of the Arab populace who were unwilling to support them. Roadblocks were set up in many places, and it was unsafe to travel without police or military escort, and even with an escort travellers often had to face the dangers of armed attack. By the middle of 1937 it was common to read in the local papers of various crimes, ranging from robbery and murder on the highway to the assassination of a *Muhktar* [Headman] suspected of giving information to the authorities.

Then, in July 1937, when the findings of The Royal Commission, recommending "Partition of Palestine", were published, conditions deteriorated from bad to worse. The Jewish population was very divided but the Arab people rejected the recommendations out of hand, for it would mean an exchange of land and population transfer – taking as a precedent the exchange of populations after the Greco-Turkish War in 1922. The Jewish population was to receive the northern coastal area, the fertile Jezreel Valley and the Galilee area, and the Arabs the rest of the country, including the less fertile mountainous areas and deserts. The British Mandate was to eventually be abolished, except for a corridor surrounding Jerusalem and extending to the coast, south of Jaffa.[1]

The Arab rebels were always referred to as Arab gangs, as at that time no one wanted to give them the dignity of referring to them as rebel patriot bands. Consequently they were regarded, quite wrongly, as robber gangs. Admittedly they did sometimes do a bit of highway robbery, by holding up cars and buses and relieving the occupants of some of their wealth, but that was not the prime reason for their activities. They were, in fact, demonstrating the Arabs' displeasure and non-acceptance of the idea of a National Home for the Jews in Palestine, and were endeavouring to make the whole country ungovernable. And, in truth, by the middle of 1938, the whole country was in turmoil and the Arab areas completely ungovernable. The Government only actually held the main towns and the army camps. The rest of the Arab areas were controlled by the rebel Arab armies, known by the general population as the *Assabi* [army], which by then must have numbered some 20,000 men and boys.

–

While at MeaShearim, I had applied to join the mounted section of the force and was eventually accepted, and so embarked on an entirely different kind of life.

---

[1] See also *Wikipedia Peel Commission, Palestine.*

Chapter 3

On the Mounted – Artuf 1937

Learning to Ride

I had wanted to join the Mounted Section of the Police for a while. My father had worked with horses in the Chatham Corporation Yard, before he joined the Kent Police, and he always encouraged me in my love of those beautiful animals. I learnt to ride a pony when I was a child, so I thought I would be able to ride a horse, and put in an application "to go on the Mounted". "Kutch"[1] Nunn gave me a test and just told me to ride across the stable yard. It was obvious to him, however, that my riding skills were not sufficient, so he said, "Have a bit more practice, and try again later."

I had a pair of jodhpurs made by a local Armenian tailor, Seraphim, and, hiring a horse from a local stable whenever I could, or borrowing a police horse, I rode around the outskirts of Jerusalem and out to the village of Nebi Samuel, about 6 miles to the north, often with my pals, Norman Carswell or Barry Boucher. I also helped in the stables in Kishleh[2] barracks in Jerusalem, cleaning the tack and grooming the horses, to show how keen I was! Some chaps there were very kind and encouraged me, including "Robbo" Robinson, "Lofty" Freestone and Bill Long, all ex-British Army cavalry who had served in India. Robbo used to let me ride his thoroughbred *Seglawi* gelding. The *Seglawi* are one of the five thoroughbred breeds of Arab horses, and Robbo's horse certainly lived up to the excellent reputation of that breed. One character I particularly remember from those days in the Kishleh was Charlie Ketley. He was about 15 years older than me and had been in the British Cavalry in India – in the Ninth Lancers or the "Saucy Ninth" as they were known. He was an extremely smart mounted man. He did not much like mounted patrol work in the rural areas though – what he really liked was riding up the middle of the Jerusalem streets on traffic duty, keeping the streams of traffic to their appropriate sides of the road. He was especially chosen for this work because he was so smartly turned out. He came to a rather sad end. After the end of the Mandate he joined an ex-Palestine Police football club, and played in goal. On one occasion he got cold and was too proud to put a coat on. He caught a chill and died of pneumonia.

On to Artuf and Har Tuv

Kutch passed me on my second assessment, and in the late summer of 1937 I was transferred to the small mounted outpost of Artuf, or, as the Jews call it, Har Tuv, which in Hebrew means "Good Hill" (see sketch map 1). This was as relief for Bill Shevlin who was on UK leave for three months. Artuf was

---

[1] Kutch means "nun" in India, where Kutch had been in the cavalry.
[2] Kishleh barracks – the old Turkish Headquarters and stables of Jerusalem Rural Division.

Practising riding on hired horses around Jerusalem.

Norman Carswell (left) and the author.

situated about 20 miles west of Jerusalem, at the base of the Judean Hills and on the edge of the coastal plain. The railway line, which ran up from Lydda to Jerusalem, was close by. On the hill across the valley to the west stood the village of Sara, which was the home of Samson, the strong man of Biblical fame, and the valley through which the railway ran was the Wadi Ara, the place where the boy David picked up his pebbles before he went forth to slay the giant Goliath. The locality comprised the Arab village of Artuf and the Jewish settlement of Har Tuv – about 100 people.

A very brief Explanation of Zionism and the Root of Conflict over Land in Palestine

These settlements came about because, amongst the members of the Jewish populations of the world, there had been for some time a strong desire to return to the land of their former greatness – which they expressed as a return to Zion. Mount Zion near Jerusalem, where once stood a fortress, became, over the centuries of the Diaspora, a metaphor for Jerusalem, and Zionism, a return to the Promised Land.[1] "Next year in Jerusalem," is the promise made each year at the Passover meal. In the late 19th century the modern Zionist movement was born. Thor Hertzl led the first Zionist Congress, in 1897, in Switzerland, and the Zionists aimed to achieve settlement, and a Jewish State in Palestine, by buying and settling on land there; and a few Jews had made the effort to do this. Even at this early time, some Arab tenants had been displaced in the formation of the new Zionist settlements. (Before the first Jewish Zionist settlements were formed, Christian settlers, mainly from Germany, developed the Swabian Templers Settlements in Haifa, and at Sarona, on land from a Greek Monastery, 4 km north of Jaffa. These were considered to be the first modern agricultural settlements in Palestine, and according to Helmut Glenk[2] the model settlement for the first Jewish immigrants. They suffered extreme hardships, and deaths from malaria, but they eventually became well-established and other settlement followed – including Wilhelma and Bethlehem).[2]

Two types of Jewish Zionist settlements evolved. One was a colonial model, where plantations were created and run, using Arab labour (as the would-be-settlers felt they would not be able to work as hard as the Arabs could, or for such low wages). Others, influenced by socialism, felt that a Jewish nation could not be properly created unless Jews worked the soil with their own labour. Not all Jews were happy to encourage this movement, and there were also warnings in the earliest modern political Zionist discussions that the Arab population in Palestine was not to be dismissed lightly. The Zionist

[1] http://en.wikipendia.org/wiki/Zion. A search for Zion was also very common imagery in Christian hymns and literature, as a search for the ideal.
[2] Ref wikipedia.org/wiki/ Sarona,_Palestine

View from Artuf. The Village of Sara is just to the right of the crest of the hill on the right.

Track to Artuf.

Artuf Personnel: Left to right – The author, Tom Coton,
Titch Reading, Stacey Barham (Cons. i/c) and "Pluto" Morgan.

Resting in an olive grove, when on patrol near Artuf.
Left to right – The author, "Titch" Reading, "Pluto" Morgan
and a visiting officer.

writer Ahad Ha'am (Asher Ginsberg),[1] in 1891, wrote that it was "hard to find tillable land that had not already been tilled" in Palestine. Also it was not correct for those "living abroad" to assume that Arabs were all "desert savages, like donkeys" who did not understand that what was going on around them could be detrimental to their situation, for many Arabs realised only too well, "but pretended not to understand." It was only that they did not feel the early activities (of the few Zionist settlers) were a threat, that the Arabs did not take action. The writer went on to say that if development in Eretz Israel continued as it was hoped, to the point of encroaching, the "native populations... will not easily yield their place." However, over the decades since 1890s, the Zionist movement grew in organisation, numbers and financial support, whereas the Arabs' tenure of land had become tenuous and complicated, and there was no outside financial support to secure the land for them. Observations of a traveller to the area in Ottoman times, Laurence Oliphant (in *Haifa*: 1887), explained the causes of the Arabs' difficulties. Excessive increases in land taxes at that time, which had to be paid in money rather than kind, forced the *fellaheen* to resort to moneylenders in Acre, Beirut and Syria – putting the ownership of their land in jeopardy. As well as the loss of land security, these excessive tax demands would have also depressed innovation, as any benefits resulting from increased productivity would have been immediately lost in taxes. (Oliphant himself had been applied to by *fellaheen* who owned land in El Lejjun, but the authorities had stopped the sale to foreigners at that time.) After the First World War the Turks destroyed all their land registry records when they left Palestine, and the new administration had to sort out the rightful owners. "Every possible publicity was given to the need for re-registering ownership of the land, and while some complied... many, through ignorance or misapprehension, failed to do so. A number of unscrupulous, educated Arabs, many residing in Beirut and the Lebanon, saw their chance and took it with both hands, registering their name to vast tracts of land to which, in fact, they had no real claim. Jewish organisations offered these absentee landlords irresistible sums for the land, so thus it was that the *fellaheen*, who had always believed themselves to be the owners of the land which their ancestors had farmed for generations, suddenly found themselves evicted and replaced by Jews" supported and funded by World Jewry.[2] The Arabs had seen some of their best land, which they had farmed for generations, sold to the new settlers, while they were left with the poorer, more difficult slopes to cultivate.

The Strength at Artuf

Life at Artuf was very pleasant. The strength of the Post was five British policemen, and an Arab and a Jewish Policeman – all constables – with the

---

[1] www.zionism-isreal.com/zionism_history.htm
[2] Geoffrey J Morton 1957, *Just the Job* p.46

senior constable, Stacy Barham, in charge. My other fellow constables were E. A. Morgan ("Pluto!"), Bill Shevlin and "Titch" Reading. Titch's father had been a surveys officer in Palestine and consequently Titch grew up in the country, becoming an expert Arabist, for, as a small boy, he had played games such as marbles with the other children down in Gaza. The Arab policeman was Ahmen Arekat and the Jewish policeman, Ouvadiah Navasolski from Har Tuv.

Har Tuv

The Jews living in the settlement, or colony as it was often called, had ancestry in Spain, from where they had been expelled at the time of Queen Isabella, and they would tell of their subsequent wanderings in the Balkans. They had settled in Palestine in about the 1880s, under an agreement with the Turks, Palestine at that time being part of the Ottoman Empire. The settlement grew crops of millet, maize, wheat and a little tobacco. The Muhktar of the Jewish colony, one Albert Bahore, had arrived there as a boy in Turkish times. He was a real character and quite a raconteur, for he would often amuse us with some of his stories, which he usually finished in peals of raucous laughter. The Elder of the Jews was a grand old man named Kanoon Levy, who was held in high regard by many of the local Arabs. I also had a great liking and respect for another old farmer, Gabriel Levy. I used to sit and chat with him and the conversations could employ four of five languages – Hebrew, English, Arabic, French and German – in order to emphasise just what we wanted to convey. I well remember him saying that the cause of all the trouble in Palestine was that there was no confidence between the Arabs and the Jews. In this he was, of course, quite correct, for the Arabs distrusted the Jews; they could see the logical outcome of the continued Jewish immigration – and the Jews understood all along that the Arabs would oppose them.

Police Work

Artuf was a typical little Arab village of about 200 people. The police work was to patrol the surrounding Arab villages, conducting the necessary crime detection and arresting offenders. We were also there, however, as a defence garrison for the Jewish colony. It had been attacked by the Arabs in 1929, when much of the settlement had been burnt to the ground. Luckily no lives had been lost, for the colonists had managed to barricade themselves into one strong building, and having some firearms they were able to keep the marauders off. Now of course, in 1937, the colony had its own settlement police, who were armed and controlled by the constable in charge of the Police Post.

Artuf Station was truly an outpost, being six miles off the main road and accessible only by a dirt track. There was no wireless transmitting set at that time, and the telephone was, more often than not, out of order. It was a free

Deir Aban, a large Arab village, a short ride from Artuf.

and easy kind of life. Rations were sent to us three times a week, but owing to the fact that the ice, which was used to preserve the food, was generally all melted by the time we received them, we were obliged to eat most of the food on the day it arrived and tighten our girths on the days in between. We kept rabbits and chickens, so we seldom went hungry. Also, on most days that we spent out on patrol, an outlying village would provide a meal. At times, when we were unable to accept an invitation to stop and eat, the villagers would be most disappointed, for Arabs are a most hospitable people and regarded our visits as social occasions. They provided us with some lavish spreads and waited on us most assiduously – except when things had gone wrong.

A nice old Bedouin lady, Fudeh, used to do our washing and earn a little money for herself. She was lame, having been born with a club foot, and could not travel distances on foot. Because of this she was not highly regarded by her Bedouin family and had been sold to the village Headman at Artuf for a wife, when she was young. She was fascinated by the tricks that Paddy McGill, the previous constable-in-charge, used to do, pretending to lay eggs! Fudeh told us how Paddy would show her his empty hands, then bending forward clucking, he would put his hands round his back and produced *"baiden minteesu"* [two eggs from his arse!]. It used to really make her laugh to think he could "lay eggs" like that.

Each of us was expected to do two day patrols and one night patrol each week. Travelling in pairs or threes, we would visit up to 10 villages on a patrol. It was pleasant country to ride over, for some villages were in the hills and others down on the plain. Deir Aban [the sanctuary of Aban] was a big village at the foot of the hills, with fertile land and open fields easy to plough, spreading onto the plain, whereas Deir Yassin was up in the hills where the farming was a bit harder and they had to rely on terraces to grow crops. One track, to Ishwa, was very dangerous to ride along, as it turned into a narrow ledge, six feet wide, with a drop of 50 to 100 feet into the valley on one side. One horse we had, Mick, would scare the wits out of me until I got to know him better. Whenever we had to traverse a narrow track or mountain path, which was quite frequently the case, he would stand on his hind legs and dance along the edge of it in playful mood. At such times I was powerless to interfere, for if I had pulled his mouth he may have stepped over the edge. The only thing to do was let Mick have his head, while I sat right up along his neck and prayed that his judgement and surefootedness were equal to that of a mountain goat. After a few 100 yds he would settle down and walk - and when it came to walking he could walk the legs off any horse I knew. After a while, however, when I knew a narrow path was coming up I would dismount and lead him. Some years later Mick was being ridden by a mounted reserve man, in Jerusalem's Main Street, when he decided to do a little dance. Unfortunately he danced right in front of an oncoming bus. His rider was thrown and badly hurt and Mick received a terrible gash which lay his chest open, exposing his beating heart. So strong was the spirit of that animal that, even with the wound, he danced through the gate of the police barracks as though being led on parade for the Derby. The veterinary surgeon took one look at the wound and decided to put Mad Mick to sleep.

Ahmed Arekat

The old Arab constable on the Post strength was Ahmed Arekat, and he was really the uncrowned king of the area. Apart from a few odd words, he could speak practically no English. While on patrol one day, and resting in the village *madafi*, or guest house, he turned to one of the British policemen and said, "You want kitchen?" meaning, "Would you like chicken for lunch?" One of us replied in the affirmative and, with a few words and a nod of the head, he made the necessary arrangements for us to have lunch there. One of the villagers then said to him, in Arabic, "Are you learning English then Ahmed?" and he replied most indignantly, "What do you mean, am I learning English? I can speak it like an Englishman!" I backed him up, of course, and chatted away to him in English, while he answered with a few nods, and squeezed in a "Yes," or "No," as he deemed fit.

Ahmed was a dear old chap and not without his share of courage. A few months later he achieved some fame, and generated not a little wrath in the eyes of the Divisional HQ Officers. He had received information that a certain man (who I think was wanted for murder) was holed out in a cave in the hills a few miles east of the Post. He drew a rifle from the armoury, saddled up his horse on the pretext of exercising the animal, and left to arrest the wanted man. As he neared the cave where the man was taking refuge, Ahmed dismounted and left his horse in an olive grove. He then proceeded, stealthily, towards the cave and picked a suitable spot from which he could ambush and capture the man. After a while the wanted man emerged from his hiding place carrying his rifle. Ahmed waited for a favourable opportunity, then aligning his sights on the man, he challenged him, telling him to drop his gun or he would be killed. The command was obeyed and an hour or so later Ahmed returned to the Post triumphant, with the man under arrest. When the incident was first reported, Ahmed was commended and awarded £5 (his monthly pay would have been £3). Later, however, when the full facts of his case became known in HQ, our hero was reprimanded for endangering his life and jeopardising the safe custody of his rifle. He pleaded that, if more police had gone out on the job, it may well have been unsuccessful, as some noise might have aroused the criminal and given him sufficient time to make good his escape. A sympathetic officer subsequently assisted Ahmed and he was permitted to retain his reward.

Scots Guards in Jerusalem – "showing the flag in Allenby Square".

Jerusalem: 1937 The Hotel Fast, Jaffa Road. A German-owned hotel,
decorated for the coronation of King George VI. A pleasant bar to frequent!

Settlement Security

In the colony the Jews had organised their own system of night guards. They had some Temporary Additional Constables (TACs) who were under the supervision of their own corporal. He in turn was responsible to the British i/c, by this time a sergeant. Each British constable was detailed to act as orderly officer in rotation. It was the orderly's responsibility to keep the Station Diary, and in the event of an attack he was to turn out the other Britishers and inform the Post commander. One night, when I was acting as orderly officer, shots rang out and I turned out all the rest of the personnel. However, it was soon found that the guards had made a sham attack on the colony. They had heard that half of the special guards were to be discharged and, by this false alarm, they had hoped to be able to keep their jobs for sometime to come. But shortly after, real trouble developed, so their jobs were secure!

Search for Arms and a Rival's Intrigue

One afternoon we had information and instructions to go to Rafat, to arrest a man wanted for taking part in a highway robbery. Four of us went out and approached Rafat from four different directions. We found the wanted man sitting just outside his house, a search of which revealed two rifles hidden under the manger.

Another incident illustrates that the honour of Arabian women is not always as infallible as we sometime hear. It occurred at Deir Aban, where there lived a man – we shall call him Sharif Awad – who was married and had three children. He was very fond of, and delighted in, the charms of a young girl of easy virtue who can be called Shelabi, also living in the village. He was, however, not without a rival for the favours of the fair Shelabi and this rival was an ex-convict and a very wily man, whom we shall call Abu Saad. Abu Saad decided to hatch a plot to rid him of his rival for a while. He had a friend who coveted the wife of his rival and the two together conspired to plant a bomb and 20 rounds of ammunition in the house of Sharif Awad. The bomb and ammunition were placed by a nephew of Sharif Awad, who hid them in some *tibbin* [chaff].

This having been successfully accomplished, Abu Saad came to the Police Post and gave information of the bomb and ammunition in his rival's house. A party was sent to check and search the house and in due course the bomb and ammunition were found. The owner was away at the time, but on his return he was arrested and held in custody, while he, of course, denied all knowledge of the incriminating articles.

Village rumours brought to our ears the true facts and after a little investigation we were convinced that our informer was crooked. It took some time to get to the truth, but eventually the nephew became frightened and admitted what had happened. Abu Saad received four years' imprisonment for his felonious intrigue, and the nephew, a boy of fifteen, was sent to Reformatory School for a spell. Two colleagues and I were awarded commendations for "averting a serious miscarriage of justice". With Emergency Regulations in force at that time, the Military Courts, which tried such cases, might well have sentenced the intended victim to death and the least he could have expected would have been five years' imprisonment. Sharif Awad showed his appreciation by presenting us with five chickens, which we cooked and invited him to dine on with us.

Social Life

It wasn't all work at Artuf, but there was very little to do in leisure time other than read and play cards. One small diversion we had was to dance with the teenage girls from the settlement, accompanied by the music of about a dozen records that we played on an old gramophone. One of the records, I particularly remember, was "Louise" which was played incessantly! It was all innocent fun, but I did strike up quite a friendship with one of the girls, Rachel Levy. She was out of the teenage bracket, just about 21, and as there were no young men of her own age at the colony, life must have been a little dull for her, so she appeared to be pleased to have a dance and a chat with me. Batshava, a younger teenager, who always wore white blouses and blue shorts, became known by us as Blue Pants, or "Bloop" for short.

During these few months while I was at Artuf, the situation in the country was deteriorating very badly, and the armed gangs were becoming stronger and bolder. We heard on the radio news of various rebel activities – including highway robbery, when the roads were completely blocked with stones and travellers ambushed. In the Hebron area the little Police Post at Dhahriya, south-west of Hebron, had been raided and all the rifles and ammunition stolen – it was believed by Eissa Battat and his band. West of Hebron, near Beit Jibrin, a British archaeologist, Mr Starkey, who was very popular with the Arabs, and was engaged on an archaeological dig at Tel ed Dwiya between Biet Jibrin and Gaza, was robbed and left murdered on the roadside while travelling towards Hebron. Attacks on all kinds of Government property were made and, nightly, miles of telephone wires and poles were pulled down and dragged away into the hills.

My few months at Artuf ended when Bill Shevlin returned. In the early part of February, 1938, I was posted back to Jerusalem Rural Division H.Q. at the Kishleh, and after a few days, was included in a large body of mounted men, and sent on to Hebron.

64

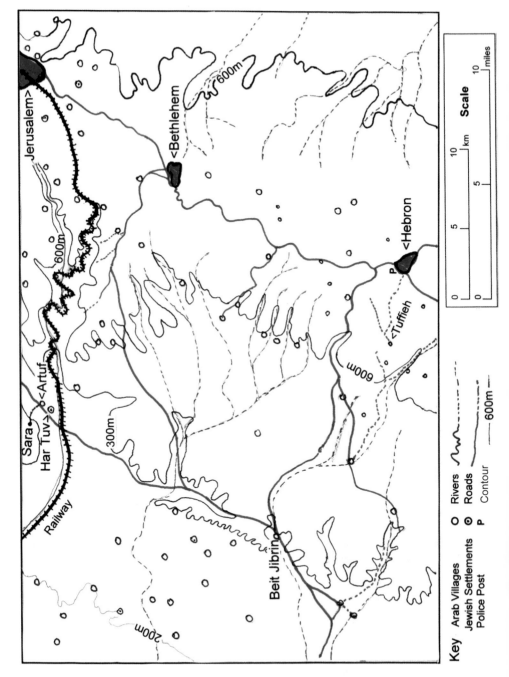

Map 1: Sketch map of the Hebron Area

Chapter 4

The Hebron Column

On a Monday morning in February 1938, our cavalcade of about 10 constables – four British[1] and six Arabs – left the Kishleh, heading south, to cover the 35 km to Hebron. The weather was bitterly cold and a biting east wind was sweeping across the Dead Sea Depression from Transjordan. The high ridge of hills of old Judea we were riding along seemed to be the only obstruction in its course, for it was nearly strong enough to blow us out of our saddles. My mount was Matey, a fine-looking horse which I had inherited from Sgt. "Burglar" Williams when he transferred from Jerusalem Rural Mounted Section to the Dog Section. "Matey" became my nickname ever after.

We arrived at the Arab town of Hebron, the town of Abraham, at 1 pm. Our horses were our first worry, for no arrangements had been made for stabling, and when a mounted man's horse is not comfortable he can never rest contentedly. The senior officers at Hebron did not seem to be concerned about us and gave us no assistance. We set about finding some place that would serve for stabling and discovered, below the house of one of the married British constables, a disused garage and storeroom. I asked the constable's wife if we might use these two places and she, being an average Englishwoman and fond of horses, agreed to our request. The remainder of the mounts were sent to the old Turkish prison cells.

Our Mission – to find Eissa Battat

During the afternoon more mounted men, 10 or so, arrived from the Jaffa district.[2] By nightfall we were over 15 British mounted constables, 15 Arab mounted constables and about 15 Additional Temporary Arab Constables, under the command of B/Inspector "Crash" Holloway, with Senior Sgt. Jimmy Sneddon, his 2nd I/C. We were really very unpopular with the Station Sergeant for we cluttered up his station accommodation and made his place extremely untidy. He seized on every chance to find some fault with us. There was insufficient sleeping accommodation and some of us were obliged to sleep in the mess hall, while the recreation area was littered with saddlery. The poor sergeant was at his wits' end, and all day long we could hear him grumbling about "these bloody mounted men!"

Sure, it was untidy, but what were we to do with our kit? We couldn't carry it around on our backs! A few days later the District Superintendent, it might have been Mr Kyle, arrived from Jerusalem, and something was done. We

---

[1] The British mounted constables included Les Parker, Jock McGuire and Tom Slattery (father of Fergus, the Irish international rugby player). Cons. Woolley joined us later.
[2] Including "Chesty" Charles, Thompson, Saunders and young Oats (nephew of Captain Oats of Scott's Antarctic team. Not long after the ambush he went to Australia).

were found new billets and supplied with heating stoves. Mounted British Inspector "Crash" Holloway paraded us to explain our task and what was expected of us. He told us that a band had been formed by an absconded offender, the previously-mentioned Eissa Battat, and that it was our job to catch up with the band, bring it to action and wipe it out.

With a patrol strength of about 40 we began by spending much time out in the villages, searching for this band, but met with no success. A few minor arrests were made, but we couldn't bring the band to action – the necessary intelligence was not forthcoming. As nothing happened for a couple of weeks or so, the strength of the parties was reduced to about 10 and more patrols were operated.

At night, we mounted constables would chat amongst ourselves, hoping that soon we would be able to complete the job, for in truth it was most uncomfortable at Hebron. We were badly overcrowded, sleeping "hugger-mugger" on the floors and wherever we could find space, but we did appreciate that we were there specifically to defeat or capture Eissa Battat and his men. Rumour had it that the band was about 15 strong, but at times reinforced by local villagers, who would often erect road blocks at night, shoot up passing cars and rob the occupants. So the sooner we could bring the gang to action the sooner we could defeat it and the sooner we could return to our normal stations.

Ambush

Then one day in the middle of March, the whole available mounted strength, British, Palestinian and Auxiliaries were detailed for patrol. While on parade at the Old Serai (Turkish Fortress and HQ), prior to moving off, the officer i/c checked all the men present, to see that they carried the full issue of 100 rounds of .303 SAA[1] and drilled us in a few arms movements. We were not told anything, but I feel sure that Inspector Holloway had been "tipped off" about something, somewhere, for word went round that we should expect some action any time. This, in general, went without saying as the Arabs were by now very disillusioned with British rule, which had become very much to their detriment.

It was a grey, overcast day, with low cloud and restricted visibility. We moved off, riding through Hebron town in sections of fours and turned west, up a narrow track, leading past Abraham's Oak (a very old tree, reputed to have been planted by Abraham, but I very much doubt that it was 4,000 years old). We then headed out into the hills, towards a village named Tuffieh. It was good grazing country, green after the winter rains, though quite rocky. When Hebron was about 4 km behind us and Tuffieh visible in the distance,

---

[1] SAA – small arms ammunition

we descended a steep, rocky hill by a narrow track which was lined with stone walls on either side.

The officer i/c halted the column and sent British Constable Thompson and an Arab constable on as advanced guard, circumventing a conical hill, just to the right of the track. He then sent B/Cons. Page and an Arab constable as flank guard up to the summit of the hill, while the advanced guard was rounding the base. Page was riding a snow-white horse and he and the Arab constable made a lovely picture as they cantered up the hillside. Just as they reached the summit a volley of shots rang out, echoing across the valley to our left. It was difficult to assess where the shots had been fired from and I thought that maybe someone was shooting partridges. However, the "Dismount for Action" order was called, and the No. 3s of each section took over the horses and led them away, for cover, to the right. The horse holders had not gone more than 30 yards when they were met with fire – bullets were flying all about them. They were then ordered to return and take cover with the rest of the party, behind the walls lining the track.

We were caught in a neat little ambush and a fatal mistake had been made. We should have either galloped forwards or back. Our commanding officer, though, had different ideas and he decided we should stay where we were. The men were fairly safe, provided the ammunition did not run out, but what of the horses? They had not been trained to lie down. Bullets were, by then, flying in all directions, and Jock McGuire shouted, "Sir, my horse has been shot." His grey horse, which carried him on Jerusalem traffic duty, crashed down stone dead, shot though the neck.

Two loose horses were kicking each other and Cons. Woolley (Cricketer Frank Woolley's son) got up, separated them and led them back. Sgt. Jimmy Sneddon shouted to Woolley, "Take cover, don't be a fool. You'll get shot!" However, Woolley, who was a very religious young man (even to the extent of refusing to play cricket on Sundays) replied, "I'm not afraid! God will protect me." (God did look after him on that occasion and he did not get a scratch. Later, however, when serving in the RAF in England, he was unfortunately killed in an air crash.) But, to return to the ambush, eight of the horses were now either shot dead or fatally wounded and had to be destroyed within half an hour, including my horse Matey, BP No 53.

During this time I was peering over the wall to see if I could see anything of the attackers, or the direction from which the attack was coming, but I could see nothing. There was a little bush growing out of the wall I was using for cover, and I think the attackers could see me, for Cons. Oats' who was with me said, "For Christ's sake keep your head down. A bullet has just snapped off a twig in that bush, and if it had been two inches lower, your number would have been up!" After that narrow escape I was a little more

Members of the Hebron mounted column at the billet of old stone houses in the town.

Army troops with Lewis gun being transported by packmule.

careful, and changed my position slightly. Just up from me a party of Arab auxiliaries were lying on their backs, blazing away at sky and clouds, and were eventually just about out of ammunition. Most of the regular force had been less wasteful with their ammunition and taken more careful aim.

Then the Inspector panicked when he saw a small party of *fellaheen* with donkeys travelling towards Hebron on a ridge across the valley to the south and called out, "We're being surrounded!" An Arab Sergeant was sent back to Hebron to inform Divisional Headquarters of the situation and to ask for help. The Sergeant gallantly mounted his horse and galloped away up the track shouting, *"Ana ibn Arab ya Shabab"*, ["I'm an Arab you young fellows"], and away he went to Hebron.

It was then decided that we should withdraw, but there was some concern about the advance and flank guards who were now out of contact. Young Cons. Saunders called out, "Give me a horse, Sir, and I'll go and look for them behind the hill." He mounted a loose horse and galloped away, bullets chipping pieces off rocks all around him and his horse, some passing under the horse's belly, but miraculously, horse and rider were unscathed. He scouted around behind the hill for the missing men but was unable to locate them. (It later transpired that they had gone up the hill and joined the other two). Some minutes later he came galloping back through the same rifle fire, still unhurt. It was a very courageous act and, personally, I felt that he should have received a King's Police Medal. For some reason or other he was never honoured, and did not receive even a commendation. If our action that day had been victorious, I'm sure that Saunders would have been decorated, but instead we had suffered a defeat and so his courage was never officially recognised.

For about two hours, it seemed, we were pinned down on that hillside and then came the order to, "Withdraw in ones and twos." So we started creeping along the wall and up the hill. There was an area without cover, across which it was necessary to run and trust in the Lord! My turn came and away I went, wearing a coat and bandolier with 90 rounds of ammunition and carrying my rifle. When I reached cover again I was breathless and threw myself down behind the wall to recover my breath. As I lay there on my back, gasping for air, I could hear the reports of the rebels' rifle fire and I actually saw their bullets flying through the air like high velocity bumblebees. I think the rebels must have been using refilled cartridge cases, charged with black powder and lead projectiles, as normally you cannot see bullets.

Then, quite suddenly, the weather changed, the clouds descended and a mist reduced the visibility very considerably, allowing the missing members of the advance and flank guards to be brought in. Cons. Page had just about run out of ammunition, for from his vantage point at the top of the hill he had been blazing away at the rebels. Then a fighter plane (armed with a machine gun) could be heard overhead, but could not be seen, and neither could the air crew see us. Air assistance had been called for when the Arab Sergeant had got back to Hebron, but it came too late to help us. The firing stopped as suddenly as it had started and the gang got clean away. Page said that he had seen about eight of the rebels withdrawing down the valley in single file. Obviously, undercover of the mist, they too had made a strategic withdrawal: very well pleased with themselves, I should think, for we had completely failed in our objective.

Woolley then caught a loose horse, mounted and rode off towards Hebron. Poor Sgt. Sneddon, not in the first flush of youth, was in a bad way, suffering from rheumatism or arthritis or something similar, for he had great difficulty in walking.

We withdrew from the scene of action and as we reached the top of the track, we met a detachment of Highlanders – Black Watch, if I remember aright. Next came Assistant Superintendent Ronny Broadhurst from Hebron, who met up with the Inspector. By now it was pouring with rain, and we were soaked through, but were obliged to wait shivering while the ASP heard all about it, asking some not very helpful questions and making some equally unhelpful suggestions. A roll call was taken and Woolley was found to be missing. On learning that he had taken a horse and ridden to Hebron, A.S.P. Broadhurst exclaimed, "What? Deserted! He should be charged with cowardice in the face of the enemy!" I almost burst out laughing, for it was certain that cowardice was one thing that Woolley was not guilty of. He had waited until the action was over and then had gone home to lunch!

We now returned to the scene of the ambush to collect the saddles and bridles from the fallen horses. What a sad duty that was. The other horseless constables and I had to walk back to Hebron carrying our saddlery.

I was a very young constable then, but learnt a lot that day. It was impressed upon me, by some who had had cavalry training and experience, that a party caught in an ambush should never remain at the ambush point. Either the party should retreat or advance and wheel left or right, wherever escape offers. Ever after, during my mounted days in Palestine, as Sergeant and later as Inspector, when out on patrol I always planned ahead. Kilometre by kilometre, I eyed the topography, forming a mental image of what I would do in case of an ambush. One day above Qalqilya, some six years later, I was bringing home a patrol from the Azzun area, and an army section opened fire over our heads, just for fun! As the bullets whined about us, I galloped my party into a small depression, dismounted and advanced undercover to the army patrol. When I realised who was shooting at us, I shouted, asking, "What the bloody hell are you playing at?" The officer apologised and said he'd never seen anyone take quicker evasive action. I replied that he was lucky he didn't get a load of lead back at him!

My New Mount, Dusty

A few weeks later while still in Hebron, the other constables who had lost their mounts and I went to Jaffa by bus to collect our remounts. I was the junior member of the party so I had no choice of the horses. I was left with the one that none of the other fellows wanted. My new mount seemed too small for me, being under 15 hands while I stood a fraction over six feet. However he turned out to be a really good little horse, and what he lacked in size he made up for in spirit. He was a real pet, sweet-natured and with the heart of a lion. Being a grey roan in colour he was called Dusty. It was a two-day trip back. We rode from Jaffa to Ramleh, where we stayed the night and then on to Hebron via Jerusalem. Ramleh was where the "Palestine Heaven Bourn" were posted: men whose fathers – it was generally acknowledged – knew Spicer (the Inspector General of Police). It was nice easy riding country – cultivated land, ditches and scrub: and the Ramleh Vale Hounds, which hunted jackals and foxes, were kept there. Nick Carter was struck off normal duties as kennel huntsman, looking after the hounds and the stables. The Chief Secretary, Attorney General, Heads of Departments and Senior Army Officers all used to like to go down there for a hunt. They also had a polo team at the Station.

On our way through Jerusalem Charlie Ketley asked if he could ride Dusty around the station yard. When he dismounted and handed him back to me he said, "That horse is the most intelligent horse I have ever ridden! I only had to show him what I wanted him to do once and he understood. If there was a Police Sports coming up, and I rode him in the Best Trained Horse event, I would guarantee I'd win!"

–

After the Hebron ambush there was a full inquiry into the affair and Assistant Inspector Jack Birch and Sgt. Buck Adams took over command at the Station. A few additional constables also came up from Jerusalem, including Michael Hook and Charlie Bessant. Tragically, A.I. Birch was killed by rebels near Ramallah just a few months later.

Sergeant Buck Adams

Sergeant Buck Adams was quite a character. He was known all over Palestine as "Abu Korbaj" [Father of the Whip], and we certainly held him in respect. He was in his early 30s and was an ex-Royal Artillery man who had seen service in India. He was entirely self-taught and I take my hat off to him for being one of the most efficient NCOs I served under. He had a rare knowledge of Arabic and an ability to understand the Arab mind. He liked and respected the Arabs and the feeling was reciprocated. He would be up early every morning, shouting his orders to the men to see that all was well and the horses well cared for. "Don't just lie there with the sun scorching your eyeballs!" he would cry. Sometimes, when asked by British constables what certain phrases in Arabic meant he would reply, "Pal, your father spent a lot of money on your education, so you should be able to do as I do and find out for yourself." I used to get on quite well with him, and in his less authoritarian moods I often chatted to him. He taught me a lot about the Arabs and their language. I remember asking him one day what a certain Arabic phrase he used meant, and he scratched his head and replied, "I'm damned if I can tell you what it is in English." Then he went on to tell me three other ways it could be used in Arabic, and even with my scant knowledge of the tongue, I understood.

The Search for Eissa Battat Continues

With these two men to lead us, we again started to patrol out into the hills, searching for rebel gangs. Our strength was reduced to some 20 men, mainly British, but our armament was increased to include a Lewis machine gun and also grenades with a grenade discharger. This would help to dislodge attackers who may be hidden behind walls or rocks. There was also a packhorse to carry the additional arms and ammunition.

By this time the rebels were getting organised all over the country, and in the "Triangle of Terror" as it was known (the area lying between Nablus, Tulkarem and Jenin) some very hot battles were taking place. In these engagements hundreds of men took part, often up to as many as 2,000 regular British troops being employed, and a few score police thrown in. The rebel bands were on average 500 to 600 strong. They, of course, had the advantage of knowing the local hills, but, even considering this, they put up some magnificent performances for irregulars. The Royal Scots Regiment lost quite a number of men, for they were extremely unpopular with the Arabs on account of the treatment they had meted out to some men they had captured, and also because of the damage and havoc they wrought in the villages.

One night in Azzun village, near Tulkarem, five Arab mounted policemen were murdered. The gang leader, Farris Azzuni, and some members of the gang crept up to a house, slugged the guard, entered the house and cut the throats of the five policemen who were sleeping there. The British Sergeant who was in charge of that party displayed great courage in managing to escape with the remaining men. They fought a pitched battle in the narrow village street and drove the gang off.

Meanwhile, we in Hebron district were spending weeks at a time out in the villages, trying to locate and engage the local gang. We patrolled days and nights, picking up information where we could, but never a shot was fired at us, though we often learnt, on doubling back, that a gang had been following. Prior information as to the gang's activities was hard to come by, but plenty of people would give us a word or two after anything had happened, hoping to keep their village in favour with the Government. It was too much to expect that the villagers would readily give information. In the first place they were in sympathy with the rebels – for they didn't want to lose their homes to Jewish immigrants. Secondly, if they did give information to the Government they could not be provided with the protection they wanted, as rebels took away informers and summarily executed them. In such cases all the police could do was discover the dead bodies.

After some months, our local rebel leader, Eissa Battat, came to a mysterious end. He had had a death sentence hanging over him for several years, and had sworn that he would never be taken alive. At the time, he was reported shot by a police patrol but, from information I gathered later, it appeared he was killed by an acquaintance of his – arranged by the District Officer. Eissa Battat was killed in return for saving the assassin's own life.

Chapter 5

Back to Jerusalem and Return to Artuf 1938

About midsummer 1938, while we were breakfasting one morning in the outlying village of Yattah, south-east of Hebron, a message came out by car to our commander, ordering him to return the whole party back to Central Police Barracks, Jerusalem. It didn't take long for us to get ready to move off! We had been living out in the villages for over four months and we had seen enough of the hills for the time being. We had not tasted alcohol and our diet was very monotonous, mostly rice and occasionally meat (though the villagers had been very good to us), so we were looking forward to seeing the bright lights again. Kit was packed and horses saddled, and in less than half an hour we had started to cover the 40 km separating us from Jerusalem-the-Golden,[1] a full day's ride. Not that we expected to find milk and honey when we arrived!

We arrived late that Saturday afternoon and what a weekend we had – every man was as drunk as ten lords! Next morning we gave our horses a really good grooming. Many of the mounted men in Jerusalem, and the officer-in-charge of the district, possibly Assistant Superintendent Noel Ford or Superintendent Munro, came to have a look at us, expecting to find our horses in a sorry state after all the work they had done. But what a shock they had, for our Sergeant, Buck Adams, ensured that good care was taken of the horses and they arrived back as round and as hard as little apples. Sgt. Adams was complimented by several of the senior officers on the condition of our mounts.

Breakdown of Law and Order

Generally speaking, from now on – for a year or so – very little mounted work was done, for it was considered unsafe for small parties to operate in outlying areas, remote from District HQ. Most of our work was done in conjunction with the military forces, and the whole country, having become completely out-of-hand, was placed under the control of the General Officer Commanding, who I think was General Dill. By late summer 1938, it can be truthfully said that the Palestine Government held only the large towns and the actual military camps. The hills and remote places were definitely "Rebel Country" and Rebel Law was enforced by the *Caid el Assabi* [Rebel Chief]. The rebels and the Arab cause had the sympathy of practically the whole of the Arab population, which also gave very active support, both in food and money, for the rebel soldiers. The gang leaders known as Caids held their own courts and tried the persons whom they suspected of giving away information or of having sympathy towards the Government, and many

---

[1] Hymn: "Jerusalem the Golden, with milk and honey blessed."

people were sentenced to death and summarily executed.

Gradually the pressure of the military began to weigh very heavily upon the Arabs. The male population of many areas was rounded up and placed in detention camps. Meanwhile, so we heard from our Arab colleagues, the rebel leaders began to force people to subscribe to the cause, though money was becoming scarce and the *fellaheen* found it difficult to pay. Those who failed to pay were often abducted and kept in captivity in disused wells until their families paid up. Many such wells harboured snakes and rats, and after a few days in such confinement the unfortunates usually found some way to raise the necessary funds.

Many casualties were inflicted on the rebel soldiers by the military and the pressures were becoming so great that the influential Arabs began to approach the Government with sources of information. They were assisted by the Government to raise their own little armies or bodyguards, which helped the Government to track down and kill or capture the rebels. One leader, Abdul Rahim, who operated in the Jenin area, was a real patriot who maintained discipline amongst his men and dealt fairly with the local populace. However, I was told by an Arab who had once been a Sergeant under this Abdul Rahim, that when their leader was killed near Qabatiya, the gang members became like a pack of jackals and many fights took place between them. The gang quickly broke up and returned to their homes.

"Mr North"

One day, when I was down in the Old City, I was approached by someone who was apparently a tourist. However, he was unusually smartly dressed, wearing a pair of corduroy shorts, a light tweed jacket of Saville Row cut and superb quality woollen stockings. He was every inch an Englishman, I thought. He asked me the way to the Wailing Wall and he chatted to me for a few minutes before starting on his way. About two days later his photograph appeared in the *Palestine Post*, over a column which informed us all that the Colonial Secretary, Mr Malcolm MacDonald, had visited Palestine incognito, travelling as a "Mr North". He was personally apprising himself of the true situation in the country and had spent some time talking to various members of the population.

Jewish anti-Government Demonstrations

Jewish anti-Government demonstrations at this time created a new diversion for us. A young Jew, Shlomo Ben Yousef, had been arrested after he had shot and killed an Arab near Rosh Pina, in the far north. He was tried and sentenced to death. Scores of Arabs had, by then, been executed for offences connected with firearms and explosives. But now Jewish women all over the country were organizing demonstrations, protesting against the execution of this young Jew. A curfew was imposed on the population of Jerusalem.

Many streets had to be cleared and a number of arrests were made. From the windows of their houses the Jews boo-ed the police as we did our job, and many buckets of slops were hurled at us. I well remember the cry of one woman, "Boo, boo, you whisky-drinking English."

Damage to the Railway

Some nights parties of police were sent down the railway line as Arabs were regularly blowing up bridges and destroying the track, a game Lawrence of Arabia had taught them during the 1914-18 War. This was by no means a popular duty for we would leave on the last train down at 5 pm, get off and lie in ambush along the track near some culvert or bridge, and wait for the early morning train to take us back to Jerusalem. We seldom saw anyone apart from a few shepherds, for the wreckers would go on a few miles further down the line and do their damage there. Often a bridge was blown further down the line so that the morning train could not get through and we were stranded for hours. Then some small Ford cars were fitted with train wheels to enable them to run along the railway and they became our patrol cars. After that we were never late for breakfast!

There was a good canteen in the Kishleh where we spent a lot of our time when off duty, though always on call, and even though there was a curfew on, the Chief Superintendent also arranged for the International Café to be always open, so that we would have somewhere else to go to other than the canteen.

Artuf Under Siege

My next posting was back to Artuf, so at about 8 am on a summer morning, around the middle of 1938, I saddled up Dusty and rode out along the main Jaffa Road towards Bab el Wad [Gate of the Valley]. I travelled along as far as Enab and there the British Inspector decided it was too risky for me to be alone. He provided me with an escort of Supernumerary Arab Police as far as Bab el Wad. There, waiting at the café, a party from Artuf had come up to meet me and escort me along the track. It was a terribly hot day, and coming down about 1,500 ft to the plains I felt the heat rather badly, as did Dusty, for we were both dripping with sweat when we arrived at the Police Post about 1 pm, and remained in this uncomfortable state until sunset.

The happy atmosphere about the place, which had struck me on my previous tour there, was now missing, and it was obvious that the monotony of the life there was putting the men on edge. There was now no village patrolling, for the strength of the rebel bands in the hills made it impossible for small parties of police to go out on patrol with any real hope of returning without loss. The personnel were used almost entirely as a garrison for the Jewish colony and they soon became bored, uninterested and lazy.

I set to work on a pile of timber which was given to me by the Jewish Muhktar, and built a set of jumps over which the horses could be exercised and at the same time provide some sport and interest for the men. The jumps proved to be a great success. In no time the men started to take an interest and soon we were holding impromptu gymkhanas. My little horse Dusty became a great jumper and a couple of years later he was famous all over Palestine at horse shows. Unfortunately, I lost him when I was promoted to Sergeant at Bethlehem, where there was no stabling at that time. Cons. "Percy" Hogg was lucky enough to get him and he and Dusty performed against the world famous White Russian horseman, Colonel Paul Rodzianko. Only on a judge's split decision did Dusty and Hogg lose first place in the dressage test. Here I have digressed, so we must get back to Artuf.

Preparations for an attack

By this time the i/c Post, still Arthur Stacey Barham, had been promoted to Sergeant – he eventually reached the rank of District Superintendent. Stacey was a very efficient policeman, and fluent in Arabic and Hebrew. He was respected both by Arabs and Jews. One afternoon a notable local Arab rode into the Post area on his grey mare and went to see Barham. He said, "I have always promised you that if you were in danger from the rebels I would let you know. Now I have come to fulfil that promise. You must get more men and arms from Headquarters. The rebels are coming to attack you and the Jewish colony and plan to wipe you out completely." He added that he had been ordered to produce 30 armed men to take part in the attack, though he did not want to do it, and, if he failed, the rebels would wreak vengeance on him and his village. He then left, saying that his advice must not be disregarded and he would not be able to visit again. He had obviously been very brave in coming to warn us.

The sergeant called me into the office and told me what he had learnt from the visitor. I was the only other Britisher fit at the time – the other three were suffering from malaria. He also acquainted the male Jewish population with the facts, stressing that the guards must maintain the utmost vigilance at night. Naturally the Jews were very concerned and they gathered together in small groups, talking between themselves in Hebrew, which I could not understand. After some time the Muhktar, Albert Bahore, approached the Sergeant, and with tears running down his face he told him that the colony had hidden some illegal arms. He added, "I know that, if you want to, you can put me in prison for this, but I think you should use these arms in the case of a serious attack, for it may well be that a few extra rifles could make all the difference between success and failure in the defence of the colony." Stacey replied, "Don't stand there crying, go and get the bloody rifles!"

Shortly after, four very good old German Mauser rifles were produced and a large milk churn full of ammunition. The rifles were covered in grease and we quickly cleaned them, made them ready for use and tested them for serviceability. Then, from a hole in a wall in a newly built house, the Muhktar produced another tin containing 50 locally manufactured hand grenades. The Jewish special constable wanted to go on leave to Jerusalem and, as he had a car, Stacey let him go and asked him to deliver a message by hand to HQ informing them that we were expecting an attack and asking for reinforcements.

That night, just after midnight, the guards reported that they could hear men approaching the colony. Every man was alerted and positioned for defence, and our fingers were ready on the triggers. We waited until the approaching men were just near our perimeter and a challenge was shouted. Our surprise can be well imagined when the challenge was answered in English, with, "This is the Black Watch Regiment. Don't open fire". We held our fire and another constable and I went down the track to meet the new arrivals and make certain it was not a trap. Sure enough it was a special platoon (about 30 men) of that famous Scottish regiment, which had come down in the dead of night and walked across the hills to reinforce the colony defenders. The officer in charge, Lt. Bernard Fergusson, was a very young man, and all the personnel of this platoon were hand picked for their shooting and grenade throwing skills. All wore soft shoes so they could move silently.

About an hour later, sounds of hammering iron could be heard coming from the direction of the railway line, about 1 km to the south. It was a bright, moonlit night and the officer could make out a lorry parked near the railway bridge through his binoculars. It was instantly assumed that the rebels were dismantling the bridge and a party went to investigate. However, on arrival at the spot we found we were on a wild goose chase. The metallic ringing came from the driver hammering on the steel rim of his wheel, having just repaired a puncture!

Next day the soldiers left for their barracks and we received reinforcements. Five extra constables[1] arrived increasing our strength to 10 men. We also received another Lewis machine gun, bringing our total to two. Now we were in a fair position, for with Jewish Special Police and the colonists, we could muster 30-odd armed men and two machine guns to give crossfire. We felt we could give a very good account of ourselves.

Attack on the Railway Station

During the night similar sounds to those heard the previous night came from the vicinity of the railway station. Our Sergeant decided it might well be another lorry driver repairing his vehicle and decided to take no further

---

[1] including Chalmondley-Spears, Max Cable, Lawrence and McDade.

Artuf 1938. Left to right: "Titch" Reading, "Matey" Martin and Lawrence. Cons. Lawrence was later killed by a young Jew during a riot in Jerusalem, the first of many hundreds to be killed by Zionist terrorists.

action. He had received orders from HQ not to leave the colony after dark but remain on the defensive. A few minutes later flames shot up from the railway station buildings, and in a short time the whole place was on fire. In the light of the fire, scores of men could be seen milling around and both our machine guns went into action. The incendiaries were driven off but the fires had taken a good hold, and after a short time all that remained of the buildings were the brick walls. Information was received a few days later that three men had been hit, two fatally, and they had been buried in the hills.

It was a fortunate thing that we had not been out to attack that night, for we learnt that the rebel leader had placed 100 men in the gully which ran between us and the railway, ready to ambush us and kill us at close range. The most we could have sent out was about 10 men, and against 100 lying in an almost perfect entrenchment, our chances of survival would have been very slight indeed. A serious attack on the colony never developed. We experienced only what might be termed nuisance raids, when a few armed men would open fire on us at a few hundred yards range.

One night, about 10 o'clock, a guard reported that he thought he had noticed something on a chalky white footpath below the colony and near to an old disused factory. A searchlight was turned on and swept the area, but nothing could be seen, and as many jackals and hyenas frequented the area, nothing more was thought of the report. However, about 15 minutes later a fire was seen in the old factory. We opened fire with the Lewis gun and soon the fire died down. Then an Arab was heard shouting orders to get the fire started properly. Most of our arms were then turned on the factory and the rebels returned the fire on us, resulting in a lively few minutes. Through it all one Arab must have made his way back to the factory and restarted the fire, for soon the whole place was ablaze. In the meantime the Arabs were calling out and cursing us as "sons of dogs and harlots", to which we replied with equally choice expressions.

The excitement died down as suddenly as it had started, and soon all was peace and quiet once more. Our sergeant was a bit upset about it all and said so to me. He had had explicit orders not to leave the colony, or go outside the perimeter fence, after dark. But, after what had happened, the Jews in the colony were whispering amongst themselves, saying that we were afraid to go out and, if we had done, we could have saved the building and machinery.

About this time, two young constables, Chalmondley-Spears and "Titch" Marchant, were very angry about the situation in the area. We used to get a weekly overseas digest of the *Daily Mirror*, and they decided to write a letter to the *Mirror* for publication, saying they were, "stationed in, and guarding the Artuf Settlement, and not allowed to go outside the barbed wire at night. We do not feel it is right to just be guarding the Jewish settlement while some Arabs are being attacked by armed bands and we are doing nothing to protect them." The letter was sent off but I do not think it was published. Chalmondly-Spears signed himself "Finch-Folks" and Marchant something like "Jack Smith"!

Another day, soon after, as the police car which brought our rations was coming along the track, it ran into a large body of Arab rebels crossing the track on foot. A brisk action ensued. Fortunately none of the police was injured but there were casualties in the rebel band. As the car party was only three strong, it was necessary for them to make a lightning strike, and move out, before the band had time to re-organise.

By this time we had been supplied with a wireless transmitter set and also an ordinary radio receiving set. Nightly, we would listen to the news, and never a day passed without some announcement being made of actions that had taken place between the rebels and the Government forces. Sometimes, heavy rebel casualties were reported and it seemed that at last the Government was gaining the upper hand.

Curfew in Jerusalem

On taking a few days' leave in Jerusalem, and arriving by bus in the city about 11 am one morning, I left my transport in Mamillah Road and started to walk towards our Divisional Police HQ. I felt it was strange that there were so few people about. I seemed to be the only one walking down the road, and then it occurred to me that something was wrong and possibly a curfew had been imposed. I was in civilian clothes, and looking up at the Old Citadel walls I saw a Highland soldier very carefully aligning the sights of his rifle on me. I was indeed, without knowing it, a curfew breaker and liable to be shot. I quickly stepped into the doorway of a shuttered shop, which gave me some protection. Each time I looked to see if the way was clear the soldier took aim. I had to stay there for half an hour until Cons. MacDonald, a British Policeman I knew, came by in uniform. He shouted to the soldier not to fire and escorted me on my way.

It was not an enjoyable leave. The rebels had taken over the Old City and the military were engaged in an operation to drive them out and restore our Government to the locality. Curfew was in force most of the time and after about four days I was glad to return with the ration car back to Artuf.

—

The old Arab constable at the post, Ahmed Arekat, came to talk to me with a look of consternation on his face. The villagers were all saying that the British Government was paying money to the rebels to keep them fighting, for it was good training for the soldiers! He asked me if I thought that this was possible. I replied, "No," but he countered that the British Government was very strong, and if it so desired the trouble in Palestine could have ended in a few weeks. However, this was a civil disturbance and not a war, and I believe the Government wanted to contain it with as little force as possible and not use all its might, so as not to alienate the indigenous population completely. I did my best to assure Ahmed that HMG would do no such thing as encourage the disturbances. However, he had sowed some seeds of doubt in my mind – for it was around the time of the Munich Crisis: Neville Chamberlain had paid his visit to Hitler and the war clouds were gathering in Europe.

Stacey and Cons. Dance were talking about the possibility of whether or not there would be a war. Stacey thought there would be one and Dance there would not. They each outlined their reasons for thinking the way they did, and when they had finished Dance said, "I don't know, talking to you and listening to your arguments, you have pretty well convinced me that there will be a war." But Stacey replied, "On the contrary, you have made me change my views and I don't think there will be one!"

Regiment in Retreat

A few days later, during the afternoon, the lookout reported heavy firing from the valley through which the railway line ran. Going up onto the roof, I saw many men moving along the railway line, across the open ground at the mouth of the valley. Through the binoculars they were identified as British troops. It became clear that the army had been making a drive through the hills and had contacted a band of armed Arab rebels. This gang had kept up a running battle, from the hills, with the soldiers for over five miles – while the troops made their way down the railway track in the valley. Then, as the troops were withdrawing from the valley and coming towards Artuf, one soldier was hit in the back and died instantly. His body was brought into the colony. Shortly after, the transport arrived to convey the regiment, of about 500 men, back to Jerusalem.

I was very surprised by the manner in which the withdrawal was effected. No covering fire seemed to have been given and it appeared to me that the soldiers had hardly fired a shot in return for the rebel fire. The soldiers were exhausted and the snipers appeared to have had a good day's sport. The incident illustrated just how strong the rebels were in the hilly districts and were a force to be reckoned with.

Autumn changed to winter and soon Christmas 1938 was upon us, to bring us a little good cheer. There was a slight, if steady, improvement in the state of public security in the country. Many of the Arab villagers, who had been pressed into the rebel forces, were becoming disenchanted with the life – especially as the winter rains set in – and returned to their villages to plant their crops. We enjoyed a lively time over the festive season, and at a party on Christmas Night, when we went to the Colony to man the strong points on the roofs of houses, we were entertained by some of the members who sang to us songs in Hebrew, Spanish and French. My old friend Gabriel Levy, in spite of his advancing years, lustily sang in French. But as the night wore on, some good voices were wasted on us as we became somewhat inebriated by an over-indulgence of good liquor. We drank right through Christmas Night until we saw the sun rise on Boxing Day. Then my old friend and Sergeant said, "It's time we went to bed."

1939 Bethlehem market.

Chapter 6
On to Bethlehem and then Home on Leave

Early in January 1939, I was promoted to the rank of sergeant and so was transferred from Artuf to Bethlehem, where a new station was being opened. The old Police Station had been burnt down by the rebels, in the height of the troubles in mid 1938, and the Arab police had been evacuated.

Station Personnel

A large house had been taken over as the new station building in Bethlehem. It was built in the Arab style with a flat roof and a large hall with rooms leading off it. The charge counter was placed across the hall and the areas behind were office and living quarters.

When I joined the Palestine Police Force at the end of March 1936, the establishment was 600 British personnel, but by the end of that year it had been increased to 1,000 men. Then during 1938 it had doubled to 2,000. The educational standard for recruits had been much reduced, as had the minimum height, from 5ft 10ins to 5ft 7ins. Many of the new intake were ex-regular soldiers. Some were excellent men but many were found to be quite unfit for police work and were discharged in a very short time and sent home to the UK. This new station was staffed by one British inspector, Inspector Adams,[1] three sergeants and 20 of the new recruits – who had only spent a short period of two weeks in the Police Training School. The senior sergeant was "Nebi"[2] Samuel, and Ben Sharp and I were the junior sergeants.

Station Under Attack

We had to try to win the confidence of the inhabitants of Bethlehem who were mainly Christian Arabs, and to this end we sergeants would take out parties of our new constables and introduce them to try to gain the people's confidence and respect. Fairly quickly we found that they began to confide in us and give us useful information, and we hoped for an early return to normality. However, we soon had a rude awakening. One evening at the beginning of March, I had gone to bed early hoping for a good night's sleep, having been constantly on call and out on active duty the previous 24 hours. Shortly after midnight, I was awakened by a terrific banging, which seemed to be caused by stones being thrown at the front-door of the station. At first I thought some constables may have been out late and were trying to attract the attention of the guards. Then I heard that the sound of banging was accompanied by the tinkling of broken glass falling to the floor, and realised that the station was being "shot up". I immediately hopped out of bed and

---

[1] Inspector Adams, one of the old-timers, had a hook for a left hand which had been blown off by a Mills-type bomb he was investigating – so of course we called him "Captain Hook".
[2] Nebi [Prophet]

A woman of Bethlehem.

Reading the news. Hard-working Jerusalem street porters waiting for customers. They worked all day carrying very heavy loads.

made my way onto the flat roof. The three constables, who were on guard with the machine gun, were peering over the parapet, and told me they were being fired on at very close range but could not see from where. Then I spotted a flash from rifle fire through the trees in our neighbour's garden. I fired a light from the Verey light pistol – which explodes like a slow-burning firework, providing a bright light as it descends – and the man with the machine gun also fired a burst.

Then Inspector Adams came on the scene and sharply ordered us to stop firing, adding that it was a waste of ammunition. Sgt. Samuel, who had come up just after me, turned to him and asked, "What! Do you think we'd better throw stones at them?" The reason for the inspector's wrath, it transpired, was that he had asked permission for his wife to come to Bethlehem, having claimed that all was now quiet and no danger existed. If I had not ordered fire on the attackers he could have kept the matter quiet, but now we would have to send an indent (order) for replacement ammunition and he feared that Police HQ would not let his wife come to Bethlehem. She would have to stay in the safety of the compound in Jerusalem.

As an NCO, and with the added responsibility that I now carried, I was really enjoying my job. Having passed my Lower Arabic, and now being able to talk to the local people and enjoy a conversation with them added greatly to the enjoyment. It was at this station that I first recorded a statement given to me in Arabic by a Bedouin who came in the night to tell me that he had just been knocked up by a gang and robbed. We then went out straight away to see what could be done. The new recruits on the strength appeared quite impressed with my apparent fluency and it earned me useful kudos and respect from them. I was only 24 at the time and many of my subordinates were several years older. They had spent years in India in the forces, and had seen action on the North-West Frontier, so it was necessary for me to know the job in order to command their respect.

Although we had now virtually been at war with the Arab people of Palestine over this vexed question of Jewish Immigration, there was a wealth of good feeling between us. Even though some of us might be shot and killed, there was no personal animosity. The local Arab Youth Club invited us to play football against them. It was not a bad match, but they were fitter and, I think, younger than we were, and they beat us five goals to two. There was no unpleasantness in the game, which I feel illustrates the point above.

Home Leave

About April, my first three-year tour in Palestine was then completed and I was due for United Kingdom leave. I delayed my leave-taking so that some very special friends[1] and I could all go on leave together. And what a leave it was! We saw the Cup Final (Portsmouth 3: West Bromwich Albion 1), The Derby (winner Blue Peter – but all we saw was the top of the jockey's cap over the crowd), a session of the World Billiards Championship (Joe Davis and Lindrum?), a Heavyweight Boxing Championship at White City and a Championship Cricket Match at Lords. Monty's uncle lent five of us a cottage in Newdigate in Surrey for a fortnight – and what fun that was. We had a peaceful time, mostly in the pub, taking on all comers at darts and shove ha'penny. The owners of the cottage were very worried that five young men might leave it in a shambles, but we, having served in a very disciplined force, spring cleaned that place as never before, even polishing all the pots till they shone. The owners later told Monty that they had never seen the cottage so "spick and span".

While in England, I noticed that many pubs had boxes on the bars to collect money for the Zionist cause. I learnt there was an association called the British Israelites which was supporting the Zionist Cause. I was astonished to find tracts and booklets on sale in churches advocating the setting up of a Zionist State in Palestine. I wondered what the Church of England was thinking of, and if they really knew of all the terrible trouble that this movement was causing the people in Palestine. Quite a lot of the Arab insurrection and violence had been reported in the British newspaper, without a proper explanation of the cause. My parents were naturally anxious for my safety, and it was hard to persuade even them, and my sisters and friends, that the Arabs were not as bad as they were reported to be in the press. People in England had no idea of the invidious situation we were in.

–

And so, as all good things come to an end, one day in June 1939, we were on board *SS Narkunda*, en route to Palestine once again. It is worth noting here that the *SS Narkunda* was carrying an IRA bomb in her hold. When she reached Calcutta the bomb blew up and set the ship's hold on fire! Luckily, she was in port at the time, and the fire was brought under control before the ship was badly damaged.

---

[1] including "Monty" Arthur J. Montgomery, "Taffy" Bryn Cole, Ray Kelly, Tom "Huck" Sawyer and "Burglar" Bill Williams (Bill had been in the British Cavalry in India and enjoyed his porridge. The word for porridge in India was *burgu* which became "Brug" and then "Burglar"!) Burg was about five or six years older than us and smart as a new pin.

Chapter 7

Jenin 1939

On arrival back in Palestine I was transferred to the Samaria District and posted to Jenin Police Station, where I remained for about four months, still as a foot policeman. The reader may recall the previously mentioned "Triangle of Terror". Jenin was at its apex. The Police Station was at that time in an old Turkish building, at the north-east end of the town, on the road to Affuleh. It was quite a large station being the divisional HQ, with about 100 Arab and British policemen on the strength – this included 30 mounted men and the rest were foot or MT (motor transport) police. ASP Paddy McGill, who replaced ASP Denton, was in charge when I first went there. Among my fellow sergeants were Mike Pattle, Dennis Toulson, "Lofty" Field, Alex Shand (who became a life-long friend) and Jack Ammonds (whom I met up with again via the old comrades association, and we continue to keep in touch).

Jenin had a population of about 3,000. The little town itself showed signs of the Government's wrath. It was in a shocking state, having the appearance of a front-line town in a modern war. Huge gaps were visible between the blocks of buildings and houses, while piles of rubble lay across the streets. This had been the result of Government action after Mr Moffat, the Assistant District Commissioner, had been assassinated at his office – it transpired on the orders of Abu Dorrah. Many men had been arrested and detained, while many buildings, including shops and offices, had been demolished as a punitive measure by the military. The Arabs had been forced to abandon their revolt and, surprisingly, a friendly atmosphere now prevailed in the town and the local Arabs, who are really a very amiable, easy-going people, seemed peaceful enough.

Small, armed gangs still roamed in the hills, however, and occasionally came into the vicinity of the town and fired on the army camp, which was situated on the north-west side of the town. When these minor attacks occurred the military usually drove off the attackers with a few well-placed mortar bombs, for they had the necessary ranges well calculated.

Village Searches

Five ex-rebels had joined forces with the police and military, and took part in village searches to identify wanted members of the population who had taken part in the disturbances. The operations were carried out in the following manner. A cordon of troops was thrown around a village in the small hours of the morning to prevent any persons from leaving; at dawn a party of police and troops entered the village and paraded all the male inhabitants at some convenient spot such as a threshing floor; then one of the ex-rebels, sitting concealed in a covered truck, indicated wanted men by tapping with a stick as the villagers were sent past in single file. In this way many really notorious men were arrested and placed in detention camps. All over the country these "cages" were full of *fellaheen*, many, I am sure, quite innocent.

At intervals officers of H.M. Forces reviewed the cases of inmates and set a proportion free. Any old man with an open, honest face was the first to be allowed out, but woe betide the unfortunate who was ugly and had a squint – for he was regarded as being the worst type and could be detained for months at a time. Pressure was applied and at times detainees were tempted with offers of release if they would disclose information as to where rebel arms caches were to be found. In this way hundreds of rifles the rebel armies had been using were located and confiscated and the Arab population was virtually disarmed.

The Circumciser

On one occasion when we were out on a village search operation, a professional boys' circumciser was detained while he was on his rounds, along with a number of other men, for screening. We learnt that he toured the country plying his skills where called for. He caused some mirth among several young army officers by demonstrating the method he used! His main instruments were an old cut-throat razor and a tablespoon, which he kept in a black Gladstone-type bag with the words "Boys Circumciser" boldly painted on the side in Arabic and English. He also produced his licence authorising him to perform the operations.

Bodies in a Grain Store

I noticed a police car which seemed to pay almost regular visits to our station, but I did not find out the object of these visits until several months later. One Saturday afternoon while I was in the station, an old Arab woman, accompanied by two young men, reported to me that her son was in a grain store near Arrabeh village. I asked the good lady why he didn't climb out and the woman replied that he was dead and there were two more bodies in the store. I passed this information onto the Assistant Inspector and was instructed by him to go out to see if the information was correct. If so, I was to return and render him a report.

I stated that I could not do this as if there *were* bodies in the store I should be bound to place a guard on it. The officer repeated the order to me and told me that if I refused he would put me on a charge. I replied that he could do no such thing because I was only obliged to obey all *lawful* orders, and if I just went and reported the bodies were there, they could subsequently be moved. The inspector, who was just walking by, asked what all the trouble was. He then went on to tell me that the police car I had seen previously had been engaged in taking out known political assassins to Arrabeh, where Fakri Bey Abdul Hadi, a powerful feudal lord, had killed them on behalf of the police, and it was likely that the bodies in question had been killed by Fakri.

I left for the grain store, which was an ancient structure cut down into the rock, possibly 20 feet deep and 20 feet across in the middle, with a narrow entrance covered by a flat stone. It was half filled with dirt and debris, on which, sure enough, were the three bodies in a state of decomposition – indicating that they had been dead for approximately two months. I covered in the store and returned to report. The old Arab woman was virtually bullied into giving a statement to the effect that she could not identify her son, and the findings of an inquiry convened were – "murder by person or persons unknown of other unknown persons." Case closed.

The White Paper, 1939

By now Malcolm MacDonald, the Colonial Secretary who visited Palestine incognito in 1938, had prepared his recommendations, which His Majesty's Government issued in the form of a White Paper. This provided for Jewish immigration into Palestine to continue at the rate of 15,000 a year for the next five years and after that it should cease completely. When this became known, the Arabs were jubilant and danced ecstatically in the towns and villages. They were prepared to accept this, as a mere 75,000 more Jews could be absorbed without causing many Arabs to be displaced. During the past three years it was estimated that 5,000 Arabs had been killed by Government forces, but now that a solution to their problems had been found, the Arabs felt that their struggle had been worthwhile.

The Death of Constable Lawrence

For the Jews it was a different story. Soon we were to find that, if not facing Arab insurrections, we were now having to deal with Jewish acts of terrorism. A young British constable named Lawrence was the first of our Force to be killed by the Jews. He served with me when I was stationed at Artuf and was a very nice young man. He was in a party of police in Jerusalem, where Jews were demonstrating against the White Paper. The unarmed police advanced to disperse the demonstrators and a young Jew pulled out an automatic pistol and shot young Lawrence in the stomach. He died almost straight away. He was the first of some hundreds to be killed by Zionist terrorists.

Destruction of the *Sinbad*

Possibly the first planned Jewish terrorist act was the blowing up of the police launch *Sinbad*. This boat was one of a small flotilla operated by the Police Port and Marine Division, and primarily used to prevent smuggling and illegal immigration. Illegal immigration had, of course, been going on for years and literally thousands of Jews must have entered Palestine in this way.

On this particular duty the *Sinbad* had left Haifa and was patrolling off Nathanya, a Jewish seaside town, when she blew up and immediately sank. The skipper, B/Sgt. King, was killed and several of the crew were injured. However they just managed to cut the dinghy adrift before the launch sank and get ashore in it. It seems that the bomb had been carried aboard the boat in a can of paint and timed to explode while the launch was out at sea on patrol. When the survivors reached the shore at Nathanya, they were objects of interest to the Jewish inhabitants, but even though several were injured they were refused a drink of water in the town.

Ambush at Jenin

At about the same time, while we were playing football one afternoon, there was quite a bit more than the usual sporting excitement. While the game was in progress, shots were heard well away to the east of the plain, towards Beisan. Closer inspection revealed what appeared to be a lorry racing towards the town at breakneck speed, enveloped in a cloud of dust. When the lorry reached the sports field it was found to contain five very badly wounded policemen. One was B/Sgt. Wilson of the Nazareth CID and the remaining four were Arab constables. Sgt. Wilson said he had gone out with Cons. King and the Arab constables to arrest a man wanted by the Beisan police. They had used an Arab civilian lorry so as to avoid detection as they neared the village where the man was to be found. On their return an armed gang had ambushed them. Constable King had stepped off the lorry to engage the attackers and was shot dead immediately. The remainder of the party had all been injured in the first volley fired at them. The driver of the lorry drove off as more shots were fired, causing still more injuries. They were too weak to be able to bring back King's body, so we went out and brought it in, but the band had moved off. Sgt. Wilson was dressed by the Government doctor and sent to Nazareth hospital, where he died that same night. The doctor remarked to me what a brave man he was to have suffered the intense agony which he must have been in so uncomplainingly.

War with Germany and a kind of Peace comes to Palestine

War with Germany, which many of us had been expecting for about six months, was then declared, on September 3rd 1939, and the Palestine Government deemed it necessary to deal with the remaining gangs. Military and police patrols began to comb the countryside and it seemed to be our lot to spend countless nights out of bed, out in the hills. However, our efforts were rewarded and in a short time these robber bands were wiped out. I noticed, by their features, that most of the robbers shot dead were former African slaves, or their offspring, from Turkish times. Although they were treated well by the general population they were regarded as lower class, and consequently found banditry attractive. Up to 1917 slavery was common and legal, but by the time of which I write, some of the dead bandits were in their middle age, their first 20 years having been lived in slavery.

Peace Overtures – an Army Band Concert!

Now that war had been declared, an attempt was made by the Government to enlist the sympathy of the Arabs towards the Allied cause and to let bygones be bygones. In Jenin, the first evidence of this new policy was an Army Band Concert in the main square to which all were welcome. The Assistant District Commissioner and the District Officer were well in evidence, and provided coffee and sweetmeats for all the notables of Jenin, and also of the villages in the outlying area. It was, without doubt, a good gesture on the part of the authorities, and although the music may not have been entirely to the taste of the Arab ear, it did at least appeal, especially the vocal rendering of "In a Persian Market" – references to "bahksheesh", of course, being appreciated and understood!

Several speeches were made on both sides. The Military Commander said he hoped there would be a friendly spirit in the town and that his troops may assist local business by making purchases in the shops. Other speeches stressed to us all the dangers of a Nazi victory. Fahkri Bey Abdul Hadi, who had been a rebel army commander, spoke on behalf of the Arabs in Jenin District. He said that while the danger from Nazi Germany lasted, Great Britain could count on the loyal support of the Palestine Arabs. The only argument they had with Britain was over the question of a National Home for the Jews, and apart from this they, the Arabs, knew that there wasn't a better government in the world than the British. It is important to note that Fakri did appear to express the general view of the population – that they did not plan to take advantage of the war to try to gain any national aspirations during the period of hostilities with Germany.

The irony of the situation was not lost on an old shopkeeper friend of mine, who had his business close to our billet. He remarked to me, "Last year you were blowing up our houses and shops, and now you are courting us with your band concert!" I once remarked on his very pretty little daughter and he agreed, saying that his wife had come from Cyprus where very pretty Turkish brides were to be found. I asked how many wives he had and he replied, just one for, *"Ma wahad besire eshway ahub"* [With one there grows a little love]. Every bride has a price, but the more honourable families keep the money paid to them safely to one side, so that if the marriage does not work out, the bride has that money to fall back on.

Yousef Hamdan

One rebel band which had caused the authorities great concern was led by

Jenin 1939: Army Band concert – a peace overture!

95

Jenin 1939: Arab District Officer and Arab Notables outside Jenin Police Mess on the day of the Army band concert.

Yousef Hamdan of Umm el Fahm village. He was, I believe, quite a patriot, but had been involved in various acts of violence and there was little chance of him receiving an amnesty. He had been on the run for months and had always been successful in evading capture. I remember going after him one afternoon with a party of police and troops, after we had received information that he was visiting his wife in a small hamlet at the back of Rumaneh, about 12 miles from Jenin. We tried to surround the hamlet but he must have had a lookout posted for, as we neared the place where he was with his lady, he suddenly rushed out of the house through a small garden and on to where he had left his mare untethered. He leapt on her back and galloped away across the rocky valley and then up an equally rocky hill. He was fired on by at least a score of men, but when he reached the summit he reined in his mount and shouted a farewell to us, "*Masalameh ya shabab*," [Farewell young men], adding he would probably see us again next week! After that bravado he rode over the horizon and by the time we reached the top of the hill, he had completely disappeared. I never managed to get close enough to see him well, but I am told that he was a very handsome, smart chap. He certainly had courage, which won my respect.

Geoffrey "Geoff" Morton, a courageous, much respected and famous Palestine Police officer – among members of the Force – detained Yousef Hamdan inadvertently one day when he was ASP in charge of Jenin. Geoff published his memoirs, *Just the Job*, in 1957. It included a description of Yousef Hamdan; I quote, "a distinguished-looking man in his fifties, very well dressed in silken robes and riding boots of exquisite quality, and with a richly decorated saddle on his fine Arab mare." Geoff was able to fall into conversation with Yousef, before he knew who his companion was – as Yousef Hamdan had given a false name and home village – and found him to be "most cultured and agreeable." He was allowed to "escape" custody and was handed over to Orde Wingate,[1] then a captain in the Royal Artillery. With a special party they "chased round each night for weeks on end, setting ambushes, at spots indicated by Yousef, but only on one occasion did they get near a gang of rebels… when Yousef called out something in Arabic… which the rest of Wingate's party did not understand … The band (which was led by Abu Dorrah – Commander-in Chief of the Northern rebels – in person) melted into the night." A while later, Geoff continued, "Yousef actually did escape … with much-enhanced prestige and a good insight into the military operational methods and returned to his old haunts in the Jenin/Haifa borders."

---

[1] Orde Charles Wingate, Major General. Organised various companies of irregular soldiers, including Special Night Squads of British soldiers and Jewish irregulars during the Arab Rebellion 1937-38, also in Abyssinia, and in Burma against the Japanese in the Chindit campaigns deploying Long Range Penetration forces behind enemy lines. Ref. Liddell Hart Military Archives : King's College, London – internet site.

To return to my story, some weeks later another operation was planned and, using troops and policemen, Yousef Hamdan and his gang were caught and killed in a valley just west of his village. Among the arms recovered that day was the revolver of Cons. King, who was killed in the ambush when Sgt. Wilson was injured. Yousef had had a good run for his money, and it was said he had made quite a pile. It was rumoured that he had been paid £50 a month by Spinneys – the firm that delivered the police rations – to allow safe conduct to those employed on the job.

The body of Yousef lies buried in the village cemetery at El Lejjun – close to Umm el Fahm. Over his grave a tombstone has been erected bearing an epitaph in Arabic which can be translated thus –

> Here lies Yousef Hamdaneh,
> He that was *hameh* [hot].
> When he saw the government forces
> He became bold and courageous,
> And when he died
> The mountains became sad and angry.

It was a fitting memorial, I feel. However, the Arab sergeant who read the inscription out to me was unprintably uncomplimentary!

The reasons for the now rapid defeat of these bands were twofold: firstly, the publication of the White Paper which had removed the Arabs' anxiety over their future, and, secondly, many bands had deteriorated into robbers, highwaymen and extortionists. Consequently, the authorities received the necessary information to track down, and arrest or kill, the miscreants. Some surrendered and were dealt with fairly leniently, but many stated openly that they preferred to fight to the end with their leaders. They chose to be decently fed and retain the respect of the population, rather than live the life of an underdog or shepherd on the hills in all weathers.

Station Sergeant

About this time Mike Pattle, the Station Sergeant, was given compassionate leave to go home as his father had died. I was now promoted from Duty Sergeant, "one of the mob" who received the instructions, to Station Sergeant, looking after the books and station registers and issuing day-to-day instructions. The considerable administrative work involved was very good experience for the future. As the disturbances had greatly reduced, normal police work resumed, and some rebuilding took place in Jenin town.

The Jenin Cinema

The Jenin weekly cinema was a very popular event in the town. The mobile unit, which used to visit the station every week, was first engaged by ASP Geoff Morton, when he was i/c Jenin. Alex Shand, a fellow Duty Sergeant, ran the cinema which was really the only form of entertainment imported into the town. The most convenient place to set up the screen was in the "lock-up" yard – a large open rectangular space with cells all around. In the evening, when it was dark and the prisoners confined to their cells, the screen was put up at one end and the forms and chairs arranged opposite it. It was mainly intended for the police but, in order to increase the gate money, the male members of the local population were also allowed in to watch the film for a small fee. Small boys were allowed in for one piastre and adult men, three piastres. Of course, many wanted to claim they were boys and so enter for a reduced fee, so a British policeman used to feel the chins of the boys. If he decided they had started to shave they had to pay the full entrance fee. The prisoners in the lock-up had a free show. Often as many as 20 faces would be pressed against the grills of their doors, hoping to get a glimpse of Deanna Durbin in "The Three Smart Girls", or Charles Laughton in "Mutiny on the Bounty". It was all good fun and helped to improve relations between police and public. Alex replaced me as Station Sergeant when I left Jenin.

Music and Entertainment

When I hear certain pieces of music and songs, they take me right back to Palestine days. For example, "The Birth of the Blues" played on the piano, takes me back to Mount Scopus when I was a new recruit. Harold Daring was playing that tune the first time I walked into the recreation room. Later in MeaShearim mess, Norman Carswell (Cons. 379) used to entertain us with "Moonlight and Roses", his signature tune, accompanied on his banjulele! After we had left Palestine, at one of our Old Comrades' get-togethers, when we had been singing various songs, someone started to sing "The Holy City", and by the time he had got to the last verse and chorus, the whole party had joined in. Since that time it has become a tradition that we always sing "The Holy City" at all our Old Comrades' meetings.

I particularly remember our Free Nights in the Jenin British Billet. Spinney, the catering contractors, would pay a percentage towards the canteen fund and when it amounted to a certain sum we would have a party. The District Commissioner and other guests would be invited. The sandwiches and a couple of drinks would be free, and various members would be persuaded to perform their party pieces – sing songs, perform tricks or recite poetry; Kipling was popular, particularly the ballad "Gunga Din". Arnold, a big Cockney driver, would be asked to sing "Cinderella". "Go on Arnold, give us '"Cinderella"!" was the general cry. "No! No!" he would reply. Later they would call again, "What about 'Cinderella' now?" "Alright," he would say, and then stood up to sing,

"Sty in me aums Cin'erella
"My be Oim tha' fella, Prince Chawmin'.

"Since Oi met you Oi'v bu' wan design,
"Yaw weddin' shoes nex' t' mine.
"Midnigh' of midnigh's an' so divine.
"Cin'erella, sty in me aums."

One song we all joined in was, "Hi, Hi, Kathusalem, Harlot of Jerusalem!" Green, an ex-public school boy, who had a great store of filthy songs, was entertaining us one evening when the Padre was also invited – possibly not the most appropriate entertainment for our guest! (Green went on accelerated promotion somewhere down in Africa, after blowing out the windows in Police HQ in Jerusalem – while experimenting with chemicals. The Inspector General said, "Get him out of here, quick!" The CID officer suggested, "Don't be too hard on him, Sir. He may have been on the verge of a great discovery!")

The Palestine Police had a very fine band that played the necessary accompaniment at recruit passing out parades, though not for our squad, which was ordered to leave with half an hour's notice - some to Jaffa and some to Tulkarem - during the time of the '36 "Disturbances". The Band not only played military music but also dance music, jazz and orchestral music. It was under the command of conductor A.S.P. Aubrey Harris Silver, a London Jew who had served in the Royal Fusiliers in Palestine in World War 1. Most of the bandsmen were Russian Jews. Occasional soloists, such as vocalist "Boop" Horward ("Boop-a-doop" was a singing style of the time) performed with the band from time to time. Boop was a fellow Sergent in the Jenin mess when I was there.

–

Being on the Foot Branch at Jenin, I missed my mounted patrols, though the Customs officer was good enough to let me exercise his horse from time to time. However, the mounted branch was beginning to operate fully again and, as I felt this kind of work was by far the best and healthiest the Force offered, I applied to re-join as I was anxious to get back in the saddle.

Fakri Bey[1] Abdul Hadi

But before we leave Jenin, I must record the story of Fakri Bey Abdul Hadi, previously mentioned as the local rebel commander. He really is worth a book to himself. In Turkish times, his family had been feudal lords, and even at the time of which I write, Fakri Bey was the Lord of Arrabeh, the village where he lived. He was a very rich man, though not all his wealth had been acquired honestly, he having at one time been a robber baron, and tales were told of him having been the most notorious robber in the whole of Samaria.

He could be a cruel and callous man as one story, purported to be true,

---

[1] Bey – Lord, Master, Sir

concerning a rifle that he had bought some years previously illustrates. Before he would pay the price asked, Fakri Bey said he must test the gun. He stepped outside the house with the weapon and spotted a shepherd on a nearby hill. Taking careful aim at the poor unfortunate, he squeezed the trigger and shot the shepherd dead. He was apparently delighted and gleefully paid the sum asked for the gun, exclaiming that it was a grand weapon and perfectly accurate!

When the 1936 rebellion started, Fakri Bey was one of the leading generals under Fawzi ed Din Kauwakji, who commanded the rebel army. He led his own command against the British troops in many a skirmish and was always spoken of as a lionhearted man. When further fighting broke out, in 1937/38/39, Fakri was again among the leaders. Later, when the gang leaders began to extort money and valuables from the general Arab population, Fakri was still very active and it was said that he was merciless to anyone who failed to subscribe to what he termed his "just demands". Even his own relatives were fleeced of their possessions, or abducted and placed in rat-infested pits if they refused or were unable to pay.

As the months dragged on and it became apparent that the Arab revolt could not be sustained much longer, Fakri decided to save his skin and move over to the Government camp. He received a free pardon and in return gave much useful information and assistance. He then returned to his life as a feudal baron at his home in Arrabeh, where he retained a strong, armed bodyguard. He entertained there, on a most lavish scale, many high-ranking Government and military officers.

Some time around 1940, a young servant girl employed in his household became pregnant and Fakri's son, Shawki, was regarded as the man responsible. One day the girl came to a mysterious end, an accident it was claimed, while she was cooking over a primus stove, and she burned to death. I had left the station by then and Sgt. Alec Shand went to the village to investigate. Suspicion naturally fell upon Fakri and his son, but no conclusive evidence could be found to support the case against them. Any member of the household who may have known the truth was scared to death to breathe a word about it. Consequently, no charges were preferred – it was just the life of a servant girl, a rich man's plaything, and what did it matter to such a man as Fakri?

However, he that lived by the sword himself came to a violent end, when Fakri was shot and killed at his son's wedding feast. The great day arrived in 1943 when Shawki was to be married. A gigantic wedding feast was prepared, and about 2,000 guests attended. They arrived by car, lorry, bus, on horseback or donkey, or humbly a-foot. Officers of the British Army were there and also many notable Government officials. Drink flowed freely, for although Fakri was a Moslem he was no teetotaller. Horsemen galloped and wheeled around in the open, calling out challenges to others to race them. Then, when the festivities were at their height, Fakri came to a similar end to that which he had brought to many a life. One of his near relatives, a young nephew named Hilmi, drew his gun and shot the great overlord dead. Hilmi was arrested and charged with murder. At his trial he was convicted and sentenced to death. Hilmi appealed against his sentence and, while the appeal was being heard, it was rumoured that he was to be reprieved. A few days later, in Nablus town, three gunmen entered a factory and shot three of Hilmi's relatives dead. A car was waiting in readiness and the three made good their escape. It must be assumed that Shawki was among the three murderers for he disappeared. After this tragedy Hilmi was reprieved and Shawki, son of Fakri, became a fugitive from justice. It was rumoured that he fled to Saudi Arabia, for pilgrims to Mecca occasionally said they had seen him when they returned.

One day in 1943, when I was stationed in El Lejjun shortly after the murder of Fakri, while I was out on patrol and visiting an Arab village, the conversation turned to his death. Many village elders had stood in great awe of him and on this day they were saying what a great man he had been. They praised his memory and the many acts of daring and courage that he had shown during his life. As often appears to be the way with mankind, we seem to remember the best and forget the worst. Shakespeare wrote, "The evil that men do lives after them, the good is oft interred with their bones." I wonder if this is true?

For my own part I will say that at one time I thought Fakri to be totally evil, and certainly he committed many evil acts. But things are not always as simple as they first appear to be, and he should be judged in the circumstances in which he lived. I once met him in the Jenin police mess. He was a handsome man, well-mannered and full of self-assurance. He was tall and slim with a very neat, small moustache, and dressed impeccably in a suit. He would have fitted the bill of a romantic bandit chief, in something like a production of "The Desert Song", perfectly. He was a man who will be remembered.

My request to re-join the Mounted Branch was granted and so, after a few months of office work at Jenin, another chapter for me was concluded when I received orders to leave for Givat Olga, a newly-built Coast Guard Station near Hadera.

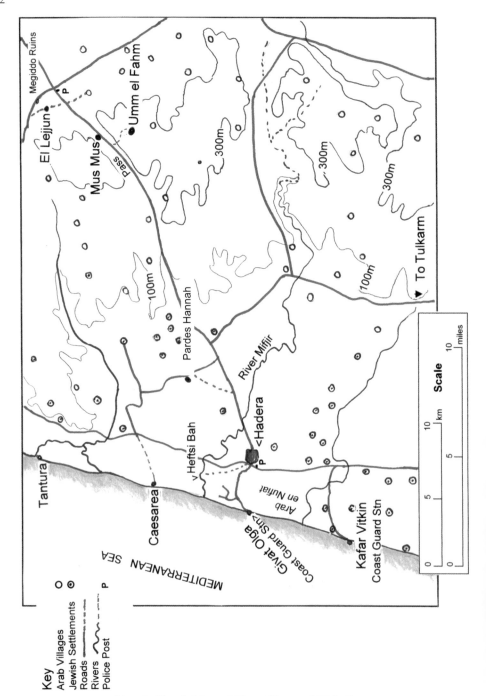

Map 2: Sketch Map of Givat Olga and El Lejjun

Chapter 8
Givat Olga – Coastguard Station 1940 –1942

Givat Olga Coastguard Station was one of four new stations built along the coast, primarily to keep a check on Jewish illegal immigration. Bill Shevlin had been there under canvas while the station was being built, but he was on the list to be married and as there were no married quarters at Givat Olga, he moved to Haifa.

Palestine in the War Zone

The stations had been planned when the White Paper on Jewish immigration was to be implemented, but now, however, with the outbreak of war, there was little illegal immigration by sea, for by mid-1940 Italy had entered the war in support of Hitler's Germany and the Mediterranean was no place for immigrant ships. Before the war many cargoes of Jews had disembarked along this stretch of coastline, and after having been in the country no more than an hour or so they would all be accepted into some settlement and the authorities would hear no more of them. However, at the time I assumed command of Givat Olga, the British Forces were being evacuated from Dunkirk and things looked very black for Britain. Our work now was mainly checking on drug smuggling and watching for likely intrusions of enemy agents into Palestine. It was felt likely that the Italians would invade the country, for it was well known that they intended to occupy Palestine and Egypt, and much propaganda to this effect was printed and distributed by them amongst the Arabs.

The Italian Airline, Ala Littoria, had a regular service between Palestine and Italy – up until the time Italy entered the war. Bombing raids were expected from Italian bases on Rhodes, so air raid precautions were taken and members of the public, British, Arab and Jew, were enrolled as air raid wardens. Shortly after this the storage tanks of the Iraq Petroleum Company at Haifa were bombed, setting them on fire and causing huge blazes and clouds of black smoke. When raids were expected, sirens sounded and wardens went into action, warning the public to take cover and not to panic. One Arab, patrolling the Kingsway in Haifa, called out as he went, *"Bikaffish, kul ishi min Allah."* [Fear not, all things come from God], to which a B/C wag replied, *"La ya sheikh, mush min Allah, min / Ala Littoria!"* [No sir, not from Allah, *ala* [from] Littoria!]

The police along the coast and hinterland were formed into air raid watches as one of our duties. A pair of binoculars was the total sum of our equipment, though we did of course have a Bren gun to shoot aircraft down, and we realised how much luck we needed. After a few weeks some enterprising Jews had devised, and persuaded the Government to buy, equipment they called "Aircraft Detectors". They were two plywood pyramids mounted on an upright and connected to earpieces, similar to those found on a medical stethoscope. I was away on a patrol when the detector was delivered and on my return I went aloft to see the new equipment. B/C Jack Dowson, a Yorkshire man with a dry sense of humour, was on duty, and when I asked him, "What's it like, Jack?" he replied, "Well *Shawish*, if you see the craft and you point this thing at it, when it gets near enough, you can hear it too!" This equipment was obviously tried out inland, where they did not take the sound of the sea into account. It amplified all sounds, including the sound of the surf, which drowned out the sound of the planes. I often wondered who it was who accepted the equipment on behalf of the Palestine Government.

With the outbreak of war the Police now came under Army Control regulations. Many British police who joined from the services, especially the Army, wanted to leave the Force and rejoin their old regiments to be with their old comrades. The OC Troops informed us that the work we were doing in Palestine was vital and we were not to leave the Force. He concluded his remarks by saying that if any left he would see to it personally that they would get the worst jobs! However, those who were determined to leave did so.

The Position of the Station and the Local People

The name Givat Olga is Hebrew, meaning Olga's Hill, and has its origin in the fact that a Jewish pioneer, one Joshua Hankin, had built a house for his wife, Olga, on the cliff nearby. It was a delightful spot, with cliffs about 60 ft high, overlooking two lovely little bays, situated midway between Haifa and Jaffa. Just behind the station were some ancient ruins, perhaps Greek or Roman, where I found a set of very beautifully made old bronze needles. The hinterland was mainly sand, which stretched up to 5 or 10 km inland. In places the sand was very loose – like quicksand – and difficult to cross. Scrub and grass had colonised much of the sand and as a result provided grazing for sheep and goats.

Sheikh Abu Fadil

The Arab en Nufiat tribe of the old Bedouin patriarch, Sheikh Abu Fadil, lived in tented camps in the sand dunes about 3 km from the station. In about 1890, the sheikh, with his new wife, had moved northwards to settle in the area. There was ample grazing for his goats, sheep and a few camels, as well as several horses. Here he pitched his black, goat hair Bedouin tent and set about raising his family away from the main tribe. His first few years were reasonably uneventful, apart from acquiring a second wife, and he watched his flocks increase while his wives presented him with several children. By the time I knew him he had four wives and his family numbered 148 souls. His wives were still producing his offspring, for he had lost a number of wives over the years, either by divorce or death, and he had replaced each one with a new, young wife as a vacancy occurred. He also had sons and daughters, grandsons and granddaughters who had married and were producing children of their own, while he, the old sheikh, continued to father more children of his own.

His four wives each had a tent and were settled at the corners of an area about one mile square. The sheikh told me that they didn't quarrel that way. He visited his wives in rotation, staying the night with each in turn. In the morning he would rest and chat with his family at that encampment, and then, after a midday meal, he would saddle up his mare and ride to the next wife. She would be expecting him and have his favourite meal ready soon after his arrival. These ladies knew his favourite dishes and always did their best to please the old man. He told me they had some special way of preparing chicken that he greatly enjoyed.

Sheikh Abu Fadil told me that he had seen both good times and bad during his lifetime, but the most terrifying experience he had known was during 1917, when the British Army was harrying the Turkish forces as they withdrew northwards, up the coastal plain. The British Navy was steaming up the coast and supporting the British troops with naval gunfire. Shells were falling all along the coastal hinterland and his famly were caught in this gunfire. "Perhaps," he suggested, "they mistook us for Turkish troops." But whatever the explanation, it was a horrific experience and he was sure his was going to die. With this thought in mind, he took his favourite wife to a small depression in the sand dunes and, clasped in each other's arms, they lay waiting for death as shells burst all around them. They agreed that if they were to die they would die together. They prayed to Allah and he answered their prayers for they survived. However, some of his family were injured and many sheep and goats were killed. With the end of the British Mandate the Bedouin have again to fend for themselves and I understand that many were driven away to the east, ever since unable to return to their homeland.

However, we will return to the Givat Olga area of the 1940s. Further inland, beyond the sand dunes, was the little town of Hadera, developed out of one of the original little Jewish settlements that dated back to Turkish times. Hadera had its own Police Post, and the sergeant/inspector i/c at that time was John Denley. Up the coast from Givat Olga was a small café, the seaside "resort" for Hadera. About 1 km inland from the café were the orange groves of Heftsi Bah plantation.

The Strength

The strength of the station was small, being 15 men. All were mounted apart from the wireless operator and Bob Barden the driver. The six British policemen included Tom Rishworth (the Second Sergeant), "Blondie" Bayliss, A. P. Cook, Jack Dowson, "Tug" Wilson and big "Ginger" Smy (a gentle giant who would sit with tears running down his face when listening to the record from the film of "Snow White" – then recently released). Sgt. Hassan Riati, a Bedu, and Corporal Farris were the Arab NCOs and there were six Arab constables. The constables were detailed as lookouts as part of their duties, and a permanent lookout of two men – one Arab one British – was posted on the top of the small tower. Sometimes at night the moonlight was so bright that Jack Dowson found that he could read a book while on watch, as his fellow lookout took turns to scan the sea. The remainder of the men of each watch were used to patrol about 30 miles of coastline. We used to patrol northwards up past Caesarea and on as far as Tantura. At Caesarea there were the remains of a very ancient port, including two marble steps going into the sea, down which, it was said, Cleopatra had walked to board a ship. There were several ancient columns in the sea that the Arab fishermen had repositioned to act as breakwaters. Up at Tantura, the village Muhktar had salvaged from a wrecked ship, *The Walls End*, the door to the saloon and installed it in his house, still with the word "Saloon" on it!

Saif

Our cook, Saif, was quiet and inoffensive and clean as a new pin, as well as being a very good cook. He had been taught his craft by Mrs. Bodell, who ran Bodell's Hotel at Port Said. He would often cook every day for three months at a time, without taking any leave. Then off he would go to Haifa and meet a few of his friends. He was not a big man, but once he had had a few drinks he would find himself engaged in a fight with a few of his companions. They would smash up a bar, so the police would have to be called, and he would finish up in court the next day before the magistrate. According to the severity of the offence, he would be charged and have to spend 7 or 14 days in prison. Consequently we were often left without a cook. I had to learn to cook so that I could help cover for Saif when he was off. Constable "Tug" Wilson had worked in a family hotel on the Isle of Man and had been sent to the London Cookery School for further training, which was situated opposite the Royal Artillery Barracks. While he was there he decided to join the Artillery and went to India instead, where he served seven years before joining the Palestine Police. He took turns to help with the catering and was able to give me some very useful cookery lessons, including how to cook roast beef, rock buns and pastry!

Sergeant Riati

Sgt. Riati had transferred from the Camel Corps section of the Palestine Police, based down in Beersheba [Bier Sabah – Seven Wells] in the Sinai.[1] Being a forward-thinking man he had learnt to speak and write English and had been advised that he would improve his promotion prospects if he switched from the Camel Corps to the Mounted Section. I got on very well with Hassan. He was about five or six years older than me and I greatly valued his knowledge and experience. It was Hassan who taught me a great deal about the stars and their Arabic names when on patrol at night. The Bedouin are very knowledgeable about the stars, as they use them to navigate the deserts at night.

There was an unwritten understanding in the Force that, in a patrol pair, the British member would be in charge, even if he was a constable and the Palestinian policeman a sergeant, but if the British policeman was not sufficiently experienced this could cause unpleasantness. I always used to ensure that Sgt. Riati would patrol with me to avoid any such difficulties. We always got on well together and developed a very good working relationship and friendship.

To begin with, Hassan's wife stayed with the tribe in the Sinai, but he discussed with me the possibility of bringing her up the Givat Olga, and hired a lorry to collect his family and his tent. At first, he pitched the tent in the station yard, but when DSP Jimmy James came on inspection he did not like the idea of the station looking like a Bedouin camp, so the tent was taken down and pitched on the sand dunes just outside the perimeter fence. It was very convenient for a water supply, as his wife was able to use the station tap, and I am sure that Sgt. Riati was happy to have his wife and family with him, but I used to think that they must have been quite lonely to be living away from the tribe.

Each man rode two night-patrols and one day-patrol each week. It was a most pleasant job during the summer months, riding along the cliff tops and seashore. We also rode inland, through the shade of the orange groves, which smelt wonderful in the spring, as far as Pardes Hannah – a little settlement of attractive houses amongst the orange groves and a very well run café. Here we would stop to rest the horses and put on the nosebags, and have a drink ourselves. Wintertime was not so easy, especially at night, for then the patrols sometimes rode about 40 miles out and back in pitch-black darkness,

---

[1] A British driver, Hawley, was sent down from Jaffa to the Camel Corp at Asluj in the Sinai, with a load of hay and fodder for the camels. He drove around all day in the featureless desert landscape, not able to ask directions, and had to return with a full load, saying, "Where's this bloody place Asluj?" He was, ever after, called "Asluj" Hawley.

1941: The River Mifr, half a mile up river from the coast, close to Hefsi Bah orange plantation.

1941: Givat Olga cove. Civil and Naval engineers inspecting an Italian mine.

1941: Sailing off Givat Olga.

without seeing even a single fisherman. At times the rivers, which we could normally cross quite easily at their mouths, became so swollen in the rains that is was necessary to swim the horses through raging torrents. Dangerous was this job then, and on one occasion the horse of Corporal Farris, I think it was, became frightened, and they were swept out to sea and almost drowned. Luckily the waves washed them back in again.

Behind the dunes, between Givat Olga and Kafr Vitkin, was a large depression that filled up with water during the late winter rains and became quite a lake. A large number of eucalyptus trees had been planted in the area to encourage drainage. It was known as the Rothschild Forest, after the benefactor who had made the planting possible. It was certainly a fine sight. In the spring this swampy area was the home to thousands of frogs who made a terrific din with their chorus of, "Quaar, quaar, quaar," like the crowd at a football match, as soon as the sun went down. But when you rode into the area the chorus would suddenly cease, and all would be quiet. Then, as you rode away they would all start up again.

The station itself was ideally situated and very healthy. Perched on the edge of the cliff top, it caught the sea breezes, so was seldom unpleasantly hot. While we were cool and comfortable, the temperature at Hadera, only four miles inland, was unbearable. The little bay below the station was surrounded by rocks and had a sandy floor. It was all that a swimming enthusiast could desire. To return from an all night coastal patrol and then dive into the sea and swim before breakfast well compensated the rider for his night's work. Much of my leisure time was spent in this "Blue Lagoon", either swimming or sleeping in the shade of the rocks.

Often at the end of a day-patrol we would take the horses in the sea for a swim. One Arab constable had a wonderful little swimming horse. This horse was so adept that his rider would set the him swimming out to sea and then slip off his back and just hold onto the horse's tail. They would swim so far out they would be almost lost from sight. Eventually, the rider would pull himself up on the horse's back, splash some water into one side of the animal's face and get it to turn round. He slipped off into the water again and holding onto the horse's tail would be towed back to shore. Swimming so far out to sea, the little horse must have enjoyed it and, certainly, it was a lovely way of keeping the animals nice and clean. I remember Inspector Ley, the farrier responsible for the condition of the horses in the whole of the Force, remarking one day as he stood at the stable door, while visiting me on inspection, "No one, by any stretch of the imagination, could describe these horses as neglected!"

Sailing boats

The Arabs had *markab shariya* [two-masted schooners] which sailed quite fast.

They have a big mainsail, foresail and three plain jibs to catch all the winds. They carried quite a lot of merchandise – and contraband when the occasion arose. Most of these boats put out from Haifa and Jaffa. The fishing boats – *felucca* – had one mainsail and a little jib, and put out from the villages like Caesarea and Tantura.

To take advantage of the pleasant nautical situation, I bought two sailing boats. The first was an old *felucca*, which I bought for £4. It had seen better days, but it was fun to take it out for a sail. However it was rather heavy, too heavy to pull up the beach in bad weather, and during one storm it was dragged out to sea by the waves and then smashed on the shore. The next boat was a little sailing dinghy I bought from Major Tinkler, of the Yeomanry, who were camped nearby, for about £6 10s, and a little book on sailing terms and techniques to learn how to sail. We had many pleasant sailing trips up and down the coast. I learnt to watch the wind, which I noticed used to go round the clock during a 24-hour period. You could tack south to Kafr Vitkin Coast Guard Station – about 10 km down the coast – in the morning, as the wind came up from there. We usually sailed back about 4 or 5 o'clock in the afternoon, while the wind was westerly on the port side. If we stayed too long, the wind would be coming from the north and you had to sail right out to sea before tacking back to Givat Olga Cove. In the late evening the wind dropped completely, and sometimes when there was no wind you had to row back. Usually, after midnight, you could feel a slight breeze begin to blow from the east on your cheek, which steadily strengthened. Then, by 6 am it would be blowing strongly up from the south again.

However, my little dinghy went the way of the first boat. Although it was light enough to be beached in rough weather, a storm blew up when I was away in Haifa one time, and no one at the station had the forethought to drag the boat out of the water to safety.

Pigeons

When we went out on patrol up the coast, 20 miles north of Givat Olga, there was no way of informing the station of anything we had seen, so I hit on the idea of keeping some homing pigeons. On chatting about this to an Arab colleague, he suggested that if you fed them sweet almonds, which they like, they would always come back. One of the constables, Jock Baines, and I made a pigeon cote, and I obtained four or six pigeons from some local people, at eight piastres a bird. Having kept them in for a while, I decided one day to collect them and take them out in the car. We drove about four miles up the coast road and let them go, hoping and expecting them to return to the station. However, they seemed to have some other interests in life and deserted us, but a few days later Jack Dowson, who was on look-out duty, called down to tell me, "The pigeons have come home, Sergeant. They have got sore feet. They've walked all the way!" I decided this scheme was not worth persuing!

The next time I tried keeping pigeons was at El Lejjun. Although I built the cote on a high post, a mongoose-type animal unfortunately got up in among them and killed the lot. One of my Arab policemen suggested that once a predator had discovered the birds, it would return again, so I did not continue the project. However, the Arabs felt that, generally speaking, keeping pigeons was commercially worthwhile, as one of them once remarked to me, "Every 40 days they will hatch a new one, and it is like the pigeon saying to you, 'Here, take 8 piastres'!"

Mines

The first Italian sea mine to be washed ashore was found early one morning by two Arab fishermen, about one mile from the station. They thought that any metal container washed ashore was likely to contain oil and were keen to recover it. They had found the mine floating by a reef and one of the men had entered the water and manhandled it between rocks. Assisted by the waves, they had managed to it get it ashore. Then, with a large pebble, one of the men had knocked off a horn so that he could look inside and see what sort of oil it contained. Being unable to get a satisfactory answer, he sent his companion to fetch a pickaxe, with which to open the steel casing. He remained on guard, should anyone come along and try to claim the prize. When, having returned with the pickaxe and used it with some force, they found that the mine still refused to give up its secrets, the pair became suspicious and reported the matter to the station.

When I arrived at the spot with the fishermen and they told me what they had been doing, I cursed them both roundly for their foolish act and told them of the danger they had been risking. They looked at me rather sheepishly and replied only with a embarrassed grin. Next day the mine was demolished by the Royal Engineers and the two fishermen were in the vicinity to watch the operation. A tremendous explosion took place and brought down about 100 tons of cliff. The look on the faces of the fishermen vividly expressed what was going on in their minds!

After this incident I drew several sketches of mines and distributed them among the local people, warning them to leave such articles strictly alone. However, I know that several other mines washed up and were tampered with by reckless fishermen, who hoped to extract the explosive – for they often used dynamite to stun fish.

The Christmas Party

Barrels containing oil and other such substances did wash up on the shores now and then. One morning in December 1941, I went up on the roof to see that all was well, and Jack Dowson, who was on look-out duty, said to me, "Sergeant, it looks as though the Christmas beer has arrived!" He was pointing to a couple of metal barrels washed up on the shore and a few more floating on the sea. We went down to the shore and manhandled a few up the dunes and brought them into the yard. On removing one of the plugs we found the contents smelt edible. We took a small sample in a glass bottle and one of my Arab sergeants, who was going to Jaffa for a few days' leave, said that he would take it to a friend of his who was a chemist and who would analyse it for us. By rights, I should have reported the barrels to the Receiver of Wrecks, but we decided we would have a party instead.

The news came back from the chemist that the oil was Indian nut oil and of a very high quality, and he would give us £5 a barrel for the five barrels we had found. With the proceeds, some beer, wine and spirits were purchased from the NAAFI manager of a nearby army camp, and the station barrack room re-arranged for a dance party. We made a bar by stacking the kit boxes; borrowed an electric gramophone and some records; and ran an electric cable from a little house nearby. We then went to the Eden Café in Hadera, run by Fanny and Rosie, and invited quite a few people to come back to the party with us. All seemed to thoroughly enjoy the event and I later heard that Mrs. Rosengarten, who was from Austria, was surprised by the civility with which she and her fellow guests had been received by the Sergeant and the other officers. She said she had never imagined that such a party could have taken place in a police station.

Drug Smuggling

While at the station, much of my attention had been given to the drug smuggling trade, for Palestine was a corridor through which drugs were conveyed from Turkey and Syria to Egypt. Hashish, opium, heroin and cocaine all passed through the country in large quantities, and the farther south they reached, the more valuable they became. Egypt, then, was the best drugs market in the Middle East, and was the subject of *The Last Plague of Egypt* by Russell Pasha, who was the Chief of the Narcotics Bureau in Egypt at that time.

On the 15th March 1941, a fisherman whom I had befriended came to me in the morning and pointed out a motor launch travelling south, about two miles out to sea. He told me that this craft had a large cargo of drugs on board, and that after keeping her under observation out at sea for sometime, he had put his boat into a creek and hurried along the coast to tell me. I took a bearing on the launch and estimated her speed; and then sent a message to Port and Marine HQ Haifa, asking for a patrol launch to check the craft. In the afternoon I received a message to the effect that the police launch, the *Sea Lion*, had taken the crew of the boat, the *Marbrouk* [Congratulations], into custody and found that she had been carrying almost a ton of opium and hashish, and 50 gallons of Syrian arrack, a cargo probably worth about £7,000 – £10,000 at Egyptian prices.

Six months later the crew were charged and tried in the District Court at Nablus, I think it was. The President of the Court,[1] prior to passing sentence, said, "Undoubtedly you will not give any information which may lead to the apprehension of the other members of this drug smuggling ring, so you will each be sent to prison for one year." Then the faces of the men in the dock showed the concern they felt at the prospect of a year's imprisonment. However, the President continued, "Or each of you will pay a fine of £100." Then smiles wreathed their faces. They actually congratulated each other while still standing in the dock!

The *Marbrouk* was confiscated, but the owner, who was present in court, was not charged and seemed in no way perturbed at the loss of his boat. He had brought along £6,000 in cash with which to pay the fines. As there were only five accused, he cheerfully paid over the £500, and then the six of them, together with their lawyer, made their exit to celebrate the occasion and undoubtedly make preparations for the running of more drugs in the future. The informant received £50 for his information. I was amazed by the whole outcome of this matter and the leniency with which the affair was dealt with.

News of the seizure was well known in the locality and one evening while I was in a café a Jew came to me and sat down at my table, quite uninvited. He asked me if I had kept back any of the drugs for myself, and went on to say, "I'll give you £200 for a slab of hashish." Apparently, everyone who could be was in the drugs racket and it was a real paying game. Although there was a lot dealing in drugs, which appeared to be mostly headed for Egypt, I did not come across much drug-taking in rural Palestine.

Local Jewish Politics

During the time I was at Givat Olga, being in a predominantly Jewish area, I was able to meet many Jews, learn quite a lot about their aspirations in Palestine, and became friendly with quite a number. Information about the situation also came from the Jewish-owned newspapers like *The Palestine Post* and police intelligence from HQ.

The older members of the community, who had actually helped plan and build Hadera more than 50 years before, were, generally speaking, very moderate in their views, and their children, mostly born in Palestine, were not particularly politically ambitious. They had worked hard, often under

---

[1] I think in this case an Arab. There were no juries in Palestine because of the obvious racial problems, which meant that safe convictions could not be guaranteed by jury. There was usually a President and two Members.

heartbreaking conditions, clearing swamps and making a hitherto malarial district into a beautiful, healthy and fruitful township, surrounded by orange groves and other agricultural enterprises. They were rightly proud of their achievements. The newcomers, however, who had come to Palestine from Germany after Hitler's rise to power, and from other anti-Semitic countries, were entirely different. Many were openly belligerent towards the British and accused the Government of having a British Gestapo working in the country against them. Menachem Begin, who subsequently became an Israeli Prime Minister, was an anti-British terrorist.

There was much division amongst the many and various political groups and factions (in 1942 there were at least eight political organisations). Jews who were non-political Zionists, and just wanted to settle in Palestine and live the religious life, as Jews had done 2,000 years before, always had my sympathy. However, I consistently failed to see how the political Zionists, who claimed the land of Palestine as a right, arrived at their conclusions. In discussing this subject freely with my neighbours, I know that I was regarded as an "anti-Semite" because I would not agree to the claims for a Jewish National Home in a country already populated by Arabs – but as Jews and Arabs are both Semitic[1] peoples, this was a rather empty criticism. What should happen to the Arabs did not concern the political Zionists. Their only suggestion was that the Arabs could, "Go over the Jordan – there is vast empty space on the other side" – no matter that over there was a hostile, arid wilderness with no water. But, in fact, political Zionists even had ambitions to claim a large chunk of Transjordan, as well as Palestine.

I suggest that the Jews are not a race – they are a conglomerate of races, having intermarried with the various nationals in the countries in which they have settled, and wherever they have lived, only religion has kept their interests separate. People of Jewish origin who adopt other religions, and there have been many conversions, are no longer considered to be Jews. So what makes the people of Jewish faith a race? Are Christians all one race or Moslems one race?

The Pre-Zionist Jewish Communities in Palestine

A description of the many diverse communities in Palestine and their histories was included in *The Handbook of Palestine* (C.H. Luke and E. Keith-Roach 1922; 1930) - published by the Palestine Government as an introductory source of information for newcomers to the country. It included a brief account of the Jewish Diaspora which followed the destruction of the Temple and Jerusalem by the Romans in 70 A.D., and the further flight from Judæa, in A.D.135,

---

[1] The Oxford English definition of Semite – "A person belonging to the race of mankind which includes most of the peoples mentioned in Genesis Ch.10, descended from Shem, son of Noah, – Hebrews, Arabs, Assyrians, and Aramæans."

after the Bar Cochba rebellion against the Romans. Some communities settled in Galilee which became the spiritual centre for a while, but with the Christianization of the Roman Empire, at the time of Constantine the Great (312-337 A.D.), the spiritual centre of Judaism shifted to Babylonia, though Tiberius continued for some centuries as a centre of Hebrew learning. Throughout the Middle Ages very small Jewish communities remained in Palestine, such as those in the towns of Safed and Tiberias. However, one community, the Samaritans, remained in Judea throughout the centuries of the Diaspora, and they continue to live in Nablus today. They regard themselves as a race apart from the modern and orthodox Jews, whom they view with suspicion and do not accept as Jews. At the time of which I write, they had many Arab characteristics and dressed in a similar manner to their Arab neighbours. While I was stationed in Nablus I observed no friction between the two communities, the Arabs regarding the Samaritans with interest and benevolence. The High Priest claimed to be a direct descendent of the High Priest of ancient Israel. At that time the community numbered only some 300 souls and the race was probably the purest in the world. In the 1940's, a marriage occurred between one of the Samaritans and a non-Samaritan girl, the first such occasion for hundreds of years in the recorded history of the Tribe.

By the time of the Balfour Declaration (see below), in 1917, the Jewish population of the country was 9.7% of the total, and only began to increase significantly after that time.

Pattern of Jewish Settlement in Palestine from 1880s-1930s

As mentioned previously, a strong movement, conceived by Theodore Hertzl in the 1880s, grew amongst the Jews to work for their return to Palestine, then still under Ottoman rule, and many, including Baron Edmund de Rothschild, known as the "Father of the Yishuv", encouraged and gave substantial financial assistance to the scheme. This was the first material step towards modern Zionism. In the early stages, this movement received the support of a number of religiously-minded Jews, who then migrated to Palestine as "A return to the Promised Land". Many settled as farmers and cultivators, with the idea of forging their swords into ploughshares and spears into pruning hooks (Isaiah 2:4), before entering the Promised Land, in peace. Har Tuv was such a settlement. From the early days there were some struggles for land, but in general, until the first Arab anti-Jewish riots of 1920, these early Zionists lived quite happily with, and had the respect of, their Arab neighbours, and normal business carried on between both peoples. Other farmers followed, mainly from Central and Eastern Europe. The main areas of settlement were the coastal plain, the Jezreel Valley and the Galilee District. The later settlements were of three types – the Kibbutz where all profits were pooled, no wages paid and control was communal; the Xratsa – co-operative bodies where each member drew his proportionate share; and the Mashar – where groups of small-holders farmed individually. Traders, craftsmen and professional people, such as doctors and lawyers, established themselves in small towns like Petah Tiqva and Hadera – which started as settlements and became towns – as well as in Jerusalem. (Tel Aviv was a small suburb in 1917 but grew as a port alongside the port of Jaffa in the 1920s.) The Jewish Agency, which came into being in the 1920s, and the National Council of Palestine Jews, were regarded by the vast majority of the Jewish community as being in authority, and as powerful bodies able to impose their will on the Jewish population.

The Balfour Declaration 1917 – a Twice Promised Land.[1]

In 1915, during the First World War, the British Government, sensing the collapse of the Ottoman Empire, "pledged to recognise and support the independence of the Arabs in all regions within the limits demanded by the Sheriff of Mecca," in which Palestine lay. The people of that area were assured that, if they supported the Allied cause, their independence would follow an Allied victory. The Arabs fought with people like T. E. Lawrence (Lawrence of Arabia) to overthrow Turkish rule. However, in 1916, a secret agreement – the Sykes-Picot agreement – was made between the British, French and Russian governments to divide up the Arab world between them, into "spheres of influence", but, with the overthrow of Tsarist Russia by the Bolshevik Revolution, this agreement became public. It was now obvious to the Arabs that the British intended to renege on their promise of independence when peace was declared. Meanwhile the Zionist cause continued to be pursued in the highest spheres of the British Government by such supporters as Lord Rothschild and Dr Chaim Weizmann,[2] the latter a lecturer in chemistry at Manchester University and a constituent of Lord Balfour's.

The Arabs had looked forward to independence for pre-1920 Syria, in which Palestine lay, but France also laid claim to that area, particularly The Lebanon. Britain wanted to maintain influence in Palestine, as well as in Egypt, to ensure security for the Suez Canal. The leaders of Zionism undertook to support the idea of a British protectorate of Palestine if Britain supported the Zionist cause. In an attempt to ensure and maintain Arab support for the Allied cause, in 1917 – before Britain had a mandate in Palestine – the

---

[1] This is a very brief, simplified summary of some very complex events, which are much better explained in *The Arabs* by Anthony Nutting, Chs 24, 25 & 27, first published in 1964. For additional reading see also *The Palestinians* 1980 by Jonathan Dimbleby and Donald McCullin.
[2] Dr Chiam Weizmann had done very valuable service to the Allies in developing explosives used in the 1914-18 War. He asked for no favours personally but that Palestine be given to the Jews.

British Government issued a declaration that attempted to please everyone, both the Arabs and the very influential supporters of Zionism. Lord Balfour, the British Foreign Secretary, in a letter to Lord Rothschild, wrote that "His Majesty's Government view with favour the establishment in Palestine of a National Home for the Jewish people, and will use their best endeavours to facilitate the achievement of this object, it being understood that nothing shall be done which may prejudice the civil and religious rights of the existing non-Jewish communities in Palestine, or the rights and political status enjoyed by the Jews in any other country." This became known as the Balfour Declaration and it was this statement which has led to so much trouble throughout the Middle East (and now throughout the world). The first part was a vague and hopeful statement to the Jews and the second part was meant to reassure the Arabs. However, the Zionists always regarded the first part as a "promise", and many went on to ignore the proviso. And, unlike the British Government, the Palestine Arabs viewed the establishment of a Jewish National Homeland in Palestine with considerable disfavour. In 1920 the High Commissioner, Sir Herbert Samuel, stated in his interim report that, "If growth of Jewish influence were accompanied by Arab degradation, or even by neglect to promote Arab achievement, it would fail in its essential purposes ... In a word, the degree to which Jewish national aspirations can be fulfilled in Palestine is conditioned by the rights of the present inhabitants ..."[1] However, 1922, there continued to be grave concerns about the outcome of this policy, as expressed by Lord Sydenham in the House of Lords, when he stated that, "the harm done, by dumping down an alien population in an Arab country – Arabs all around in the hinterland – may never be remedied. What we have done, by concession, not to the Jewish people, but to a Zionist extreme section, is to start a running sore in the Middle East, and no one can tell how far that sore will extend" (*Hansard,* June 1922). As Morton commented, Balfour did not explain how large numbers of foreigners could be allowed to enter the country *without* prejudicing in some degree the civil rights of the existing communities. Perhaps large numbers of immigrants were not envisaged, as in 1917 Hitler was still an unknown corporal and Zionism, with little or no positive attraction for world Jewry as a whole, was the dream of a handful of idealists only.

Arab Rebellion – 1920

The first Arab demonstrations against the policy of a National Homeland for the Jews in Palestine were staged in Jerusalem in 1920. At that time Haj Amin Husseini was a young political leader and he fled, with other members of his party, to Transjordan. Then the Jewish/British High Commissioner (the Governor of Palestine), Sir Herbert Samuel, sent for Haj Amin, welcomed

---

[1] H. C. Luke and E. Keith-Roach (1930) *The Handbook of Palestine*

him back and appointed him as Grand Mufti of Jerusalem. The following year, 1921, saw anti-Jewish riots in Jaffa. In 1922, the British Government announced that it interpreted the Balfour Declaration to mean: "not the imposition of Jewish nationality upon the inhabitants of Palestine as a whole, but the further development of the existing Jewish community in order that it may become a centre in which the Jewish people as a whole may take, on grounds of religion and race, an interest and a pride" – a statement which Morton[1] felt left no one any wiser. Immigration steadily increased, reaching a peak in 1924-5, and then fell sharply, until the "rise of Hitler and Nazi persecution … turned the eyes of German Jewry to the Promised Land. .. Then Immigration rapidly increased and … the Arabs viewed with dismay the speed with which Arab areas were quickly changing to Jewish colonies."

Then in 1929, after serious incidents at the Wailing Wall, riots broke out all over the country. Much of this unrest was caused by untrue propaganda, to the effect that Jews had attacked and entered the Mosque of Omar in Jerusalem. Although the propaganda was false, a party of young Jews had incensed the Arabs at the Mosque by behaving in a very truculent manner. From then on there was a complete lack of confidence between Arabs and Jews – and the wave of anti-Semitism which was sweeping Europe, resulting in immigrants arriving by the thousands, only added to the troubles. The year 1933 saw very serious riots in Jaffa. Up till then the riots had been anti-Jewish, but now the patience of the Arabs was running short and the riots also became very anti-British.

According to Sir John Hope Simpson's Report to the Secretary of State for the Colonies in 1930[2] (which summarised land use and population and made recommendations) the population of the country was Mohammedans 692,195, Jews 162,069, Christians (many of whom were Arabs) and others 91,727. From now on the Arabs had determined to resist the policy of a National Home Land for the Jews in Palestine at all costs, and to fight for the country which had been their homeland for 13 centuries. This state of lawlessness continued into the late 1930s, as I have previously related, until the publication of *The White Paper on Palestine*, which restricted Jewish immigration and land sales. This brought some measure of content to the Arabs, they accepted the terms, and peace *almost* descended upon us. But peace was to be denied us. The Jews now commenced their demonstrations against The White Paper proposals, and the Militant Revisionist Party started to indulge in anti-British terrorist activities.

---

[1] *Just the Job.* 1957 Geoffrey J. Morton
[2] http://domino.un.org/UNIPALNSF/O *Hope Simpson Report on Palestine 1930.*

The Revisionists

The Revisionist Party were a group of people with extreme views whose aim was to convert Palestine *and* Transjordan into a Jewish state by mass immigration and by using any means to achieve this end. From this extreme party sprang two even more extreme and violently criminal branches. One was the Irgun Zvei Leumi. The Stern Gang was the other, being an offshoot of the Irgun.

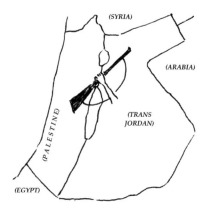

Revisionist Banner

The Threat from German Forces – Illegal Home Guard Activity

However, it must be said that, with the war raging, and Germany having great successes with its various advances, the Jews were in a very nervous state in Palestine. The Germans were about a two-day march from Cairo and knocking on the doors of Turkey. I thought it highly likely that the Middle East would be overrun in a pincer movement. I wondered if I should ever get home and thought that I would probably be killed in the fighting or taken prisoner. Ironically, because of this threat, I was able to enjoy two years of work at the Coastguard Station without undue concern from Jewish terrorism.

The Jews, nevertheless, *were* preparing for a more active form of self-defence as the following incident will illustrate. It should be understood that those involved were not terrorists but were training themselves as a sort of unofficial Home Guard. An Arab policeman and I were out on patrol one day when the unmistakable whine of a bullet was heard overhead. This was followed by a second, and my first thought was that we were being fired on from an ambush. Together we cantered forward towards cover, while two more bullets whizzed by. We put our horses into a hollow in the sand dunes and I then crept up the bank hoping to find out just what was going on around us.

I discovered I was directly over the targets and butts of a temporary rifle range, while at the firing point about 20 men were lying on the ground and taking aim at the targets. I shouted to them to stop firing and as I approached some men disappeared into the orange grove with their rifles. On arriving at the firing point I informed them that, under Emergency Regulations, the practice was taking place illegally and asked who was in charge, but no one replied or would take responsibility. When asked what rifles they were using, I was told .22, but I had torn off a piece from one of the targets and it was plain to see that .303 bullets (a forbidden calibre of gun) had pierced it. I informed them of the obvious, that unauthorised rifle practice like this could easily result in inadvertent wounding or death.

I then attempted to take the whole party to a nearby orange fruit farm, Heftsi Bah, where the manager, Alfred Joseph, was a friend of mine, so that with his help I could find out and confirm the names of the people. My Arab sergeant had gone to fetch the horses, so, being on my own, I lost about two-thirds of the party on the way, as they slipped among the bushes and disappeared. When I went to find them, more disappeared. It was all quite laughable. With the help of the manager, however, I was able to list those present and told them that they would be reported for taking part in illegal military training under the Emergency Regulations. One of the group asked the manager to offer me £5 to forget the whole matter. Alfred was so incensed at the suggestion – that I could be bribed – that I thought there would be a fight between them.

I sent a full report to my local HQ, with a list of names of the people participating, but the only action was a disciplinary charge. It emerged that a Jewish Settlement policeman had arranged the whole thing, and he was dismissed as a consequence. That probably made little difference to him and, likely as not, he carried on as before. None of the participants was charged, even though they had clearly committed an offence under the Laws of Palestine, which rendered the perpetrators liable to a sentence of 10 years imprisonment, a sentence, in my opinion, that would have been carried out if the perpetrators had been Arab. For my action many Jewish acquaintances let me know of their disapproval in no uncertain manner and again accused me of being "anti-Semitic". I found that, if any non-Jewish Government official upheld an unpopular regulation, as far as the Jewish population was concerned, he would be accused of anti-Semitism. Yet, one friendship did result from the incident. Wolf Aaronson, a Russian Jew from Kharkov who took part in the shooting practice, was so pleased I would not accept the bribe that afterwards, whenever I met him, he would always invite me to stay and share a bottle of wine. I learned from Alfred of Aaronson's great generosity, for every month, after he had received his wages and paid his living expenses, he gave the remainder to charity.

There was of course some justification for the Jews to want to practise the use of firearms, as Rommel's Army was threatening. The general gossip, passed onto me, was that some of the Arab youths were boasting of which Jewish girls they were going to take for their pleasure as soon as the Nazis arrived. Rice and flour had been stored and cattle earmarked for slaughter for a feast to welcome the German visitors, who, luckily, never quite made it.

Alfred and Mia Joseph

Alfred and Mia had come from a small village in Bavaria in Germany. His father was a farmer in the village and Alfred worked with the horses. There was a German artillery battery nearby, and their guns were all horse-drawn, so Alfred, with his interest in horses, had quite a lot in common with the soldiers and spent much time in the soldiers' mess. Mia was a schoolgirl in the local convent, and first noticed Alfred while she was in school and looked out as he walked by with the horses. In time they got to know one another and became special friends. When the anti-Jewish riots and atrocities began to take place in Germany and things became very difficult for the Jews in the early 1930s, Alfred decided that Germany was no place for a Jew to live a happy and contented life, so he made enquiries and arrangements and went to Palestine. When Mia left school, and when she was able to do so, she decided to follow Joseph and married him. Alfred was a manager of a group of orange groves at Heftsi Bah belonging to about two or three people, employing a predominantly Arab workforce. These groves were about two or three miles from the Coastguard Station and we had a very pleasant ride through the groves to get there.

While the war was on, people of German nationality were interned in camps for enemy aliens. The German colony of Sarona (near Jaffa) was surrounded by barbed wire and became one such camp. German Jews were considered anti-German and were able to remain in the community. Although Mia was a Christian German, she did not have to be interned but had to report at intervals to the police in Hadera. Even though Mia was anti-Hitler and anti-war, she was proud of her countrymen, and while the war was still on made the comment, "You have to admit that, as a fighting force, the Germans were something to be reckoned with!"

I used to speak to Alfred in Arabic and to Mia in English, and they spoke to each other in German. They were a very happy couple and appeared to be much in love. I spent a pleasant 10 days' local leave staying with them and their two sons, relaxing and sketching, when I was later stationed at Lejjun. I went down to Hadera by bus, with my case and a crate of beer as a gift, which they both enjoyed. It was my fortnightly ration, which I had been allowed to take with me, and was a source of some interest to my fellow bus passengers. I hired a horse and a two-wheeled cart in Hadera and drove out to Heftsi Bah. Abu Fit, Joseph's Bedouin worker, drove it back.

A German Submarine

One image from this time remains very vividly in mind. Sgt. Riati and I were making our way down the coast to Kafr Vitkin Coastguard Station one dark, moonless night, and at one point we had to leave the sandy shore and make our way up onto a little hill. From the hilltop we could see down the coast to Tel Aviv and Jaffa 20 miles away, though they were not lit up because of the blackout. To our surprise we could hear a faint boom of a gun and saw shells being fired from a submarine which had surfaced. Six or eight shells followed one another, like shooting stars, into the electricity power station at Tel Aviv. It appears that the submarine had hung about for a couple of days previously, hiding below a rock shelf. A while later I met another policeman who had also been on coastal patrol at that time. He had seen a large, submerged dark patch, just out to sea, which he took to be a shoal of fish; but after hearing about the shelling he realised the dark patch was the submarine.

Caesarea and Mishmar Village

Mishmar Hyam [Watch on the Sea] was a small Jewish fishing kibbutz near Caesarea village, and the members were very ambitious, hoping to make a small settlement where, at the time, they lived only in tents and huts. For years, the inhabitants of Caesarea had cultivated a fairly large tract of land next to their village, which they rented from the Latin or Greek Patriarch in Jerusalem, and it was their only good piece of arable land.

After the inhabitants of Mishmar Hyam had established themselves and been there over a year, they negotiated with the Patriarch for the hire of the land, and when they went out to plough, trouble started. Neither party would desist from interfering with, or cede to, the rights of the other. The Jews then brought in an Arab, one Mukbil, from Samami village, a soldier of fortune, to protect their rights and intimidate the villagers of Caesarea. He had, in fact, fought with the Arab rebels but had also taken part in many negotiations between Arabs and Jews relating to the sale of land. Such Arabs were naturally despised by their countrymen but, as Mukbil had also been a rebel soldier, he commanded a certain degree of respect. On the day that he arrived to protect the Jews while they cultivated the land, a battle royal ensued. The people of Caesarea, who were mostly Circassian by descent (Moslem people from the Caucasus), refused to be overawed by a "mere Arab" and both parties came to blows. This stopped work on the land for a while, but later the Caesareans re-established themselves by cultivating the same plot. Up until then, they and the Jews had got on very well, and could often be seen paying friendly calls on each other. However, by bringing in Mukbil, the members of Mishma Hyam Kibbutz earned the contempt of their Caesarean neighbours.[1]

Bedouin Wedding

One day I received an invitation from the Bedouin patriarch, Sheihk Abu Fadil of the Arab En Nufiat tribe, to attend a wedding feast at their camp. This tribe retained the Arab love of horse racing, and many Arab guests were expected to arrive on their fiery steeds that day. The old sheihk hoped that we would also arrive mounted. I had a little conference with the Arab policemen and they assured me that we should be challenged to a race on our arrival. Sgt. Hassan told me that he had seen Baby, Constable "Tug" Wilson's mount, beat the best horses of the Beni es Saker tribe near Beisan a few years previously. Baby was always a good horse to go and if there was any chance of a gallop he would take it.

We left for the Bedouin camp, Tug riding Baby; and what a "Baby" he was, with the strength and heart of a lion, full of courage and fire. Tug was quite small and weighed about 10 stone, so horse and rider suited each other well. Sgt. Hassan had insisted that we must win with this horse, for the Bedouin declared that police horses were "*ihkdaish*" [commonly bred – not thoroughbred like Arab horses] and held our horses in contempt. As we neared the camp a young Bedouin on a fine chestnut stallion, came out to welcome us. When about 40 yards from us he reined in and called out, "*Marahaba ya kheiyal*!" [How do you do/ Welcome, horsemen!]. He turned his horse to throw out a challenge to race in the customary manner, and waited for this to be accepted. I then said to Constable Wilson, "Right Tug, show him the way home!" At the touch of a spur, Baby leapt forward and was almost immediately in a full, striding gallop. The challenger whipped his horse and streaked away towards the encampment, with Baby a full five lengths behind but gaining at every stride. After a few hundred yards, as they neared their destination, they were racing neck and neck, but on going up the slope and passing the black tents of the Bedu, Baby steadily forged ahead and then pulled away in front, the undisputed winner! The whole assembly stood yelling their heads off, thoroughly enjoying the spectacle, which to them was as good as the Derby and did much to liven up the festivities.

I galloped in with the rest of our party and dismounted at the *madafi*, the guest tent, where we were made most welcome by the chief, who then introduced us to the elders of the tribe. They must have been sorely disappointed to have had one of their best horses beaten by a mere police horse, but they put a brave face on it. To provide entertainment and keep the company happy, we raced our horses against theirs, and after they won a couple of races their

---

[1] In 1963, Leslie Farmer in his book *Land of the Gospel* described the Arabs' "empty shattered houses (of Caesarea)… some hundreds of years old, and soon to be removed for a new Jewish city that is to be built there."

spirits rose; but Baby's victory would have been hard to forget.

To ride in a race against an Arab under their own rules is a hair-raising experience and no ordinary affair with equal chances for all. A race is run over any piece of open ground. It is the aim of the rider to get in front and to stay there at all costs and by any means, including swerving across the path of any who may try to pass him. It has been known for a confederate to help his partner win by slipping off his horse and sliding his legs between the forelegs of the most serious challenger's horse. The Arab is no respecter of rider or horse, and should he cause a man's death it is, "The Will of Allah." If he kills a horse he is not the least concerned, for he concludes that, "The horse is better dead than beaten in a race." During the afternoon of the wedding, several men and horses bit the dust, but luckily none was seriously hurt. After riding against a few of them I became a little more careful about whom I accepted a challenge from.

Sad News from Home

In May 1942 I received a telegram from home telling me that my father was ill, and then did not hear anything for several days, so I hoped and assumed that he was recovering. But when I was cleaning my saddle one morning, Jock Baines came out and said, "I'm sorry Sergeant, it's bad news. Your father has died." I rested on the saddle horse and shed a quiet tear, as I realised I would never see my father again.

After two years of command at the Coastguard Station, I was placed in an invidious situation, for my assistant sergeant, Tom Rishworth, was transferred to Zichron – a little Jewish town up in the hills from Hadera, well known for its vineyards and its wine. His replacement was a man who was senior to me but not well-regarded by the Divisional Superintendent, who informed me that I should not hand over my command to him. He said he would "arrange things" – but nothing transpired. I found this situation difficult so I applied for a transfer. Fortunately, I had a friend in Police HQ, Norman Cressy, who dealt with these matters, and I was soon moving on again.

1943: Springtime at El Lejjun, the police Tegart Fort in the background.

Rusty BP 236 – a real gentleman.
(Sketch by Cons. Peter J. C. McLaughlin)

Chapter 9
El Lejjun 1942 – 43

In mid-1942 I was transferred from Givat Olgar to El Lejjun Police Post as Officer-in-Charge. I must regard myself as a lucky man for just over a year later, Givat Olga was attacked by Jewish dissidents and blown up by a large bomb, the sergeant i/c at the time being badly injured. A firm of Jewish builders was contracted to repair the damage and, while doing so, built a time bomb into the watchtower. This exploded a few months later, causing many further casualties among the personnel.

Tegart Forts

However, we will return to Jejjun, which was the first Tegart Fort I had served in. The post was on the coastal plain, about 2 km from Lejjun village, 15 km to the north east of Jenin, and at the northern end of the Mus Mus pass – one of the routes used by Lord Allenby's columns as they advanced through Palestine into Syria at the end of the 1914-18 War. On a clear day, at certain times of the year, you could see the snow topped peak of Mount Hermon, about 65 miles to the north-east. The graveyard where Yousef Hamdan is buried is close by, near to the ancient ruins of Megiddo – the old biblical city which overlooked the Plain of Armageddon, part of the Jezreel Plain. In ancient times Megiddo had been the stronghold guarding the mouth of the pass which, for centuries, was one of the main routes south to Egypt. In the two years previously the ancient pass had been made into a modern highway and thousands of troops had passed that way.

The post, or fort, was a small version of one of a dozen others built throughout the country on the recommendations of Sir Charles Tegart, of Bengal fame. He had visited the country in 1938 to advise the Government on ways to put an end to the disturbances. Most of the forts were completed and in service by 1942. They were designed by C. Wilson-Brown, director of the Public Works Department, and built of concrete. Each post was constructed in the form of a square, with two defence towers at diagonal corners and jutting out from the main walls, to give a view of fire along all four walls. The main and frontal block contained the offices, lock-up and armoury. The two barrack rooms were on the ground floor, while the first floor provided married accommodation for the British rank in charge. Each wing comprised of a kitchen, dining room and recreation room, one wing being for the British and the other for the Palestinian police. There were two married quarters for the Palestinian personnel and, finally, there was a block of stables at the rear of the post, which completed the square. The garages, tack room, stores and Spinney's canteen and bar were in the centre.

Living conditions in the Fort

Being billeted on the premises, we were always liable to be called out on duty at all hours of the day or night, and these occasions were frequent. I found the concrete building very unpleasant during the summer months, for the walls absorbed the heat of the sun during the day, only to slowly discharge it during the night. We slept on the verandas but it was rarely possible to sleep before 2 am. In the winter, the concrete construction of the building made it very cold and uninviting and, as there were no fireplaces, evenings would find the men huddled over oil stoves, having to tolerate the unpleasant fumes, in order to heat the rooms to a near-comfortable temperature. Luckily the really cold weather only lasted for about six weeks. The building was designed predominantly with a view to defence; consequently, the windows were small and placed up high, thus allowing no view and making it rather prison-like. However, the window bars were so placed that they could be used as ladders! One evening a friend demonstrated how he could go down from the second floor to the ground and back in less than 40 seconds.

Boxing Enthusiasts on the Strength

I had an Arab sergeant and six British and six Arab constables on the strength. Bill Hutty was the driver of the armoured car, B/C Jock Lockwood, B/C AE Lewington and B/C "Basher" Bates were amongst the mounted constables. Bill Hutty was keen to box and asked if he could spar with me because he wanted to get some practice in for the Inter-Services Championship. I found that I could more than hold my own but, while we were sparring I noticed Jock Lockwood sitting quietly, watching. Jock then said to me, "Will you spar with me, Sergeant?" I thought, "Hello. Hello. What's this chap up to?" I replied, "What do you want, light spar Jock, or do you want to know who is boss?" He said, "No. Just light spar, Sergeant", but as soon as he started I knew he was good. After a couple of rounds I said to him, "You've done a bit of this in your time, Jock," and he replied, "Yes, I was a schoolboy international, and I boxed for Scotland." Bill Hutty went on to do quite well in the Inter-Services Competitions

Sergeant (Abu) Ahmed

The Arab sergeant at the post, Abu [Father of] Ahmed – as we used to call him – was a real character and a very good policeman. I freely credit him with teaching me an awful lot about the job. He had served for more than 20 years in the police and still possessed the same ideas that had been popular in Turkish times, when "third degree" treatment was harshly used. He would even beat those he suspected of withholding information until they decided to talk, but we Britishers never knew him to beat an innocent man. His reputation among the local villagers was well-known and not many would try to get the better of him. While chatting to him one day, he said that a policeman must act like a doctor, treating all the different cases individually. Some, he said, need a few kind words and sympathy when they are in trouble, others respond better when treated like gentlemen and offered a cigarette and cup of coffee. Others again must be allowed to talk so much that they even give away their innermost secrets, while nervous people will nearly always speak the truth from fear when confronted by the police. But he admitted, "There is always a tough character who cannot be cracked!"

He had contempt for the English law (the New Criminal Code Ordinance, which replaced the Ottoman Penal Code in December 1936) and methods of investigation, claiming that they were too complex for country people and at the same time open to manipulation and abuse. In Turkish times public security was maintained in the district by two officers – using much more Draconian methods – whereas the British needed 200! Abu Ahmed said it would be quite usual for a Turkish officer to send a message out to a village Muktar, or notable, to come and see him, and then leave the man sitting outside his office for three days before the officer would talk to him. He knew the Koran well and could quote the Prophet's teachings, which he could use to his professional advantage. On many occasions he was able to persuade unwilling elders into being of assistance to the authorities, supported by an appropriate quote from the Koran.

Abu Ahmed was married with three wives and had 10 children. There did seem to be a lot of trouble among the wives in the married quarters. He said that if all Arabs had large families, like him, there would be no room for Jews to immigrate into Palestine and the problem would be solved. I was never able to ascertain his real age, though he claimed to be 45. With his hair and moustache dyed black, he often looked and acted as a younger man, and young and courageous was how he liked to be thought of. But at times, when working on a difficult case and making no progress, he became worried and then looked like a real old man. He certainly had plenty of courage. In 1938 he had been injured by a bullet in the chest, and as a result one lung was badly impaired, but even on the most strenuous jobs he would never spare himself.

Rusty, My New Mount

Soon after arriving in Lejjun I decided to change my horse because Cyril, the one I had inherited, was a nice enough animal but a bit idle and always acted as though he was out for a gentle Sunday afternoon stroll. I telephoned Jack Ammonds, the Mounted Sergeant at Jenin, and asked if they had any good horses spare. He replied that they had two or three, but there was a rumour that one of them had kicked and killed someone in Beisan. I went down in the armoured car to take a look and took out Rusty, BP 236, the one who was rumoured to be difficult. I put the saddle on him and rode him up a nearby hill. He went with plenty of energy and initiative – "Well on the bridle," as they say – and I decided to have him. A few days later, I rode Cyril the 15 miles down to Jenin, left him there and brought back Rusty. Opposite Lejjun Station there was an empty army Mule Corps camp, where some manèges had been made for the schooling of horses – which the officers rode. I was able to use them to school Rusty and took my staff there so they could also school their horses. Rusty was a bit head heavy, tending to have his head too far out in front of him, but he schooled extremely well as he was intelligent and willing to learn. I managed to get his centre of gravity back so that he stood with his head back and up. I rode him in two or three gymkhanas and won four cups with him, and we became very good friends. Often when I was out on patrol I wouldn't tie him up but let him wander around to find some grazing, though I made sure he did not eat any of the crops. When it was time to move off, I would call him and he would come like a dog, which fascinated some of the village people.

Paddy McLaughlin, a constable at Qalqilya, made a very fine drawing of Rusty for me. He was an excellent artist and appeared to be aided by a photographic memory for, if he was talking about someone, to illustrate what that person looked like Paddy would draw a picture which would be a perfect likeness! He said he just imagined the face on the piece of paper and drew lines round it!

Surrounding Villages

The post area contained 12 villages and 14 hamlets. Umm el Fahm [Mother of Charcoal], home of Yousef Hamdan, was the largest with a population of nearly 4,000. Rumaneh, with a population of about 300-400 was out on the plain. Zububa, another village down on the Jezreel Plain, always struck me as a rather poor village – the land was good but the wealth the village generated seemed to go to absentee landlords. We were out in the district all the time and occasionally a patrol would develop into a gazelle hunt. We counted ourselves lucky if we made a kill, for our rations did get somewhat monotonous at times.

Cattle thieving was the most serious crime at that time and was difficult to check, for the rustlers mostly drove the stolen cattle across the Jezreel Plain to the Jewish butchers in the settlements, who then quickly slaughtered them and sold the meat. We discovered who the chief offender was but did not have sufficient evidence to bring him to court. However, we put such close surveillance on him that he decided to buy his own herd and became almost a respectable citizen. It was a case of prevention being better than cure.

Tragedy at Umm el Fahm

I found Arabs to be prone to exaggeration and consequently, when complaints were made to the police, they were not always accepted as entirely accurate. Trifling injuries were often reported as very serious assaults, and so on, and one could never be sure until arrival on the scene as to what would be found. One Sunday afternoon I was informed that a boy named Tewfic Musa of Umm el Fahm had been stabbed and was likely to die. I left with the Arab Sergeant and a party of constables by car, and on arrival we found the village in a state of uproar. Tewfic Musa *was* dead, so there was no exaggeration this time. The clans of the dead youth and the accused lad had had a pitched battle with sticks and stones, and two neutral families had stepped in to try to preserve order until the police arrived.

The mother of the dead youth was marching up and down with her dress ripped down the front and exposing her breasts which she flung around in a wild frenzy. All the while, she shrieked out for vengeance against the boy who had stabbed her son. She repeated the wail, *"Lazim idba el bandook,"* [Cut the throat of the bastard] as a rhythmic chant, accompanied by other female relatives. The accused boy was sheltering in the house of his uncle on the outskirts of the village and on my arrival at the house to arrest the lad, I found a large crowd from the victim's family, all clamouring for the boy's life. All the windows of the house had been smashed in by rocks, and several people inside had been injured. I ordered the attackers to withdraw, but it was not until I had struck a few with the butt of my rifle that they returned to their own quarter of the village. I then took the boy, one Mustafa Jarore, into custody. He was so full of what had happened that he blurted out a full story of confession to me immediately. He was a lad of about 14 and it appeared that Tewfic, the deceased, who was 19, had been in the habit of bullying him. On this day when they met, Tewfic had grabbed Mustafa by the hair and cursed him and his family. Mustafa had drawn his dagger and stabbed Tewfic in the chest, and he had collapsed and died shortly after.

It appears that there is a great deal of "hot blood" in Arab culture, and actions and reactions are violent and hysterical. The lad, Mustafa Jarore, was later sentenced to three years in a reformatory school. I had the opportunity to get to know him quite well and under ordinary circumstances he seemed to be a normal and likeable boy. It is a tragedy that these crimes most often result in long-standing blood feuds, when first one party kills and the injured party then kills in revenge. In this case, before peace could be arranged between the two families, much damage was done to the property of the accused family by the family of Tewfic. Three houses were burnt, three cows shot dead as they were being driven out of the village one morning, and dozens of trees were cut down.

Eventually, peace was made – after ridiculous sums of *diyet* [blood money] had been claimed by the victim's family. At one time, more than a £1,000 was demanded. I was present with Abu Ahmed at this meeting and he quoted from the Koran that *diyet* should in no case exceed the equivalent of £330. The aggrieved party then lowered their claim to one of £400, which they stated should be allowed, owing to inflation and the high cost of living because of the war. In retrospect, this seemed a fair claim.

A collective fine levied on the deceased's family in respect of the damage caused to the accused family's property almost cancelled out the value of the blood money. In addition, after a feast and peace meeting had been arranged, the cost of the food also being paid out of the *diyet*, the victim's father complained to me that all the money he had received in *diyet* had been wasted on the feast. After the affair was over, my Arab sergeant commented, "I don't know what all the trouble was about. The deceased was a homosexual and not worth a shilling."

A Case for the *Sharia* Court

Many and varied were the complaints lodged at Lejjun Police Post, but one was most extraordinary for a Moslem area. A young married man complained one day against his mother-in-law, whom he stated was in the habit of taking his young wife to Haifa, where she was being temporarily employed as a prostitute in a brothel. On this occasion I refused to take any police action and informed him that he could take his case to the District Officer and the Religious Courts [*Sharia*], where, if true, his case could be dealt with by a sheikh. (It has often been said by our judges that, "Our Courts of Justice are not courts of morals.")

A Slighted Husband Seeks Revenge

Another young fellow came one day and informed me that his father-in-law was in possession of a rifle and ammunition and offered to take me to the house. So after dark one evening, a couple of Arab policemen and I left with him, and after trudging across about five miles of track, we arrived at the house. We carefully deployed ourselves and then I knocked on the door. A constable who was peering through a crack in the window shutter saw an object thrown into a corn bin as I rapped. This object soon proved to be the rifle and the ammunition was also produced. I later found out that the young man's wife had returned to her father as she could not live happily with her husband. The father would not compel the girl to return to her husband so to avenge his hurt pride, the son-in-law had given information about the rifle and ammunition. Luckily, the father got only a light sentence or I would have felt very uneasy about it.

Illicit Arms Dealings and a Foretaste of New Terrors

Just at this time much publicity in the papers was being given to a case being heard in the military court, in which some Jews were being tried on charges of "Buying, and having at some time been in possession of 300 rifles and 100,000 rounds of ammunition". These arms and ammunition were alleged to have been stolen from the British Army, having been sold to the Jews by British soldiers, including some members of the Dominions Forces. There was much talk of a "Big Boss", who always appeared masked when dealing with the soldiers concerned; also of a flat – rented and supplied with a mistress for the men – when the transactions took place.

The Jewish public of the Palestine population took a very poor view of the publicity given to this case. With the War raging, it was considered very thoughtless of the Government to make the facts surrounding these illicit arms dealings known. Thefts of rifles, machine guns and mortars from military camps in the country occurred regularly. At one camp in Haifa, a complete armoury was stolen, including 400 rifles and 14 machine guns. It was obvious that this was no work of the Arabs. The public were being given a foretaste of what to expect in the future. By this time, General Montgomery's push from El Alamein had been successful. The American Forces had landed in North Africa and the threat to the Middle East had been removed. The Jews had now lost their dread of Nazi occupation and Menachem Begin and his Revisionist Zionists began their terrorist campaign – with the aim of forcing the hand of the British Government to drop the policy of Malcolm MacDonald's White Paper for Palestine.

A Wartime Break in The Lebanon 1943

In late May or early June 1941 the Vichy French in The Lebanon had been defeated by the British and Australian Forces. They had occupied all of Syria to the apparent delight of the Syrian and Lebanese people, for the French, obviously under duress, had allowed German military advisers into The Levant. Until the Allied occupation it had been apparent that German Forces could fly in at any time. The occupation was not a walkover, for the garrison of the French Vichy Forces stayed loyal to Marshal Pétain and put up stiff resistance for a while. The French had gun emplacements in the hills above Merj Ayoun and along the hills overlooking the coastal road, and having meticulously surveyed the countryside were able to use their guns to great effect. However, the campaign was not a lengthy one and after some three weeks the Allies were in control, right up to the Turkish border. Colonel Collett, a French Cavalry officer – who had an English wife – commanded a cavalry regiment in The Lebanon. He decided to come over on the Allied side and during the first night of the invasion led his regiment through the hills and crossed the frontier into Palestine. When fighting eventually ceased

Palestine Police Sgt. Arthur Callan, who was detached to the military as an interpreter and general liaison officer with the rank of Sergeant Major, proudly led the victorious allied troops into Beirut on a motor cycle.

While I was stationed at Givat Olga I saw a lot of horse-drawn, Vichy French transport and troops, which had been brought down from The Lebanon housed near Hadera.

By September 1943, while still at Lejjun Police Post, I was certainly due for some leave. Taffy Cole, who had been posted as Frontier Control Officer at Ras en Nakura, where the coast road crosses the frontier from Palestine into The Lebanon, had a very pleasant, educated Lebanese police colleague who had joined the Palestine Police Frontier Control. A member of his family had recently opened a hotel in Hamaneh in the mountains east of Beirut, so we decided to spend a couple of weeks leave there. Taffy, having many contacts in Beirut, was an ideal companion to travel with. Taxi travel was very cheap, for one could get a seat in a taxi for the 70 mile journey from Haifa to Beirut for around 5s (5 shillings). Taffy was waiting for me when I reached Ras en Nakura and together we went on to Beirut. There we negotiated for another taxi to take us to Hamaneh, about another 20 miles up into the mountains. We were to spend a week of quiet rest in beautiful countryside, with peaceful evenings and early nights, which was to be followed by a week in Beirut, with its nightclubs and general big city entertainment.

Our journey through the hills to Hamaneh took us first past beautiful Aleh, with its gorgeous houses and palaces belonging to Lebanon's millionaires and other wealthy princes and sheikhs. Steadily we drove on through the valley, climbing ever higher, until we reached our destination, a pleasant and modest country hotel of about 20 rooms set in an orchard, with the grounds terraced and tables and chairs arranged under the fruit trees. The view was magnificent, straight down the winding valley to Beirut, visible in the distance with several barrage balloons tethered above it. They were for a defence against Italian air force planes, for Italy was still then allied to Germany, though not for much longer – during our week there Italy broke its alliance with Germany and changed sides.

There were only about 10 other guests staying at the hotel, including, I felt sure, a Madam and four of her girls, perhaps on holiday from months of hard work with the troops in Egypt.

Taffy and I enjoyed some very pleasant walks through this lovely countryside in the cool of the morning, enjoying the breathtaking views. The warm afternoons were reserved as siesta times to avoid the tiring heat, and evenings were spent sipping the very good quality arrack, from nearby Zahleh, under the stars in the garden.

I found the railway line most interesting, for it was a rack-and-pinion track which enabled the engines to cope with the steep hills, both coming up and going down. Huge cogs ran up the centre between the lines. These engaged with the cogwheel on the engines enabling the drivers to control the trains better on the steeper slopes.

The kitchen of the hotel was, as was usual there, away from the main building and open onto the garden area, where we ate while enjoying the lovely summer weather. The activities in the kitchen provided some unexpected excitement, for as we were breakfasting one morning, several chickens with their throats cut were hurled out of the kitchen onto the gravel of the garden path, flapping around in their death throes among the tables and chairs where we were eating. The excitement continued the following morning when an animated altercation between the cook and the kitchen boy was heard coming from the kitchen. Then out shot the kitchen boy, closely pursued by the cook, wielding a huge carving knife. Away went the boy, leaping down several of the terrace walls, with the cook yelling fearfully and hot on the chase. I think that the youthful vigour of the boy outlasted the energy of the elderly cook – who had to give up before he could commit murder. Tempers must have cooled subsequently for lunch was prepared on time.

By the time we departed for Beirut, our time at the hotel had fulfilled all expectations of rest and relaxation and left me with lasting pleasant memories. Beirut was, in those days, a most beautiful city, and known as the Paris of the Middle East. It had everything – striking French architecture; lovely palm-tree-lined avenues and promenades; and a vibrant nightlife. France had had a great influence in the city for centuries, and especially during the 19th century, well before it had been granted the League of Nations Mandate at the end of the 1914-18 War. French fashion was very evident among the ladies, even amongst the veiled Moslem women, who wore fine, transparent black silk veils through which their, often striking, beauty was visible.

The French influence could also be seen in the flashing neon lights which proclaimed M A R I K A, the foremost bordello in the heart of the city. Madame Marika's establishment was then under the protection and control of the military, while Madame Jeanette ran an "Officers Only" house not far away. There was also Anzac (Australian and New Zealand Army Corps) Harry's Bar and Restaurant, run by an old soldier from the '14-'18 War, a well-known watering-hole; and the Kit Kat Club which operated a nightclub cabaret. There we saw some very creditable song and dance and variety acts. I was particularly intrigued by some belly dancing. Another act appeared to be a Balkan dance performed by two girls in costume. After their performance they came down from the stage and approached our table. Speaking to us in perfect English, they said, "You're English, aren't you? May we sit with you? It won't cost you a lot of drinks, but will protect us from those awful men over there who are looking for a dirty night out." We agreed, of course, but I was surprised to find two English girls taking such risks, following the calling of a nightclub dance act, in such a place as Beirut. They were certainly courting trouble. Apparently they had arrived in Beirut just prior to the War and found they could not get back. Later, they made their way down to Cairo, via Palestine, and telephoned us in Jerusalem, at MeaShearim Police Station, on the way through. From Cairo they would have, eventually, been able to make their way home to England.

It was in Beirut that I had my first and only view of sewer rats. Like many other people, I had heard of these rodents being present in the London sewers but had never seen any. One evening, while sitting on the sea wall overlooking the small bay, I glanced down on the sandy shore and there were two of the animals, literally the size of large cats, just like those we had heard of in the song, "The Quartermaster's Store"! Taffy was as astonished as I was. We watched them forage among the flotsam and jetsam at the water's edge for some 10 minutes or so until they moved towards the wall, jumped down a large drain and disappeared.

Poor Beirut, how you have suffered over the past half century! From being the once glorious Paris of the East you have sunk to infamy. Now you are famous for kidnappings, murder and other atrocities – the massacres of the Palestinian inhabitants of refugee camps. Tragedy has followed tragedy as you have suffered death and destruction in the Israeli/Palestinian wars, even up until 2006. You, who showed such generosity and compassion to your neighbours – in opening your borders in 1948 to the Palestinian refugees surging in by land and sea, having been driven from their homes when the new State of Israel was formed – now suffer the consequences of that generosity. The tragedy was that, in allowing the boys of the Palestinian Liberation Army to use your land as a training ground – for boys they mostly were – in order to try to regain their rightful lands and home, Israel has been provoked into such violent responses. Israel, with all its modern firepower, has advanced right up to Beirut and smashed it with artillery and aerial bombardment. Slowly, you rose from the ashes only to suffer again. But all this was far into the future when Taffy and I visited The Lebanon. They were peaceful times in the Middle East, but all over the world, elsewhere, death and destruction were raging on land and sea.

New Inspector General

Col. Alan Saunders retired as Inspector General of the Palestine Police Force and was succeeded by Capt. Rymer Jones of the Metropolitan Police. Then, many were the new orders and instructions, which issued from Jerusalem Headquarters. It seemed that this Inspector General had come to instil a new spirit into the force. He was soon to find out, however, that this command was very different from the one he had just left in London. After some few months (in March 1944), he arrived at his Headquarters one morning to find that the Jewish terrorists had attacked it during the night and blown a wall in, murdering Asst. Sup. John Scott[1] and several members of the Basuto Rifles Regt. which was the HQ Guard at that time. Capt. Rymer Jones was heard to remark, "This is not like the Metropolitan Police!" Too true. It wasn't! He had, I believe, a Jewish wife and seemed to be inclined to believe a lot of Zionist propaganda. However, we will return to Lejjun and my life there, which was more peaceful than Jerusalem at that time.

Village Life

El Lejjun was the first post where I had been solely in command in a purely Arab area, and I was able to learn much more of the characteristics of the *fellaheen*. The villagers lived a simple, rural life, but they had a shrewd and knowing sense of how to look to their own best interests. The men lived leisurely and enjoyed a life of agriculture and animal husbandry. The older generation were fatalistic to a man and submitted to the will of God, and on any occasion, be it good, bad or indifferent, their main comment was always, "*Il hamdulilah*" [Thanks to God]. Apart from their fear of the realisation of "The Jewish National Home" in their country, their village life was their only real concern.

The village affairs were run by the *Muhktar* and the village committee, which usually worked very well in dealing with trouble and friction amongst the various clans. When the elders and the other members of the committee were honest and upright in their dealings, they received the respect of the majority, and any decisions made by them were accepted and abided by. Unfortunately, there were many villages that were blighted by feud and it was impossible for workable committees to be elected in these villages, so no agreements could be made between aggrieved and aggrieving parties in these cases. In such long-standing feuds it was best if village committees did not intervene, as the aggrieved party would always exact its own vengeance, and other efforts would be wasted. The avenging act, in most cases, was some form of agrarian crime, such as burning of crops, cutting down of trees, barking of olive trees (which causes them to die) or uprooting of plants, while stabbing, poisoning or shooting cattle or sheep, would be another form of "squaring" an enemy. However, I found that during my time in Palestine the younger men deplored these destructive crimes committed for the sake of feud, which did no more than give one party some temporary satisfaction,

---

[1] John Scott, "Scottie", who was about two years older than me, was a very good friend of mine. I met him when he was a young recruit in MeaShearim Station in Jerusalem. He was a grand chap, very efficient and capable, and had a very nice character.

while they awaited further retaliation. Unfortunately, many of the elders spurred the youth to commit these acts by taunts and gibes, declaring that it was honourable for a family to wreak vengeance in this manner.

The boys and young men loved to make themselves conspicuous as "young bucks" in the eyes of the womenfolk by swaggering around with a pistol or a dagger, where the women gathered to draw water, and to this end risked a good prison sentence.

The larger villages were divided into *hamile* or clans, which were, in most cases, large families. Each family had its own *Muhktar*, who was a sort of clan council chairman. It seemed to me that it was this clan structure that worked against progressive ideas. Often, the large majority clamoured for improvements in the villages – such as water systems, roads or schools – but owing to some feud, petty or great, one clan would refuse to enter into the discussions. In these cases the improvements had to be put aside, for the majority were not prepared to work for a scheme that would benefit all, unless everyone subscribed to participate in the planned project.

Another block to progress, it seemed to me, was the dividing up of the lands by all the members of the family on the death of the father. Where a 100 years before a man might have owned 100 acres, by the 1940s it may have been split up by 100 descendants so that each then owned only one acre. However, though the agricultural methods used were very traditional, the land appeared to be well cultivated and in good heart, and many *fellaheen* were very hard-working farmers, endeavouring to improve with new ideas.

Hake Bidhu Allah [So God Wills]

Unlike English farmers, who must of necessity "make hay while the sun shines", the Arab *fellah* generally had no anxiety over the reaping of his harvest, steadfastly refusing to adhere to the old proverb, "Never leave till tomorrow what you can do today." He had another proverb – "There's always some work for tomorrow." An incident which occurred in 1942 will illustrate the extent to which the *fellah* relies on the set seasons of the country and never counts on the rains coming until, at least, the middle of October.

I was in the habit of riding out to Lejjun village in the afternoons to exercise my horse and have a chat with the villagers to improve my Arabic. In September of that year the corn had been gathered and threshed on the threshing floors in the usual Middle Eastern manner – by driving horses or cattle round and round in a circle over it, so as to tread out the grain. On each occasion that I visited, I noticed great piles of chaff and grain had been heaped up to form conical shapes on the threshing floors, to await the right winds for winnowing. When speaking to the elders one day, I suggested that it might be a good thing to start winnowing, as cloudy weather seemed to herald early rains. One old fellow spoke up and said, "No, Sergeant, it is not necessary. The rains are still at least 40 days off, and after harvesting the men are tired. Apart from that we are still in the Ramadan Fast." I replied that I appreciated that I was not *Ibn beladhum* ["a son of their country"] but the heavy cloud and lightning at night was a fair warning of rain. The following Sunday afternoon, the wind began to blow at gale force and then the heavens opened, and for a couple of hours the rain pelted down in a torrent. Next day I visited the village to find a large percentage of the wheat grain spoilt. The huge piles of grain and chaff had become saturated overnight and the grain had "shot", rendering it useful only for chicken food, and the *tibben* [chaff] – which was also very valuable for winter-feed for cattle – was useless. The monetary loss for the village was estimated at £15,000. I met many of the farmers as I walked around the threshing floors, and, mostly, they lamented the fact that one year's harvest was almost completely lost, but some of the older men stroked their beards, and said, philosophically, "*Hake bidhu Allah*" [So God Wills], and took it all in their stride. All looked askance at me when I reminded them of our conversation of a few days earlier!

A Rural Wedding

Serving out in the rural areas, I received many invitations to village weddings, so I think I should include here a description of such a ceremony. When the son of a village notable weds, guests can be seen arriving on every approach road and track. They come by taxi, lorry, horse and wagon, riding horses, camels or donkeys and others come on foot. It is a pretty sight for the country women wear their grandest and most colourful apparel – reds, blues and greens being the most popular colours for their clothes, while many favour white or yellow for head scarves. The men also leave their drab clothing behind and wear striking, long gowns in creams and blues. The wee donkeys struggle along under heavy loads, carrying presents for the bride and groom.

Official negotiations have taken place between the families beforehand and today the celebrations take place. In the village all is a-bustle and the small children are wide-eyed and agog with excitement. As the guests arrive they are all invited to the various guest-houses, while the youths gather in the village squares and open spaces to dance and gossip; much of the gossip concerning the bride price – and is she worth it? Many were the ribald remarks made regarding the nuptial bliss to be shortly enjoyed by the couple soon to be wed. The women usually remain secluded and gather at houses and courtyards, surrounded by high walls, from where they can be heard singing, trilling and ululating. The young men quickly start dancing, accompanied by shepherd boys on their reed pipes. The dances have some very intricate steps, but the music seems to be a repetition of a few bars, which the pipers blow for hours on end. Now, the young bucks of the village, and the guests who have arrived on horseback, get busy cinching up girths for a race or two, while the old men sit around in anticipation of the sport. (Horse racing was dying out at that time of which I write, but, whenever the occasion presented itself, several riders would endeavour to arrange a few races, and much interest was centred on the event.) Now, suddenly, everyone becomes excited as two horsemen go galloping across an open field on the edge of the village. Racing neck and neck, each rider tries his utmost to put his mount in the lead. Spurs with wicked rowels rake the horses' flanks, until, at times, their skin is flayed so badly it looks like beefsteak. Another pair comes forward, and then another, and so the entertainment goes on, until all the riders and horses are streaming with perspiration and the animals blowing badly from such vigorous exercise.

The bride, by this time, has been taken away by the village maidens for her bath. They scent her body, and dress her hands and feet with henna. The youths have also taken away the bridegroom for his bath (which is just a scrub) and dressed him in his wedding clothes. After the ceremony of the bath has been completed, the bride is taken by a procession of women to her new home. She is, of course, heavily veiled. The journey is accompanied by much singing, hand-clapping and beating of tambourines. When the bride has been installed in her new home, the bridegroom is taken to her. With the most solemn expression upon his face, clad in new garments and garlanded with flowers, the groom sits astride the finest mare that can be found in the village and his procession towards the house then begins. Escorted by his friends and relatives, he is surrounded by singing and dancing, and sometimes growling, like angry dogs, to drive away any evil spirits. Shots are also fired into the air to signify his manhood. On arrival at his new home, the bridegroom is ushered into the presence of his bride and they are left alone together, where they should remain for six days and nights. As the families arrange the weddings, many newly weds barely know each other, so this period is considered most necessary to help the couple become speedily acquainted. It is known as the "honey month".

Now comes the time for feasting and leaving the couple to their nuptial bliss. A meal may consist of mutton on mounds of rice and surrounded by roast chicken and pigeons all stuffed with rice and spiced meat. These dishes may be accompanied by salads and yoghurt [lebben]. Flat loaves of bread are handed around, which can be torn into pieces and used as eating implements, and the guests squat around and eat their fill. Then may follow a sweet made from cheese, honey, nuts and spice, which is really quite delicious. For the first time in the day, quiet descends upon the village while the guests eat – and how they eat! The speed with which the affair ends, once the meal is over, is amazing. The guests leave the houses in which they have feasted and after a few farewells, start out for their own homes. Soon the village has returned to normal.

Runway for Liberator Bombers

I was at Lejjun a little more than 18 months and during that time I witnessed a large runway being constructed on the Jezreel plain below, between El Lejjun and Affuleh. Before I left, building work was completed and large Liberator bombers of the American Air Force were using it. I saw bombers take off from there, which then flew out over the Mediterranean to bomb the German Forces in Tobruk, just before the victorious Eighth Army (the Desert Rats) drove Rommel and his army out of North Africa.

New Command

During this time, I was promoted to First Class Sergeant. One day, soon after, I came back from patrol at Umm el Fham to find that Supt. Cafferata had been and left a message. I was to leave immediately and proceed to Qalqilya Station to take command as officer-in-charge. I had to bid a speedy farewell to all the personnel, especially Sgt. Abu Ahmed, and also thank him for all the support and help he had given me, and set off on my way, having made arrangements for the armoured car to bring the rest of my kit later.

—

But before we start to ride down the Mus-Mus Pass on our way to Qalqilya, I will mention the story of the police informer who also acted as a double agent, and the mischief that such an informer can cause.

I learnt from an informer that a man, long wanted for murder, was living in one of the remote villages, working for the *Muhktar*. We made preparations to arrest him and arrived at the village after dark. With my constables covering the house from all angles, I approached the door and knocked – only to find the house empty and that our bird had flown. It later transpired that the informer had visited the village and let the wanted man know that we were coming after him. The poor chap had been involved in an honour killing in his own village and had fled to find sanctuary in this village, where the *Muhktar* had given him employment. He had been living there for about 10 years, and had married and raised a family. Now the interfering informer had led us on a wild-goose chase and caused the man to flee in search of another sanctuary.

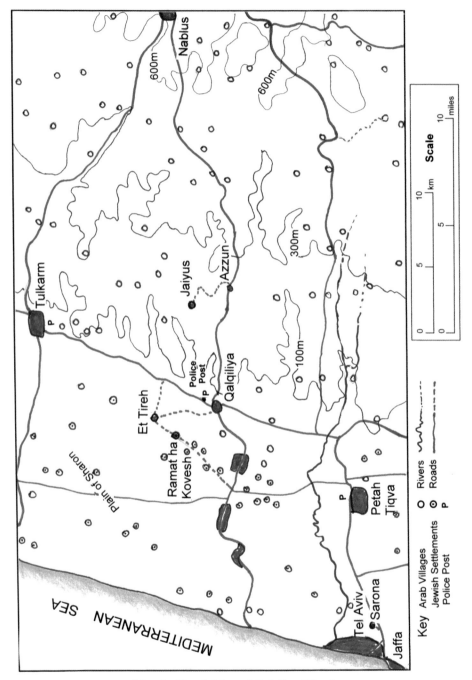

Map 3 : Sketch Map of Qalqilya District.

Chapter 10

Qalqilya 1943-44

Feuding Clans

I had only been at my new station for five days when my first murder occurred in the town during wedding festivities. Inspector Nicholson remarked, "They didn't give you much time to settle in!" Qalqilya was a real "Hill-Billy" town, full of feuding Martins and McCoys – though they went by very different names. There were about six clans in the town and the feuds were very serious – with whole areas of the township almost at war with one another. Five years previously, the Mayor of Qalqilya had been murdered by two local gunmen, who subsequently fled the country and obtained temporary sanctuary in Iraq. Sufficient evidence was collected against these two men and an extradition order was applied for to the Iraq Government. Some years later these murderers were arrested and brought to Palestine to stand trial for the crime. Both were found guilty, sentenced to death and executed in Acre prison. This murder of the Mayor, of five years standing, was the root of much of the feud in Qalqilya. It was believed to have been engineered by a man who wished to become the Mayor. The feud had amalgamated two warring clans against a third clan. We now return to the wedding, where two rival factions had been invited as guests by a third, neutral party. This latest murder had occurred whilst dancing was in progress and the factions had come into contact. Harsh words were exchanged and one of the dancers, Hassan el Hirsh, then drew a dagger and stabbed another, Abdul Latif, in the heart, causing almost instant death.

The culprit then ran off and was hidden by relatives for the remainder of the night, while the elders of the clan conferred to weigh the evidence and prepare his defence. Into the early hours, we searched houses, barns and orange groves, trying to effect his arrest, but were unsuccessful. His relatives gave him the utmost support, but next morning he surrendered to the police, escorted by a lawyer who had been engaged on his behalf and who brought him in. Now, many members of his clan also came to the police station, claiming to have been engaged in an affray the previous evening, and produced medical reports for many minor injuries sustained. This was done in order to influence the court hearing the charge against Hassan el Hirsh, in the hopes of reducing the charge of murder to one of manslaughter – on the grounds that the act had taken place during an affray, and was not premeditated. It was true that an affray had occurred, but it had happened after the killing and resulted from it.

Some weeks later the accused was tried for manslaughter at the District Court and acquitted. The President of the Court, in giving judgment, stated that the court was unable to believe all the evidence of the prosecution witnesses and this was understandable for they were nearly all from the clan of the dead man, with "an axe to grind". Many of their testimonials were bad, for being so determined to have their pound of flesh, the witnesses had told the truth, and more – including additions which were lies.

More than £1,000 had been raised by the accused's clan for his defence, and there was a strong rumour in the village that the judges had been liberally rewarded. Well over 200 people from Qalqilya were present at the court that day, both inside the courtroom and outside. It was as if a Bank Holiday had been declared, and when the acquittal was announced there was a shout of triumphant jubilation. Hassan el Hirsh was taken home in style and those of the clan who had remained at home lined the streets to welcome back their doubtful hero. The fact that the judgment had been in his favour and the accused set free was not the real issue. What they were celebrating was the victory over their enemies.

A feast was prepared and during the evening there was singing and dancing, and the womenfolk were also performing with great zest. The father of Hassan el Hirsh went to the party of the women and warned them not to be so joyful, adding, "You'll probably be weeping and wailing for him in a few months' time." His words did not quite come true, for it was an uncle who paid the price, as you will read later.

Blood Feud in Jayous Village

Blood feuds were not confined to the town of Qalqilya; the surrounding villages had their share. An old farmer in Jayous village had a grudge against a neighbour, and one morning his son waylaid the neighbours' cattle and shot and killed three cows. I was called to the spot and made an examination of the scene, where I found empty cartridge cases and footprints of an assailant. The cowherd, who had fled when the shots were fired, came to my station and gave a statement in which he said he had not recognised the man who had killed the cows. However, on arrival back at the village, under pressure from his elder brother, he then said he recognised the culprit as his neighbour, Ahmed Samha, who had previously denied having been near the spot for days.

To clear any doubt in my mind, I sent for the police tracking dogs. On an identification parade, which included the accused, the police dog, having been given the scent of the footprint I had found, pointed to the accused by putting his paws on the Ahmed Samha's shoulder. Many of the villagers had gathered on a nearby bank to watch the police dog working, and, when he pointed to the accused, a shout of delight went up from the watchers – like a cheer from a group of football supporters at a match.

However, after the conflicting statements of the cowherd, Ahmed Samha was acquitted on the grounds of insufficient evidence. A few weeks later the brother of Ahmed Samha was killed when playing with an unexploded mortar bomb he had found after military exercises had taken place in the vicinity of the village. It was whispered among the villagers, *"Shugal Allah"* ["God's Work"] – "Allah is great and exacts justice himself."

Revisionist Escape from Detention Camp at Latrun October 1943

During the preceding 12 months, about a score of known Jewish terrorists had been detained and incarcerated in a detention camp at Latrun. There, they won the confidence of the officer in charge of the camp, who had been much struck by their diligence in tending a flower garden which he had given them permission to make. Little did he know that under their hut, the detainees were tunnelling an escape route and the garden they were tending with such conscientious care was steadily growing bigger with the excavated soil from the tunnel. And so, one morning at reveille, when the detainees failed to parade, a guard entered the hut and found it empty, for during the night the Revisionist Terrorists had all escaped. At Qalqilya, we were on the edge of the coastal plain, which was the most thickly populated Jewish area, and I knew that we needed to be very much on our toes in guarding against Jewish attack.

Fred Edwards B/Sgt. 559

After I had been at Qalqilya for some months, I came back from patrol to find that Sgt. Fred Edwards had been ordered to report to Police Headquarters in Jerusalem. Next day he returned to collect his kit and personal belongings and told me he was transferred to special duties at Jerusalem forthwith. He departed and that was all I knew at the time. Many years later, about six months before he died, Fred called to see me. While we chatted, he asked me if I remembered when he had been hurriedly transferred from Qalqilya to Jerusalem, and then proceeded to tell me why.

The Palestine Government had ordered a huge consignment of specie (coin and notes) from the UK, and en route to Palestine the ship carrying it had been sunk. It was imperative that this loss was made good somehow, and the police had been requested to assist. Someone at PHQ had checked on Fred Edwards and discovered that he had trained as a printer before joining the force in 1936. He was summoned to Jerusalem, sworn to secrecy and employed to print enough money to keep the Palestine economy running. Printing machinery was installed in some type of cellar accommodation at HQ and a permanent guard posted to keep people away from the vicinity. Fred went to work and printed millions of £Ps worth of paper money. I asked him, jocularly, if he had managed to salt away a little for a rainy day. "No, not a piastre!" he replied.

Station Garden and "Small Holding"

The station was a large Tegart Fort, newly built and like an abandoned building site, so in the early part of the year I made a garden in the station courtyard, as I had also previously done in Lejjun. I obtained some young trees from a Government agricultural station about 12 miles away and planted four conifers at the corners and spreading trees for shade in the middle. I also planted a few bushes and shrubs, and grew some annual flowers such as zinnias.

I inherited some chickens, which I housed in a substantial hen house inside the perimeter fence, around the back of the stables, where they could scratch away all day in the dung maxon. Gifts of live fowls at Christmas-time from people in the village added to the flock. One time I had a turkey hen sitting on 30 chicken's eggs when I was summoned to Jerusalem for an Appeal Court hearing. As we were away for two nights, I asked one of the constables to keep an eye on the turkey to see that she did not desert the eggs. I knew that if she was let out of her brooding coop she was inclined not to return to the eggs but sit in a nearby thicket. On my return to the station I walked around to look for the turkey hen, and my fears were confirmed when I found the eggs uncovered. I picked the turkey up out of the thicket and put her back on the eggs, wondering if she had been off the eggs for both nights. I kept my fingers crossed, and hoped all would be well. Luckily, the weather was very warm at that time of year and even the nights in Qalqilya were hot. Eventually the turkey hen hatched a brood of 28 chicks and I felt the Lord was on my side! The cockerel of this flock was a very proud bird, and may have had something of the Australorp breed in him. He slowly strutted around his territory, head up, and with very deliberate, extended strides. As the young male chicks grew they began to challenge him, and there were some very noisy confrontations, but he always maintained his authority.

One of my worries at Qalqilya was keeping the grass cut, for the police station stood in about two acres of ground. I hit on the idea of buying half a dozen calves to graze the area and sell off after the month of May, when the rains ceased and the grass stopped growing. I had struck up a friendship with an Arab cattle dealer, the Haj Ahmed, who used to borrow money from me from time to time when he went off on sheep and cattle buying trips. He would say that if I lent him £50 or so, it would make his journey so much more worthwhile, and he would give me a little profit a couple of weeks later. *Haj* was the title bestowed on him for having made the pilgrimage to the Holy City of Mecca. At first, I doubted the wisdom of lending my hard-earned money, and I asked Cpl. Mustafa what he would advise. Mustafa was pretty certain that the old Haj would not let me down, so I took a chance and lent the money. The old chap was completely trustworthy, and also became a useful friend and confidant – as travelling to Syria, Transjordan and The Lebanon on buying trips, he got to know a lot of what was going on and would pass useful items of intelligence on to me.

I gave Haj some money and he bought the calves for the station for me. They were very effective at keeping the grass and weeds down and the area tidy. On one occasion when a senior officer inspected the station, he found several calves asleep up against the wall and was too surprised to say anything; but I think he was quite pleased to see the place tidy and well cared for. I explained the purpose of the calves and said they would soon be gone. When the time came to sell my little herd, which had put on some weight during the spring growing season, the local butcher would not offer me a reasonable price, and it looked as though he was trying to pull a fast one at my expense. I discussed this with my old friend, the Haj Ahmed, and he suggested to me, "Don't sell them to him. I'll butcher two each week and sell the meat in the market myself," – which is what we did, and between us we did fair business. Afterwards the old Haj said to me, "To think of the butcher trying to cheat you, and me, of all people! Why, before I made the pilgrimage to Mecca and became a Haj, I was the biggest rogue in this area. I have twisted them all and he thought he could cheat me!"

What with chickens and calves around the station, one Arab sergeant said to me, "You should leave the police and set up a small holding on your own. You could make a lot of money!"

—

The growing of oranges was a very important agricultural enterprise in Qalqilya, as it was in all of Palestine, wherever the altitude was appropriate and there was an adequate water supply. If there wasn't a good natural stream boreholes were sunk for irrigation. However, it was a very time-consuming business, directing the water down all the little irrigation channels between the rows of orange trees in turn – whatever the source of water.

Qalqilya Geese

The geese of Qalqilya were very amusing and entertaining. Many of the townsfolk kept a small flock, and each morning, at dawn or soon after, they would be released from the courtyards of the houses and make their way to the surrounding countryside, where they would forage about, eating whatever was available to them. Come sunset, the birds would all foregather in an open space at the north end of the town in a flock several hundred strong. Then as the sun sank beneath the horizon, the flock would walk into the town and down the main street. As each small flock reached its own gateway, it would separate, and the members would all turn to the main flock and call gently, with a few, "Quack-quack-quacks," as though bidding their fellows, "Good night", while the remaining flock would answer, likewise.

This would continue down the whole length of the main street, perhaps one kilometre or so, until the last little flock had reached its house. I used to love to watch this nightly ritual, and no one will convince me that they did not bid each other farewell for the night.

A Jealous Brother

Dissension between two brothers helped in no uncertain fashion to bring a dangerous criminal to book. On 28th November 1943, I received a telephone call from Petah Tikva Police Station. I was informed that armed men had fired on a motor van on its way to Kafr Kassim village, obviously with the intention of robbing the three Jewish occupants. Luckily no one was hit and the van, though damaged, was able to keep going.

I left for the scene and found two empty .303 cartridge cases near the track, which were marked and kept for future reference. Some shepherd boys in the nearby hills were questioned and though they gave conflicting stories, it was evident that a certain Hassan Aloush, an army deserter, had been in the party which had attacked the van. My next job was to find the wanted man. With a party of mounted policemen, we scoured the hills for nearly three days and nights, sleeping in the villages and resting in orange groves, in search of him. Our efforts were in vain and we were forced to return to the station to rest both men and horses, for all were very tired.

I had not long been in to rest, when during the evening, well after sun down, an Arab came to the station and told the orderly that he wanted to see me personally. I took this man into my office where he told me that Hassan Aloush was in a small hamlet near Azzun Village. I detailed a party, leaving by car for the hamlet, but when still two miles off we had to leave the car and take to the hills on foot, for there was no road. Upon reaching the ridge of a hill, I was able to see the hamlet silhouetted against the starry sky, about a kilometre to the south. Then, taking the party downwind, to avoid disturbing the hamlet dogs more than necessary, we worked our way around. The house in which my man was supposed to be sleeping was pointed out to me by the informer, and I gave orders to surround it, while with one constable I made for the door.

From the information I had collected, I understood that Hassan Aloush was in possession of a rifle and a revolver, so the operation called for some caution. The door was locked and I was unable to force it open, so, standing back from the door-post,[1] I knocked on the door, holding my revolver ready for action. The door was opened by the owner of the house and I slipped in past him to find the wanted man still asleep, with his rifle at his side. The British constable (possibly Bert Rowberry) took the rifle and I roused the

---

[1] Some while previously ASP Drummond had been shot and killed as he had stood in just such a doorway of a house containing a wanted man.

man, pulling him to his feet while I ordered him to raise his hands. Instead, he fumbled for his pocket and not wishing to die in that place from a bullet from his revolver, I knocked him unconscious with a left hook to his jaw. A quick search of his person revealed that he had no other gun, and before he had fully recovered consciousness he had a pair of handcuffs on his wrists. When charged with the offences committed – firing on a motor van on the Kafr Kassim track – he confessed, but denied having fired with intent to harm. CID experts furnished conclusive proof that the empty cartridge cases picked up by me at the scene of the shooting had been fired by the rifle found in the possession of the accused. At his trial he was sentenced to two years hard labour.

I learned later that Hassan Aloush had gone to a certain man asking for shelter for the night. This man sent him to his brother's house and then sent the informer to me. He hoped to get his brother charged with being an "accessory after the fact" and punished with imprisonment. With his brother out of the way he hoped to gain his dead father's young wife, who at that time had a distinct preference for his brother, with whom she had been living.

Zionist Terror Attacks Escalate

A case worked on and brought to a successful conclusion is a very satisfying outcome for a police officer, but the Political Zionists' terrorist outrages, which began with vigour in 1944 after the escape from Latrun, were an entirely different matter. Lack of Government action to suppress these crimes caused many a diligent policeman to lose interest in his job and resign. (I heard later, on the best possible authority, that Prime Minister Churchill had given orders that action was not to be taken against the Zionists for fear of losing the support of America in the War, which was then still raging.)

Listed below are some of the acts of terror which took place in 1944, while many more occurred in the succeeding years.

February 1944   Detective Insp. Green and a B/Det Cons. killed in Haifa, while attempting to arrest Jews carrying explosives.

March   Jerusalem HQ badly damaged by explosives and ASP John Scott murdered by attackers wearing police uniforms.
Haifa CID HQ damaged, three constables being killed.

Jaffa CID billet brought to the ground by explosives – luckily the personnel escaped just in time. (Some police, returning to the billet, saw the bombs being planted and were able to raise the alarm.)

Mr. Brown, HQ Chief Clerk, murdered on his doorstep. B/Cons. Caley and Langtrey murdered in Tel Aviv.

	P (Palestine – Jewish) /Cons. Zeev Flesch murdered at Ramat Gan (13th March)
April	Jewish CID Sgt. murdered.
May	P/Det. Cons. Haim Guttewitz murdered in Rehov Hayarkon.[1]
June	Jerusalem CID HQ blown up.
August	Attempted assassination of the High Commissioner, Sir Harold MacMichael, on the Jaffa Road. Attacks on three police stations by mortars in Jaffa and Tel Aviv.
September	Attacks on Police Stations at Qalqilya, Katra, Haifa and Beit Dajan. Mr. T. J. Wilkin Senior CID Officer murdered in Jerusalem.
October	ASP Weeks assassinated in a street in Jerusalem.
November	Assassination of Lord Moyne in Cairo. Lord Moyne supported the Arab's cause and the terms of *The White Paper for Palestine*.

After the attack on the life of the High Commissioner, Sir Harold MacMichael, a Jewish quarter on the outskirts of Jerusalem was collectively fined £500 for failure to give assistance to the police after assailants fled into the area. Loud were the protests of the Jewish community voiced in the press, claiming that the inhabitants were being unjustly dealt with. The Arab population could not understand at all the leniency with which the Government treated the Jewish population, who were obviously harbouring criminals. They remembered only too well the stern measures which the Government had taken against the Arabs during 1936-39 whenever an outrage had occurred in an Arab area. The reader will remember the destruction in Jenin when I first went there – a result of the punitive action against the Arabs, following the murder of Mr. Moffat, the High Commissioner. "What is this?" they now asked, "High Commissioner only worth £500! How can the Government expect to stop trouble with a policy such as this?" One old man said to me, and rightly too, "An Arab would be fined a similar amount for contravening the Food Control Regulations by moving a ton of sugar. Is the High Commissioner only worth a ton of sugar?"

---

[1] Report in Palestine Post May 1944 "... Stencilled leaflets [were] posted on the hoardings last night in which the 'Fighters for the Freedom of Israel' (the Stern Gang) proclaimed that the police detectives [P/Cons. Flesch and Guttewitz] had been assassinated because of treachery to the Jewish cause. The leaflet also listed nine other persons in Tel Aviv and Haifa, including six detectives, whom they threatened with death if they continued their operations against the Stern Gang."

Local Press Comments

In the Jewish local press editorials appeared condemning the imposition of a curfew in Tel Aviv, and the Jewish areas of Haifa and Jerusalem, after the bomb outrages of March 1944. Jewish passers-by in the streets were now openly hostile to police searches. Many bombs had been made up in suitcases, and one man carrying a suitcase ran off when called to stop. The police opened fire and shot and killed him – but then the suitcase was found to contain only barber's tools. The Jewish press exploded with accusations against the police for taking what they chose to called "Unofficial Reprisals". A Jewish girl when entering a hospital, and asked by a policeman to open her case for inspection, indignantly replied that the constable would be better employed guarding the Government buildings than interfering with innocent citizens. In her anger, she completely failed to appreciate that that was precisely what the policeman was doing.

There were a small number of Jews who did not agree with the aims of Political Zionism and were sympathetic to the Arabs' situation, but 90% of the Jewish population showed their ire when searched by the police, and the expression of satisfaction on their faces when they eyed the damage to the buildings indicated sympathy with the perpetrators of the various terrorist acts, though they would express abhorrence of them. The Jewish press continued to denounce the outrages as detrimental to the Jewish cause and blamed the police and "Guardians of the law", for allowing such atrocities to happen. However, such articles invariably excused the Yishuv for failing to give information and assistance, which would have been helpful to the Government. One such article is quoted below – taken from the *Palestine Post* for Friday, 25th August 1944.

TERRORIST OUTRAGES CONDEMNED
Government Authorities and Yishuv Criticized

Commenting on the latest terrorist outrages in Tel Aviv and Jaffa, the Hebrew press criticizes both the Yishuv and the Government authorities for their approach towards the problem.

The terrorist activities place a trump card in the hands of the Yishuv adversaries, says "Darar", the Labour daily. It is true that there are not many measures at the disposal of the Yishuv but it must not view these crimes as an incurable disease.

The failure of the government authorities, however, is incomprehensible, it adds. It is obvious that their task is not easy, but they are confronted by a small gang in a small country, and the failure to break it up cannot be explained merely by the difficulty of the task. Before the government accuses the whole Yishuv, it ought first of all examine the inefficiency of its own institutions.

The "Mishmar" (left wing daily) states that the persons directing the terrorist acts wish to conquer the Yishuv from within and impose their rule upon it. The existence of such an ultra-nationalist group among a people who have suffered from Fascism is tragic, but more tragic still is the indifference of the people who fail to evaluate the danger.

The terrorists know from the history of India and Ireland that Britain cannot be intimidated; therefore the heart of Zionism, rather than the British Empire, is their aim.

When I read this, I felt that the authors must have held their tongues firmly in their cheeks while stating these views.

It was impossible for me to believe that the general public knew nothing about the hideouts and activities of the terrorist groups, but very little of this information was given to the police. I had hoped that, because of the efforts the Jews had put into the land of Palestine – the many swamps drained and the barren hills made productive – some solution to their problem could be found. However, during the year of 1944, as a result of such mocking commentaries quoted above and the general terrorist situation, the sympathy that I previously felt for the Jewish cause died within me and not a spark remained.

One editorial in the *Palestine Post* featured an obituary for Joshua Wedgwood, shortly after his death. Wedgwood had for years been against the appeasement policy of the Chamberlain Government towards Hitler, and he went on to equate appeasement of the Arabs in the same light, which he felt would bring despair to the Jews of Palestine. As a result, the tenor of the article was one of appeasement for the Jews, which would result in despair for the Arabs in the threat of the loss of their own land.

Departure of Sir Harold McMichael, High Commissioner, 1944

The arrangements for Sir Harold McMichael's departure together with his wife and daughter were published, stating the date and time His Excellency would be departing from Jerusalem station, and an invitation was sent to many officials and residents, who duly congregated at 5.30 pm on Wednesday 30th August 1944. Shortly before the scheduled time, it was announced that the programme had changed and that HE and his family had already left by air.

A few days previously the High Commissioner made a farewell speech over the radio to the people of Palestine, in which he recalled some of the pleasanter days, "before the madness in Germany". He also referred to the political turmoil which reigned in the country and added that he left with mixed feelings.

The day after his departure another interesting article appeared in the *Palestine Post.*

JEWISH VIEW OF FAREWELL BROADCAST

In his farewell address Sir Harold McMichael referred to the years preceding the madness in Germany as the, "Pleasant, friendly world which many of us love to remember." Commenting editorially on the High Commissioner's broadcast, the Hebrew daily "Haaretz" says, "Fortunate are those who have such memories, for to us Jews, even in those days, the world was not pleasant and friendly, this simple and cruel fact must be taken into account for an understanding of what has happened in the Yishuv in recent years.

"Those bitter years could have been great ones", the editorial continues, "had Palestine been given the opportunity to render assistance to the people linked with her, when they were being slaughtered by the enemies of the whole world. The opportunity was not given and the years became years of many 'Strumas'.[1]

"We know," the paper states, "that the main decisions on Palestine are made in London. The White Paper was written there and Sir Harold McMichael was sent here to implement that policy. Whether he could have carried out this policy in a manner other than that he adopted is of minor importance against the decisive fact that his term of office were the years of the "White Paper".

"Because his term of office was a time of bitter experience for the whole World, 'Haaretz' prefers to leave account-taking to quieter days, for in an atmosphere of the 'mixed feelings', to which Sir Harold referred, it is hard to arrive at just conclusions."

The Arab press gave high praise to Sir Harold and hoped that his speech would reach the ears of "interfering persons in America."

And so left Palestine a man who had done his duty and taken a very active interest in the peoples of the country.

For the time being the velvet glove policy was pursued and the Arab police, and public alike, grew to view the British Government with contempt. The Britishers were hard put to carry on with any feeling of pride in the Government, and the taunts of both Arabs and Jews grew very wearing. A Government that, with the aid of her allies, was able to plan and bring Germany to her knees, now seemed unable to handle the situation in the Holy Land. Many of the Jews were openly proclaiming that the British Government officials were afraid to take drastic action against the Jewish population for fear of incurring disfavour in the USA.

---

[1] The *Struma* was a boat carrying Jewish refugees which sank in the Black Sea, about 1941.

And so, while waiting for Lord Gort, who was to succeed Sir Harold, and, hopefully, an accompanying improvement in the situation, the state of security seriously deteriorated.

Attack on Qalqilya Police Station

On the night of 27th September 1944, my own command, Qalqilya Police Station, was attacked just a few minutes before midnight. I had been out to a nearby village, Et Tireh, with my Arab corporal, working on a theft case. As the police horses were all in quarantine owing to African horse sickness, we had gone out by armoured car, and on arrival at the village I had sent the vehicle back, instructing the driver to tell the Station Sergeant that we would return on foot.

Late in the evening, having completed our task and with two culprits in custody, we set off to walk back the 7 km to the station. As we neared the station we met the car coming out to look for us. The British constable in the car told me that instructions had been received to put first degree security on the building.[1] A lorry-load of explosives had been found in the Jerusalem area, so it was obvious that attacks were being planned on police and Government buildings, and we were to take all precautions. As I entered the station I found that the Station Sergeant, Ernie Madigan, had doubled the guards and detailed half of the British police to sit up and be ready to go into action with arms at hand. A Bren gun team had also been detailed to standby in case of attack and Cons. McLaughlin detailed for prowler duty – moving around on the inside of the station and checking the men on the lookouts.

I made several tours of the building, checking on the tower guards, and spent odd periods on the roof, looking and listening. Just before midnight, as I was crossing the stable yard, McLaughlin came to me and said very quietly, "It's come, they're here. I saw six men inside the perimeter fence – all armed with Tommy guns." This surprised me as they must have cut through the fence just as I came off the roof and probably saw me silhouetted against the sky – but if they had fired then they would have given their position away. "Right, Mac," I replied, "Call all the sleeping men and get them off the verandahs." Then armed with my rifle, I went into the north-east tower and, looking through the firing slits in the darkness I saw six or seven men, all dressed uniformly and cautiously moving in towards the building.

I challenged them and receiving no reply, I thought, "I know who you are," and immediately opened fire. Two turned and ran for the gap they had cut in the wire fence, marked with white cloth. The other attackers opened fire

---

[1] An inspector of another police station received the same message, but he ignored it, put the message in his pocket and went out to a café. The station was attacked, the armoury blown up and the arms and ammunition stolen by "The Fighters for the Freedom of Israel". There was also an attack at Biet Dajan but the attackers were driven off.

Qalqilya Police Tegart Fort.

Explosives and other equipment left by the "Fighters for the Freedom of Israel" after attacking Qalqilya Station. Note the Revisionist symbols at the top of the notices.

on me and I could hear the bullets spattering against the wall around my firing slit. Several of the attackers then started to throw bombs over the wall towards the open verandahs, where the men had been sleeping. Some of the bombs landed and exploded in front of the station, but luckily none actually landed on the verandahs. The wireless aerial was blown out of its socket while a message was being sent, and all the windows in the front were smashed, but there were no injuries, even from broken glass.

The Arab Corporal W/T (wireless/telegraphy) Operator very calmly repaired his set and sent out a message that we were being attacked, and asked for help. He had, perhaps, a little overestimated our danger, but his message did no harm. Stn. Sgt. Madigan, with his Bren gun party, had gone into the south-west tower and there engaged another party of attackers which had established itself in a small fruit orchard. This had obviously been meant as a diversionary attack, while the men on the other side carried out a demolition raid on the north wall. Meanwhile, although I had been blazing away at the attackers, they, with great deliberation and not a little courage, had advanced in a crouching position to the wall. However, my fire appeared to have been pretty accurate, for I saw three of them fall, then rise and stagger off into the night. I kept up my fire and then, looking along the wall, I saw what appeared to be a crouching man whom I assumed was tinkering with a bomb. "What! One more persistent bastard still there!" I said to myself; but as I squeezed the trigger and fired, a blinding flash and a thunderous roar resulted, and I realised that I had hit and exploded a very large bomb.

Smoke and dust obscured my view of the wall, and I wondered, "What shall I see when the smoke clears away?" A few seconds later I was much relieved to find the wall still standing, for it worried me greatly that I should find the northern corner blown in. Having seen some of the damage caused to the various Government buildings in Jaffa and Jerusalem, I had expected to find similar chaos.

With Cons. McLaughlin providing cover, I cautiously made my way outside the wall to inspect the damage and found cans of petrol and a supply of "thunder-flash" bombs. It was apparent that, by our diligence, we had thwarted what would have been a very serious attack had we been caught napping. The large bomb had been placed against the wall, on the other side of which was an open recreation area, and once blown would have given the attackers direct access. They could then have doused the stairways and corridors with petrol, and when set on fire, would have penned us in while they rifled the contents of the armoury, which I am sure would have been the main objective of the attack.

After the attack was over, quiet reigned for a while; then a lorry was observed coming at breakneck speed from the direction of Tulkarm. The road ran right in front of the station, and just after the lorry passed the station entrance, a series of explosions occurred and flashes enveloped the vehicle as it came to a standstill. Some minutes later, a second vehicle was seen coming from the same direction, and when still a couple of hundred yards off, suddenly stopped. This vehicle proved to contain Assistant Superintendent Archie Pitt from the Divisional Headquarters in Tulkarm. He blew his whistle and then shouted out for me saying, "Martin, are you alright? The road here is covered with mines." He had discovered a notice on the road, put there by "Fighters for the Freedom of Israel", saying there were bombs on the road. He came in on foot and I went out to meet him. Together we went to see what had happened to the first lorry. As we neared it I shouted, "Who are you?" Then occurred the inevitable comic piece of the scene, as the driver replied, "*Ibn Arab ya sidi*," [We are Arabs, Sir], and continued, "*Shu hada? Bin ruh ila Yaffa*," [What is all this business? We want to go to Jaffa.] We found the lorry driver and his mate unhurt and quite unperturbed after the explosions – as only a genuine Arab can be – fatalistically leaving all to the will of God. They had driven right through the first lot of mines without touching a single one! Cons. Bob Forest – who had been on a course to learn how homemade bombs were put together – then rendered the mines safe by removing the detonators. The excitement over, all but the detailed guards were stood down to rest, but there had been a little too much action to allow many to get to sleep.

At dawn the next day, Superintendent Shadforth arrived to view the damage and direct operations. We searched around the area and found a large number of handmade gelignite bombs and hand grenades of Polish origin. It appears that the "Fighters for the Freedom of Israel" had been badly shaken to have left so much behind, unused. The dogs arrived from Jerusalem and were given the scent from the footprints and trailed, first through a banana grove where more bombs, a haversack and discarded field-dressing packs were found, and then across open country. The trail continued on for a couple more miles, to the gates of Ramat Hakovesh, a Jewish settlement of the most militant kind. There, some strongly smelling substance like solignum had been poured on the ground to drown the scent of the attackers and confuse the dogs. The inhabitants were openly hostile and told the superintendent that they resented his presence in their colony. A quick search of some tents produced military training pamphlets, sketchbooks on the making of bombs and a sketch plan of the attack on Qalqilya Police Station. As we left the settlement, the inhabitants – both men and women – lined the route and chanted monotonously at us, "Bravo Gestapo. Bravo Gestapo," while others threw stones.

That day, two Arabs came to tell us that during the previous night, while they were out on their land, they had seen a party of Jews withdrawing from the action, and moving up to Ramat Hakovesh carrying two bodies on stretchers; which appeared to be seriously wounded or dead. The attack on my station had certainly been a well-planned action, but I had always known it would happen, being so near Ramat Hakovesh, which was very strongly Revisionist and in fact, I had never been to my bed before 3 am each morning for the six months prior to the attack.

That night there had also been an attack on one of the police stations in Haifa Town, in which an Arab constable was killed, a British constable wounded and the building damaged. There were also casualties among the attackers. One attacker sought shelter in an Arab's house, but a citizen's arrest was made and he was handed over to the police.

Continuing Unrest and Lord Strabolgi's Parliamentary Statement

In October 1944 Assistant Superintendent Weeks was assassinated while walking in one of the streets of Jerusalem. A taxi stopped quite close to him and two Zionist terrorists occupants riddled him with bullets from their Tommy guns, before making good their escape. As usual, the public "co-operated" with the police to their fullest that the only useful clue of the assassins' identity was given by the victim himself before he died. (The attackers were recognised Haganah members, who were killed in a later similarly violent incident.)

A curfew was imposed on certain areas of Jerusalem, but lifted after a few days as a result of various outcries against it in the press, which alleged that 70,000 persons were being seriously inconvenienced by "this unjust curfew".

While these things were happening in Palestine, they were being discussed by Parliament in England. On 13th October 1944 the *Palestine Post* published the following statement by Lord Strabolgi in the House of Commons.

> All my Jewish compatriots condemn these acts of violence as I do myself. They are doing a lot of harm to the cause of Zionism in Palestine. At the same time, while not condoning them in any way, we have to realise the background. Arab gangsters succeeded in getting certain concessions before the War, and were appeased, and this small minority of violent young Jews apparently think they too can get concessions by the same methods. The ground would be cut from under their feet if we could get a satisfactory solution of the whole Palestine Problem, which I think is long overdue."

It seemed to me that, far from calming things, this statement was more likely to fan the flame. Could it not have occurred to Strabolgi that the Arabs were fighting to preserve their homes in much the same way that the English would have done had Hitler's army set foot on England's shores?

Et Tireh Village

In spite of all the serious incidents I had had to deal with, I always enjoyed patrolling Qalqilya district and getting to know the area well. One of my constables there, Fred Canter, recently reminded me how beautiful the hills and valleys around Qalquilya were. He remarked on the grey-green of the hills and the beautiful wild cyclamen that flowered in the stony valleys between the *ejbel* [hills or mountains]. I particularly enjoyed the ride to Kafr Kassam along the foot of the Judean hills, with views across the coastal plain to the Mediterranean, only about 15 miles away. There we could stop for a rest and chat to the *Muhktar* and several of the well-respected elders before moving on. The village nestled at the base of the hills, with mango trees growing amongst the houses and olive groves around the edge. The village arable land spread out over the plain.

Et Tireh was another interesting village we visited, but not for the buildings particularly. It was almost joined onto the violently Zionist settlement of Ramat Hakovesh, though the Jewish colony had a wire fence around it. I doubt very much if Et Tireh exists now, for it was on the frontier of the mainly Jewish settled coastal plain. I expect, with the formation of Israel, the Arab villagers have been moved, or frightened away, to live in what is now called the West Bank, and the village destroyed. When we stopped there, the men would automatically draw the water for our horses from a water point, pumped up from a borehole. However, word of our arrival appeared to quickly go around the village, for in no time the women began to make their way to the water point to fill up their large pitchers. Then began a competition between the women and girls to see who could attract the most admiring glances. The ladies would parade before us, balancing their pitchers on their heads, often filled with more than a gallon of water. Some would use two hands to steady the pitchers, some would manage with one, and some could balance the jar unaided. The real experts, however, could balance the jars unaided at an angle – often as much as of 60°! Then, with a graceful movement of their hips, and a stately upright posture, they paraded round before walking back to the village, showing us just what they could do! Even little tiny girls of four, five or six, would accompany their mothers carrying little *chatties* as they practised the art of balancing pots on their heads. This way of carrying loads must be the reason why the *fellaheen* women have such a graceful posture.

I often wondered why so many women came to gather water when we stopped there, and was told they came to see us and be seen by us!

Chapter 11

Qalqilya 1944 continued

Dar Zaid Seeks Revenge.

The state of emergency necessitated much extra work in the security of the station, and permanent guards continued to be posted day and night. However, terrorist activities were not to be my only worry, for now certain Arabs in Qalqilya decided that the time was ripe to take vengeance – for the killing, by Hassan el Hirsh, at the wedding feast previously mentioned.

A party of men, including this presumed assassin, were returning from the guest house to their home one evening when they were fired on only a few yards from the entrance to their courtyard. The uncle of Hassan was hit in the chest and died almost instantly, and a guest from the neighbouring village was seriously wounded. Hassan, who was, of course, the main target, escaped uninjured – the Devil taking care of his own. Someone came running for us and I soon left for the village with my Arab investigating corporal, Mustafa Samara, and found the usual pandemonium, as I expected. Every one of the 60-odd men crowding around was giving instructions, but no one made any attempt to do anything useful. I could see that one man was beyond help and already dead, but the other was wounded and needed urgent medical treatment if his life was to be saved. I told someone to fetch a van, and the word was passed on to the next, and so on.

"Where is the van?" I shouted.

"Now coming," was the reply.

"Who," I asked, "went to fetch it?"

"*Wahad*," [One] was the reply.

Eventually, I ascertained that no one had gone to fetch any transport, so I hurriedly despatched an unfortunate with a well-placed kick to the seat of his pants to ensure that he appreciated the urgency of the situation. This must have had the desired effect for, in about five minutes, my messenger came back with a lorry, and we loaded the dead man and the wounded one onto the back of it.

Meanwhile, neither the corporal nor I had been able to gather any information as to who had committed the murder, nor who had witnessed the act. I left for Tulkarm (Divisional HQ), where I saw the medical officer, informed him what had happened and asked for a post mortem examination on the dead body. On my return to Qalqilya at about 1 am, I learned that several witnesses, having come forward had sworn to having seen the murder and recognised the murderers, had been arrested and detained. Previously, it had seemed that the only witness was the uninjured Hassan el Hirsh.

In actual fact, a meeting had taken place amongst the elders of the dead man's clan and, with a promise of remuneration for their services, they had briefed certain individuals to act as witnesses. Dar Nazzal, the victim's clan, was strong and powerful in the town, and its members were badly shaken that others had the audacity to shoot and kill any of them. Personally, I regretted that Hassan's uncle should pay the price for his nephew's misdeeds, and that Hassan himself should escape unhurt, for I was convinced of his previous guilt.

The following day the dead uncle was buried during a large, solemn gathering in the cemetery outside the town. The women, who had been previously celebrating with joy just a few months before at the acquittal of Hassan, were now truly weeping and wailing – as Hassan's father had foretold. Prior to the internment, a large crowd of mostly neutral clan members had been waiting at the cemetery to pay their last respects and sat around and solemnly witnessed the digging of the grave. Many sat on the other gravestones, while one old man went to sleep in the sun, with a grave mound for his pillow. When at last the body was brought to the cemetery, most people stood up to watch. After the body had been placed in the grave, the Imam intoned the last rites. He addressed the corpse, telling it that it had gone ahead and the rest would soon be following. He instructed the dead person on what should be said at the entrance to Paradise, how he must swear to have followed the teachings of *Sidna* [Our Lord] Mohammed during his time on this Earth, and then bade the dead person to *"Ma Salami"* [Go in Peace].

In a few hours, Dar Zaid, the clan responsible for this murder, had collected well over £1,000, to pay for the defence of the accused. Next morning, the father of Abdul Latif, Hassan el Hirsh's victim, was seen to smile for the first time since his son had been killed, because someone else's life had paid for the death of his son.

Lord Gort's Arrival, the Death of Lord Moyne and Mr Churchill's Views

Lord Gort arrived in the country on 30th October 1944. The usual speeches of welcome were made, to which he replied how pleased he was to have the great honour of being appointed as High Commissioner of Palestine. He soon began to tour the country and won the approval of the Hebrew press for doing so.

Shortly after, on 6th November, Lord Moyne, the British Resident Minister of State, was murdered in Cairo by two Palestinian Jews who when caught, confessed to belonging to the Fighters for the Freedom of Israel. They stated that it had come to the notice of their organisation that Lord Moyne was working on proposals detrimental to the Jewish people and they had been sent to Egypt to assassinate the Minister.

At last some steps were taken in an attempt to force the Jewish population to co-operate with the authorities in the apprehension of members of the terrorist groups. Statements were issued by the Officer Administrating the Government and the General Officer Commanding, blaming the Jewish population for their failure to assist the authorities and warning them of the serious consequences of failure. The action to be taken by decent people was clearly published in the press.

Mr Churchill, then Prime Minister in Britain, made a statement warning the Jews to uproot terror from their midst, and that if assassinations were to be the results of the efforts put into Palestine by HM Government, then a few people like himself, who had been a friend of the Zionist cause, would have to reconsider their ideas.

Chaim Wietzmann Arrives

Dr. Chaim Wietzmann arrived in Palestine, apparently in an endeavour to influence the general Jewish population and change their misplaced sympathies. Several meetings were held by various committees with a view to combating the terrorism which had taken such a strong root. It was decided to excommunicate all terrorists, to give them no shelter and to discharge them from employment. This rather gave the lie to the previously expressed position, where responsible bodies had professed ignorance of the membership of the terrorist organisations. Now the Jewish population, who had previously been in sympathy with and, in a measure, grateful to the terrorists for having brought the Palestine problem to a head, stated that they wished to call a halt. Supposedly secret meetings were held, and it was agreed that in case of further outrages, reprisals would be taken against the terrorists, and for any member of the Jewish community murdered, some of the terrorists would also pay with their lives.

Prominent Jewish personalities sincerely hoped that such an event would not come to pass for fear of a minor civil war breaking out amongst the Jewish people. In such circumstances, the previously professed unity of Palestine Jewry would be revealed to the world as the myth that it really was. The Revisionists stood for open revolt, demanding mass immigration into Palestine and Transjordan, and advocated armed force against any authority opposing it. The more moderate Jews were for settling down peacefully and were prepared to accept that "half a loaf was better than no bread". One Jew said to me, "Most of the Jews in the world won't want to come here to Palestine in any case, and as all we really want is a name (of a country to belong to), what does it matter whether the National Jewish Home is small or large?" (Many Jews did come to Palestine, only to leave again, especially in the early 1920s, before Hitler's rise to power.) The Jewish Agency was, however, unable to voice such an opinion for fear of losing the support of the majority who considered that the Agency should demand the maximum. The general opinion and expectation was, none the less, that partition of Palestine would be the ultimate result of British policy and 80% of both Jews and Arabs would settle down to accept it.

Meanwhile….. Police Sports

Life in the Qalqilya station was not all work and no play. The Palestine Police was a good sporting force. This had been particularly encouraged by R.G.B. Spicer,[1] the Inspector General of the force when I first joined, as he felt that sport made men's minds and bodies fit. It also encouraged constructive camaraderie and kept men from drinking too much in their time off! At my interview, Spicer noted that I had done well in athletics at school, having won the victor ludorum twice, and said to his fellow interviewers, "This young man should do well in the athletics team" – but we had no athletics meetings for six years, due to the Arab rebellion and then the War. However, when conditions permitted, I did occasionally put on my tennis shoes and go for a four or five mile run when at Qalqilya.

All the team sports were played – rugby, soccer, hockey and cricket, as well as boxing, gymkhana events; and polo – as mentioned earlier, for the well-connected Palestine "Heaven-Borns" at Ramleh, on the coastal plain near Lydda. You had to play to a very high level to get into these teams – Monty (Arthur John) Montgomery played football for the PP in the inter-service matches, which were played with all the services – Army, Navy and Air Force. Apart from the Force teams, the bigger stations had their station teams, and the five stations in Jerusalem used to play for the Station Clock! As I was generally posted to outstations, I did not get much chance to play in these team games, but I did enjoy taking part in equestrian events.

We of the mounted section of the Force arranged gymkhanas, where the various Districts and Divisions invited their neighbouring formations to compete in jumping, tent-pegging, dressage and other equestrian events. It was all very enjoyable and kept the personnel interested and lively. On two occasions, I took my horse to compete in the jumping events at the Jerusalem Horse Show. This was a big occasion as, at the beginning of the War, there were about 40,000 horses in the country, brought in by the Yeomanry, as well as the regular cavalry regiments – the Scots Greys and the Royals. The armoured cars were to follow the Yeomanry, so the horses were sent to Palestine to keep them busy until the armoured cars arrived. It was felt that if men had been sent out with nothing to work with, the morale would have collapsed.

---

[1] Mr Roy G. B. Spicer was a great modernising force for the PP. He survived an assassination attempt in 1937, and was not allowed to return from leave in late 1937. He was succeeded by Major Alan Saunders, who, in 1943, was succeeded by Captain John Rymer Jones. Colonel William Nicol Gray was the officer commanding the Palestine Police from 1946-48.

The highlight of these shows, for me, was when Jock Lockwood and I won the pairs jumping at Nablus. It was a well-organised competition and it had been decided that it would make an additional interest if a Totalizator was run. Jock and I were competing against all the expert cavalry riders and not much fancied by the punters. We were the last pair to ride in the event and, riding two grey horses, we completed a clear round and obtained maximum points for staying perfectly together. Only one man had the confidence to put any money on us and the Tote paid out to him 50 to 1. As can be imagined, he was highly delighted.

One of the very few times I visited Beisan, where the Jezreel valley runs in to the Jordan valley, was when Jock Lockwood and I attended a gymkhana there. We rode to Nablus from Qalqilya, where we spent the night, and the next day went on to Beisan. Beisan was where the equestrian HQ of the force was based. The Transjordan Frontier Force had a depot there which had been taken over by the Palestine Police Mounted Section. There was the necessary stabling for a fair number of remounts, as well as manèges and a riding school. Beisan itself was a poor little Arab town, the living conditions being rather harsh.

To begin with not many Arab riders took part, but as the years went on several became more interested in the art of equitation – the development of "legs of iron and hands of silk" – and one or two became excellent competitors. There was also a famous Jewish farrier from the northern district of the Force, Mordecai Medallia, who was an excellent tent pegger.

A Truthful Lover of Justice for the British Government

While I was at Qalqilya, murders among the local Arab population were a regular occurrence, happening about once a month. One, however, was of unusual interest, so I will include it here.

Mahmoud Abu Doleh was a hardened and evil criminal, and during his lifetime had been sentenced to terms of imprisonment totalling 32 years for robbery, murder and manslaughter. One sentence was for 15 years and the other two were for 10 and 7 years respectively, though he probably only served half the time he was sentenced. While serving his second sentence he escaped from prison and joined forces with the notorious robber, Abu Jildeh. The two were together one day in the hills of Nablus District when they met with an Arab police corporal and an Arab constable. Abu Jildeh shot and killed the corporal and would have also killed the constable if Mahmoud Abu Doleh had not protected him and threatened to kill Abu Jildeh if the other policeman was shot. Abu Jildeh disappeared and during the ensuing hunt for him, Abu Doleh gave information and assisted the police in the capture of the fugitive, and later, at the trial, he gave evidence against his former partner. Abu Jildeh was convicted, sentenced to death and later executed in Acre Prison.

For his assistance, Mahmoud Abu Doleh was granted a pardon, but while he was free he decided to rob some of his former enemies. Now his luck ran out, for after firing one round of ammunition his rifle jammed and he was taken prisoner by those he set out to rob. This escapade landed him back in prison with the seven-year sentence.

While Mahmoud Abu Doleh was serving this sentence, his daughter, Bakrieh, was placed in the care of an aunt, who appears to have provided very poor supervision of the girl, and by the time she was 16 she had had affairs with several men, including her uncle. When her father was eventually released from prison he took the girl to live with him in Qalqilya, and in due course she was married to an acquaintance of his, with a dowry of £50, a small sum, in consequence of her past history. Ahmed el Hamawi, her new husband, was over 60, a shoemaker and well-respected among the people of Qalqilya as a hard-working and decent old man. He had settled there some years before, hailing from Hama in Syria. At the time of her marriage, Bakrieh was about 18 and they all lived at her father's house. Bakrieh soon tired of living with this old man and asked to go and live with her aunt. Her husband would not agree, but he rented a small house in another part of the town and took Bakrieh to live with him there.

On 27th August 1944 I received an anonymous letter sent through to me by the ASP at Tulkarem, who instructed me to investigate. The letter read as follows,

"I have to inform you that it has come to my notice that a criminal gang exists in Qalqilya town. A certain Abu Hamawi was married to the daughter of Abu Doleh and lived in the house of Ali Abu Diab.

This criminal gang decided to rob Hamawi of all his money, and while his wife was away at her father's house, took this opportunity and robbed him. And as the certain criminals were known to him, one by one they became afraid the robbery would appear. So they decided to kill him, and they killed him and buried him in his house. The only member of the gang who has appeared before me is Haj Mahmoud el Khudruj, but if I find anything further from my investigations I will let you know.

Signed, A truthful lover of justice for

the British Government.

Anonymous letters are not usually taken at face value, but they need to be investigated before they are dismissed. I went to work making enquiries in the town, but no one seemed to be able to say more than that they knew Ahmed el Hamawi, the shoemaker, and had not particularly missed him. Quite a few did not even know him. I went to see Haj Mahmoud el Khudruj, whom I found to be a delightful old man, well over 70, with a snowy white beard, grand, open expression and a twinkle in his eye. When I informed him of the contents of the letter, he just could not believe I was speaking the truth and was convinced I was having a little joke with him.

I next went to call on Abu Doleh and asked him if he knew where his daughter's husband was. He replied that he understood that Ahmed el Hamawi had gone to Jaffa to buy some leather and had said, "Don't worry if I'm away awhile." Abu Doleh further informed me that Bakrieh was living with him while her husband was away. He seemed a little nervous and I took him to the house where the body was reported to have been buried. A careful search, both inside the house and around the garden, produced no evidence of a body having been recently buried. The garden was overgrown with weeds, some to the height of 3 ft, and I could not find any trace of freshly disturbed soil.

Returning to his house with Abu Doleh, I called for his daughter and took the pair back to the station for more interrogation. I kept them apart so that they could not converse and concoct a story. Abu Doleh repeated what he had told me previously, but added that he had not seen Ahmed el Hamawi before he left for Jaffa – Bakrieh had told him what he knew. Bakrieh was then questioned by Abdin Bey Husheimi,[1] District Superintendent of CID HQ, with a female wardress in attendance. She said that her husband had left her about two months ago, saying that he was going to visit a relative in Syria. She added that she had no idea why he had stayed away so long, and had received no news of him since.

After these conflicting stories, like the proverbial Constable Plod, I became suspicious and felt there was more than a grain of truth to the letter – Hamawi had been killed, but not by a gang. I considered the possibility that the old man had been killed by his wife and her father, for his money. However, I had no dead body and no real evidence of a murder, and consequently no authority to detain them. Taking a party of police to the house where Bakrieh had been living, I had all the loose earth dug over. Working by lamplight until 3 am, the party excavated all the likely spots, and there only remained one patch of ground which was so overgrown that it looked as though it had not been disturbed for months. Next day, we went back to dig this last, overgrown patch, and there, barely six inches under the surface, a human skull was uncovered.

I sent for Bakrieh and her father, Abu Doleh, and told them what we had found. Then Abu Doleh said to his daughter, "Now, what have you done? I

---

[1] DSP Abdin Bey Husheimi was an officer in the Turkish Forces and was a member of the party that came out to welcome the British Forces as they made their way through Palestine at the end of the 1914-18 War. He was a real gentleman – about 5ft 10in, late middle age, with real presence. He was officer i/c CID Jerusalem H.Q.

have spent many years in prison and I don't intend to go back there for what you have done. You had better tell the truth."

And so it was that Bakrieh made a full confession. She said she was tired of living with the old man – he coughed and lay down all the time. She was young and needed a lover, not a sick old man. She asked him for money but he would not give her any and they had had angry words. Then, one day after lunch, when he had gone to sleep, she went into the garden, where she had been working, and brought in her hoe and hit him on the head three times with it, until she could see his brains – then she knew he was dead. She was tried for murder and sentenced to death, but subsequently reprieved. I heard later that she was regarded as quite an authority on gardening in the Women's Prison in Bethlehem where she was detained! She'd had some useful experience!

The Price Paid for Dishonour

In the nearby village of Et Tireh, there lived a family under a cloud of dishonour, for one of the unmarried daughters had become pregnant and so brought shame upon the family. Honour could only be restored to the family by the shedding of blood. The man responsible and the pregnant girl must die. The duty of the killing would normally have fallen upon the son of the family. Sgt. Abu Hassan had informed me of the situation. The man in the case had long since fled the village and his whereabouts was unknown, but Sgt. Abu Hassan told me that, according to rumour, plans were being made to have the girl killed. In an effort to try to prevent any killing taking place, I arranged with the Arab District Officer, under the administrative laws, to have the father and the uncle of the erring girl bound over (in a sum of money that would have to be paid if the girl was murdered) in an attempt to ensure no harm befell her. However, our efforts were of no avail, for shortly after the girl was shot dead, and the male members of the family all had perfect alibis – they were away in Jaffa in a brothel at the time, with plenty of witnesses to support their claims. It was such a barbarous way of carrying on. The girl was quite a handsome lass, and I felt it was a great pity that her life should have ended in that way. It had even crossed my mind to marry her myself – at least that would have saved her life!!

I later heard that the young thug, Hassan el Hirsch, had carried out the murder for £50. No one would give any information which could be produced as evidence before a court of law, and so the crime went entirely unpunished.

A Performing Baboon

Luckily, not all our days were spent with such macabre and tragic affairs – many was the hearty laugh we also had, such as when we went to a gypsy encampment out on the plain. Some of the local Arab farmers had come in to complain that the gypsies had stolen and eaten one of their sheep. They also added that, when they went to see the gypsies, a performing baboon had attacked them and threw hot embers over them. I arrived there with a few policemen and found the baboon in the centre of the encampment. He looked a ferocious beast and started to prowl around us. I said to the gypsies, "Chain up that beast or I will shoot it," for I didn't relish having a lump of flesh bitten out of me. We searched around and found some mutton bones and some sheepskin. I thought it would be best to deal with the matter on the spot, so I said that the gypsies must pay some compensation to the owner of the sheep. They, of course, denied that they had stolen the sheep, yet none-the-less, they started to collect money to pay the fine. Then an old man took a one-string fiddle, collected the baboon on its chain and started to sing a narrative accompanying himself on the fiddle, while the baboon performed the actions described.

He sang, "We travelled here from Jaffa, but we didn't steal a sheep," while the baboon trudged around gravely, shaking his head. Then he sang, "We were very tired and we went to sleep," and the baboon lay down. "We rode our horses out of the village," he continued, as he handed the baboon a stick. The animal placed the stick between its legs, like a child riding a wooden cockhorse, and skipped around in a circle. We were all so amused with the act that we paid money into the collection that was being gathered to pay the compensation, and then handed it over to the farmer who had lost his sheep. It seemed such a bizarre situation – the police paying into the compensation fund, but really it was worth it.

Food smuggling

Owing to the Food Control Regulations, smuggling was a prevalent offence, for this was the fifth year of the War; it was also very difficult to prevent. Flour, salt, sugar and eggs were the main commodities smuggled in from Transjordan, and probably came down from Turkey. Personally, I could never regard this as a serious crime, a little black market food helps out rations during war time: but the Palestine Government viewed it very seriously, as it was regarded as likely to completely upset the economy of the country. The smuggled goods were mostly brought in by pack animals, though sometimes vehicles were used. It was very difficult to catch the smugglers – with their load-bearing donkeys, horses or camels – red-handed, as they used small tracks and paths by night. Our night patrols managed to pick up a few poor, unfortunate individuals who were trying to make some money by supplying the black market, but I am sure our catches were only a small percentage of the amounts smuggled. I knew several of the local Arab smugglers and was on good terms with them. They regarded this form of smuggling as a bit of a joke, or sport even. Once one of them, a likeable character called Ahmed el Basha, said to me, "*Shawish*. I'll tell you what I am bringing in and when I

Jerusalem: Street performer with animals, including a young baboon.

am bringing it, and I bet you £5 you won't catch me!" I think he "bashed" me with his smuggling activities for I never caught him. Generally, the whole population was in favour of the smuggling, for sugar, salt and coffee were scarce and rationed, and Arabs have a very sweet tooth and also rely on salt.

Corruption in Port and Marine HQ

Hashish and opium smuggling was an entirely different matter and could not be treated so lightly. Corporal Mustafa Samara was a very astute, knowledgeable officer, and was excellent on these cases. He had a good nose for drugs and was quite fearless in following leads. He was a tall, very handsome man, who should have been an inspector at least, but apparently there had been some question of him having taken a bribe in the past.

Several cases of drug smuggling were successfully dealt with in Qalqilya. A particular case bears a special mention, though the senior officer in particular would, I suspect, have been glad if it had been forgotten. However, he died some while ago now, and will not be affected by the telling of this tale.

One evening we had a police roadblock near the station, primarily checking vehicles for the movement of Jewish terrorists with explosives, for their attacks were continuing in a more arrogant and aggressive manner. Corporal Mustafa Samara was with the party on the checkpoint when a police vehicle arrived. It was a Port and Marine Police pick-up from Haifa, and was driven by Arab Constable Tewfic Khatib, who actually hailed from Qalqilya Township. As he was approached by a policeman on the checkpoint he said, "Is this the road to Jaffa?" Then Corporal Samara, on smelling the substance, shouted, "Hashish! Stop him!" As the driver tried to slip into gear and drive off, British Cons. "Pop" Grant jumped onto the running board with a drawn revolver and forced him to stop. The vehicle was found to be carrying eight four-gallon petrol tins filled with hashish. When questioned, Cons. Khatib refused to explain what he was doing, but did say, "I will not make any statement, or say anything about this matter until I have seen Mr. Horsbrugh," (the Deputy Superintendent in charge Port and Marine).

It was late at night by then, and Tewfic was held in custody. Next day DSP Frank Horsbrugh came down from Haifa and, being senior to ASP Denis Toulson, who was i/c Tulkaram Division, was allowed to see Tewfic in private. After he had interviewed Tewfic, Horsbrugh went to see ASP Toulson and told him, "He'll give you a statement now." Then when charged with being in possession of hashish, Tewfic replied something to the effect that, "I picked up the hashish in Haifa harbour and was told to take it south. I was told that on the road I should be stopped and I was to use the passwords, 'Is this the road to Jaffa?' I would then be told what to do with the hashish." He did not incriminate or implicate any other person or persons and after the preliminary enquiry, Tewfic was remanded for trial by the District Court. At about the same time DSP Horsbrugh applied for, and was granted, overseas leave to Australia – which was a surprise to me. (It was impossible to go to England at that time.) Tewfic Khatib was tried before the District Court at Nablus. He pleaded guilty and was given a fairly lenient sentence. The Arab President of the Court said at the time, "Tewfic, we feel that you are carrying out orders and shielding someone higher up in the Service. If you were to disclose the full facts, we could deal with you even more leniently."

During a recess, the Arab Crown Council prosecuting at Tewfic's trial said to me, "Why did the officer, Mr Horsbrugh, go on leave to Australia? As far as we know, he has no relatives there, or other connections. We all feel there is something very fishy about this case." I also felt it was "fishy" and believe Police HQ Jerusalem were like minded.

An Art Exhibition

At one time, Corporal Mustafa Samara and I had to appear before the High Court of Appeal in Jerusalem. We travelled to the city by bus and after our business at the court was concluded, I had decided to go to the Annual Jerusalem Art Show in the Mamillah Road – an open exhibition for members of art clubs etc. where one or two policemen had entered their pictures. I mentioned to Cpl. Samara that I would like to have a look at the exhibition, and appreciated that he might like to do something else, so we could meet up later and return to Qalqilya together. To my surprise, Mustafa said he would like to come with me, so off we went. Walking around, my attention was particularly drawn to a lovely pastel of some flowers. Mustafa, however, was not very impressed with the impermanence and fragility of the pastel technique, and remarked, "It's not as good as your pictures," (I dabbled in watercolours). "Look, it comes off," he continued, as he gently touched the paper and showed me the pastel on his fingertips! I was a little anxious that some damage had been done, but luckily that was not the case, and no offence had been caused, so we enjoyed looking at the rest of the exhibition together, and then made our way back to Qalqilya.

Locusts

Locusts were not a plague that visited Palestine regularly, but every 25 years or so a swarm would appear, having migrated from Arabia. It so happened that a swarm came up in 1944, and as far as I could gather, the last major swarm had been in the very early 1920s.

From Qalqilya, lying as it does at the edge of the coastal plane, the land behind it rises steadily to the heights of the Samarian hills on the eastern side and then drops away to the Jordan valley and the Dead Sea Depression. In two miles, the road to Azzun winds its way eastward, and climbs up these hills to an altitude of 700 or 800 ft. One afternoon, when a small party of us were making our way towards Azzun in an open-top jeep, we encountered a swarm of locusts coming over the foremost brow of the hills towards us, and soon we were in the thick of it, as the insects made their way down the hills, westwards, towards the sea, flying no higher than 10 or 12 ft above the ground. Fat locusts smashed and squashed themselves against the windscreen of the vehicle, so that it was impossible to see through the glass. However, by peering over and around the windscreen, the driver managed to see well enough to reach the brow of the hill, and there we stopped, right in the middle of the swarm. Then, looking back, westwards down the hills, I saw one of the most beautiful sights I have ever seen. The iridescent wings of the locusts, reflecting the rays of the afternoon sun, filled the whole valley and clothed the hillsides with a scintillating opalescence. It was as though a beautiful, shimmering mist covered everything, as far as the plain, some three miles or so away. The scene was of such breathtaking beauty that I was held spellbound, and reluctant to think of the disaster that would follow. I felt truly lucky to have witnessed one of nature's great spectacles, and lingered awhile, taking in the whole scene, as the swarm flew on its way towards the coastal sand dunes.

Beautiful though it was, death and famine can follow in the wake of a locust swarm. I was told that this was a small swarm – compared to those that occur in the Red Sea area and the lands of the Horn of Africa – but there must have been millions of insects in it, and while moving it probably measured a mile or so wide and three or four miles long. I would find it hard to imagine a larger swarm. In appearance, locusts are very similar to large grasshoppers, and, when swarming, the bodies of the females are reservoirs of eggs, each containing up to 150. They fly along until they find a suitable sandy spot and then alight upon the ground. Here the females bore their bodies into the sand and die, leaving the eggs to incubate and hatch in the sun-warmed dunes.

The swarm that I observed eventually settled about five miles from the coast, where they buried their eggs. When the swarm is travelling it spells disaster for the crops where it settles, for it does immense damage, eating everything where it lands. However, when it flies off again, adjacent areas are spared. The truly dangerous stage occurs soon after the eggs hatch, when the juvenile locusts appear like small ants. As they emerge in their millions, they start to devour any and everything in their path. They grow at a phenomenal rate from the "ant" stage to the hopper stage, and then develop wings and begin to fly. As an old Arab farmer aptly put it, "Once they hatch, they start to move eastwards, back to the land of their fathers," in Arabia. Unless they are controlled, they eat everything they can while they continue their journey. I was told of a baby left in a cradle in the fields while the mother tried to drive a swarm of locust from the crops. The poor mite was killed by the locusts, which ate out its eyes and bit its skin so badly as to cause death.

Our Divisional Inspector, Inspector Nichols (who we all knew as "Old Nick!"), was appointed Locust Control Officer, and with the Agricultural Department, he set about the destruction of the newly-hatched swarms. Poisoned bran and meal was spread in the path of the newly-hatched insects as they advanced eastwards. They soon died after eating the bait, and others following ate the bodies of the dead locusts and died in their turn. The dead creatures piled up in drifts, as snow does when driven by the wind, and some of these drifts were 2 ft. deep. Where locust are able to land and lay their eggs in unfrequented areas, the swarms can reach such proportions as to leave large areas desolate.

I am told that the fully-developed females, ready to die, make a very savoury meal. Although I have never had a dish, I can well imagine this to be true, for the egg masses look much like hard cods' roes.

Danger from Old Turkish Shells

Near the village of Azzun was an old Turkish army ammunition dump. It was supposed to have been cleared of artillery shells after the 1914-18 war, but the clearance could not have been thorough enough for, from time to time, the *fellaheen* ploughing in the area would unearth an old Turkish or German shell. These shells were often used in family feuds, and during my time in Qalqilya I had several such cases, which usually occurred in the following manner.

In a typical Arab village house, often horses, cattle or sheep would be lodged on the ground floor of the house, and the family would live and certainly sleep on the first-floor ledge or mezzanine. The kitchen was usually built very near, but separate from, the living quarters. The kitchen fire was fuelled with wood and cow dung and the hearth contained hot embers for 24 hrs. of the day. If an old 3 or 4 in. shell was placed in the embers, after some time it would heat up and explode, blowing the kitchen to smithereens. So, when trouble was afoot and someone wished to pay off an old score, one of the ways of doing it was to dig up an old shell and place it in the kitchen ashes during the still of the night. Then, during the small hours, there would be a loud explosion and one of the feuding families would awake in a state of alarm to find the kitchen had been demolished. Luckily no casualties were reported in my time at the station, but one poor innocent old mule was injured.

Hitler's Persecution of the Jews, Arab Sympathy, but Fears for their Homeland

During this time of which I write, Hitler was still in power in Germany and controlled most of the rest of Europe, and thousands, if not millions, of Jews were being transported to Concentrations Camps and suffering genocide in the notorious gas chambers, and by neglect and starvation in work camps; we continually read of these atrocities in the daily *Palestine Post*. The Arab press, *El Falastine* and *Hiwadeth*, also reported the fate of the Jews under Hitler's Nazi forces. Arab sympathy for the Jews was greatly aroused and generally they were much incensed that the Jews should be so treated. I vividly recall a conversation I had with an Arab notable in Qalqilya, Hassan Abu Amsha,[1] who was horrified at the news of German atrocities against the Jews. He said to me, "Those poor Jews in Europe! Why, oh why, does Hitler treat them so? They all want to come to Palestine now, but if they all come here, from where shall we be able to grow our food and eat?"

In view of all that has happened to Palestine and the Palestinian Arabs since that conversation, I feel I must include here the fact that the Arabs were not, and are not, anti-Jewish. They were, and are, only fearful for their survival, and in Palestine it is now plain that their worst fears were well founded. There is no justice and only might is right. Jewish propaganda had poisoned public opinion in the Occident, where there is also very significant Jewish control of the press. With the support of America, they have become the most powerful and most feared people in the Middle East. In 1982, the Israeli Government exposed themselves as heartless and barbaric, in Beirut it sanctioned the massacre of hundreds of poor defenceless Palestinian refugees – old men and women and small children, by the so called "Christian" Militia, the Falange – virtually getting the non-Moslem Lebanese to do their filthy work for them. God will never forgive them.

Jayous village

However, I must go back 40 years now and continue the story of my time in Qalqilya. One of the villages in the station area was Jayous. This was a very special village, unique in the locality for it was famed for its supply of government servants, involving practically the whole of the male population between the ages of 20 and 50. The civil service, army, police, tax collectors and customs, all had their quota of men from Jayous. The houses were mostly built like fortresses, with high windows to prevent prying eyes. When I visited the village on mounted patrols, I never saw any young men – only very old women. The young girls and middle-aged women were kept very much under lock and key, only going out from their houses to take the air once or twice a week in a party, all chaperoned by the old ladies of the village. One time my patrol came across the young women and their

---

[1] Hassan Abu Amsha liked to tell about the time when, as a young man, he had been conscripted into the Turkish army. His parents tried to get him out but he was very willing to go, for he felt it would be a good opportunity to travel outside Palestine. He enjoyed the experience and was selected to become his Commanding Officer's batman. He came to live in the CO's house and fed very well.

chaperones while out walking, and they quickly drew their veils across their faces to hide themselves.

I was told a rather sad story of this place. Some years before, a Bedouin sheikh camped in the valley below the village – and he had a beautiful young daughter. One of the youths of the village saw the young girl and fell in love with her. The old Bedouin let his daughter be married to the young man, and so she went to live in the house of her husband's family, where after years of nomadic wandering she was kept very much indoors. After a few weeks her father came to visit her, but was told that now she was married he could no longer regard her as his daughter, neither could he see her. He went, but then stood nearby, and called his daughter's name, and soon she appeared at a window. She told him that her life was like being in prison, and she was very unhappy, which made the father very sad. He came back next day with his rifle and called to her, and when she appeared at the window he shot her dead, and gave himself up forthwith. When he was taken to court he said he had no regrets for what he had done, for he was sure that his daughter was better off dead than shut up like a caged bird.

Transfer to Nablus

I had, by this time, done nearly all my service as a sergeant in charge of outstations. The District Superintendent visited me one day, and asked if I was happy at the station. I replied that I was happy wherever I was, but I had been in outstations for almost six years, and I would appreciate some time at the Divisional or District HQ. So it came about that I was transferred to Nablus as the mounted sergeant of Nablus Rural Police Station, the HQ of the Samaria area, about 60 km north of Jerusalem.

176

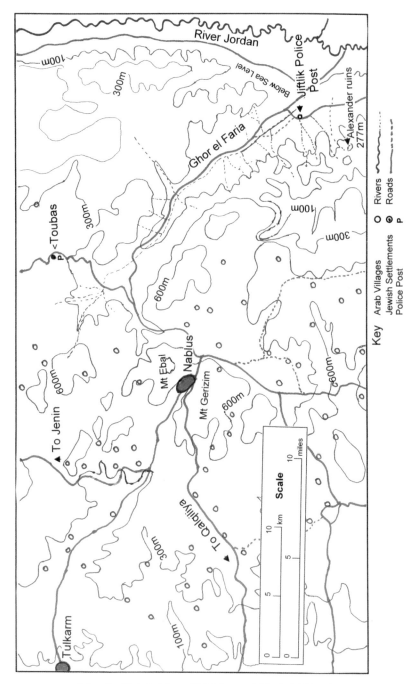

Map 4 : Sketch Map of Nablus and Toubas Districts.

Chapter 12

Nablus 1944 – 1945

Nablus station was quite an enjoyable change for me. It is always said that the captain of a ship is a lonely man, and in some ways the NCO in charge of an outstation can be a lonely man too. At Nablus, I now lived in the Sergeants Mess, and had all the other sergeants for company – some became friends of mine for many years. One was Sgt. Drayton, a very big fellow – about 6 ft 3 in. His father was the Police Sergeant at Charring in Kent, when my father was the Police Sergeant in the nearby village of Lenham. The world is a small place. I met up with Beattie here and Gregory "Greg", who was the Store Sergeant.

Now my duties were very different and, I might add, so much easier. Instead of being responsible for everything from A to Z, I was really only responsible for the stables, horses and the work of the mounted personnel. I found I had much more leisure time, and in addition we had a police club across the road from the station, complete with billiard table, restaurant, pleasant bar and lounge – and more time to make use of it. A different district area added to my new interests, and I was able to choose which areas I undertook to patrol. Naturally, in due course, I visited each and all of the patrol areas, and soon knew the entire district.

The station at Nablus town, which included the stables, was the rural HQ and was housed in an old Turkish building. The town, Shechem of the Bible, was situated in a valley between two big hills, Ebal and Gerizim, mentioned in the Bible. The hills came right down to the back of the stables of the station. It has a very pleasant climate, being not too extreme in temperature. The slopes around the town had once provided wonderful grape-growing conditions, but during Turkish times the people of Nablus had upset their Turkish rulers in some way, and they were made to grub up all their grape vines and plant cacti on the terraces instead. This had left the hillsides around the town very bare, except for cacti. A few people lived out of the village in little hamlets, or *khirbet,* with their farmland around them, but most people lived in Nablus town and had to make their way down to their land and crops, one or two miles away on the Samarian Plain. The road out to Jiftlik led eastwards down to the Jordan River and was consequently on a busy smuggling route.

A German Parachuted Party

In a late effort to swing the War in their favour, the Germans dropped some officers and a few Arabs (who had fled to Germany in 1939 and 1940) by parachute into Palestine. These included one, Hassan el Salameh, who had been a rebel leader in the Nablus area during the 1936/39 insurrections. Like Lawrence in the 1914-1918 War, these German officers had brought huge quantities of gold coin with them. The idea was that the parachute party, aided by the gold, would foment trouble among the Arabs, using Britain's past broken pledges as a reason to cause them to again revolt at the idea of the Jewish National Home. Troops would be required to quell an uprising and in doing so would have to be drawn off from Italy, where they were being used against the Germans.

With the threat of this in mind, one of the operations I was concerned with was to comb the area between Nablus and Ramallah, with the aim of driving any of the parachuted party who may be there into an area prepared for a trap. Over a period of about a week we patrolled to a timetable, sleeping out at night and eating in the villages. Our mounted column – along with columns from other stations – moved towards the "trap area" in the south west. It all went to plan and at noon at certain map reference points on the appointed day, Very Lights were fired from six different hill tops, by six different mounted patrols which had converged on the trap area. However, in spite of the success of the co-ordinated plans no one was caught in the trap. In fact, the German officers were taken in a cave in the Jordan Valley, not far from Jericho, by the TJFF a few days after they were dropped, and much of the gold was also captured. The Germans lost one bag of gold and that had given the show away. It so happened that a Bedouin found the gold scattered where the bag had burst. He tried to keep it a secret, but gold coins started to appear in the market place and soon the word was out. The *Palestine Post* reported that one of the parachutists was "over six feet tall, speaking Arabic, German and Scandinavian, as well as English with an American accent."

-

It may be of interest to include here another incident involving Germans in the desert of North Africa that I learnt of a few years later. My informant was Thompson, an intelligence officer who had been in the Palestine Police before the War, and I met him again after the War in Nyasaland. He was promoted to the Uganda Police and seconded to the British Army in the Western Desert during the War. After the Germans had been driven from North Africa it was hoped that the air route across that region would be safe. The route from the Middle East to the UK followed the North African coast to Gibraltar, where the planes refuelled, and they then flew out over the Atlantic and on to England. However, there had been several mysterious losses of various Allied aircraft taking this route. Mr Kingsley Heath, the Deputy Inspector General of the Palestine Police, was lost on one flight, and some weeks before that General Sikorski, a Polish General from the Free Polish Forces, was also shot down over North Africa. No one knew how the Germans were able to launch these attacks, but it transpired that they had managed to develop a small, but very effective, fighter air base behind enemy lines in the North African Desert. An Arab came to Thompson one day and reported to him that he had seen a group of Germans and some aircraft in the desert. "How do you know they are not British?" Thompson asked. The old man answered that he knew they were not British because they did not swear like British soldiers. "British soldiers are always saying f---ing this and f---ing that, and these airmen did not talk like that!" he explained. So, they made arrangements to take the old chap with them on a raiding party at dawn. When they came to the sand dunes, just before the fighter base, they left their vehicles and went on foot, taking the automatic machine guns with them. Over the brow of the dunes they saw a small group of aircraft and tented accommodation for the personnel. They opened fire on the aircraft and damaged a few but as a result of the action the pilots came dashing out of their tents and climbed into the planes – and one did get away. The other airmen were taken into custody, but not before their wireless operator tapped a massage through. The British wireless operator tried to continue the message, in the hope of finding out where the signal was coming from, but the receivers must have realised by the different rhythm of the message being tapped, perhaps, that it was a different operator and terminated the transmission.

Storks – A Spectacular Display

When journeying north from Africa to Europe and Western Asia, Palestine is on perhaps the most important of the three main spring migration routes that birds take. The return journey southwards is equally important but less spectacular. When I was first in Palestine, I remember one spring day in Jerusalem watching storks fly north all day long. (The Arabs have the same story about storks bringing the babies as we do, and consequently the stork is known as *Abu Saad* – Father of Saad – Saad being quite a common name.) A few storks make their homes in the villages of Palestine and drop out from the main migrating flock, in little groups, but most continue northwards.

When I was coming back from patrol in the Nablus area one day, I saw a sight which has remained vivid in my memory ever since. I was riding eastwards, towards the town, with the setting sun behind me, while a couple of miles off, up in the sky, I saw a flock of several hundred storks flying above the western edge of the Jordan Valley. They wheeled around sportingly, as though playing "follow my leader", and at times they would form a spiral and steadily dive in a corkscrew, down towards the earth. The underside of the wing is dark, and does not reflect the light, while the upper, white feathers reflect it very brightly. At times, I could see bright specks of white, like stars, and then as the storks turned, with the dark undersides towards me, they disappeared, only to suddenly reappear again moments later. As they spiralled down, they appeared like silken threads floating down from above.[1] It was such a beautiful sight that I reined in my horse, so I might watch and enjoy it.

As I watched, an elderly Arab farmer came towards me along the track, holding a bunch of newly-developed corn ears in his hand. He had obviously been to inspect his fields and was taking some ears back to his village to show his fellow farmers how the crop was coming along. As he neared me, I greeted him, and indicating the distant aerial spectacle I asked, "Have you seen the storks flying in the sky behind you?" He turned to look into the eastern sky, but as he did so my horse, Rusty, stretched out his neck and cleanly bit off the corn ears the farmer was holding, leaving only a bunch of short stalks protruding from his clenched fist. I shall always remember the look of sheer amazement on the farmer's face as he turned back and looked at the corn stubs, for it happened so quickly; but luckily he was a man with a good sense of humour and entirely appreciated what had happened.

-

On writing of nature's spectacular displays I should mention the wonderful sight of a flock of starlings that I saw one winter evening when stationed at Lejjun. The birds, on their winter migration, had congregated in an enormous flock flying above the Plain of Armageddon, just south of Nazareth. They made a shape like a huge, long sausage, and then, as though someone had pulled some plugs, they poured out of this shape at both ends and also in the middle. Then they flew all around and up into the sky and formed a perfect sphere, like a football. Then once again they all fell out of the bottom of the sphere and flew around to form anther shape, before eventually flying off to roost.

The Young Haj

One Arab shopkeeper I knew had made the pilgrimage to Mecca and so became a Haj. I called on him soon after his return to offer my congratulations. He invited me in and, after the usual offering of coffee, he related to me an account of his journey and the sights he had seen. He told me, in particular, of a public execution he had seen in Mecca. It seems that a member of a sect had been observed deliberately fouling the Holy Stone, the *Kaba* of Mecca, by smearing human excrement on it. The man was arrested and admitted the offence forthwith, saying that he had travelled from some remote area of Iran for that express purpose. The Iranian Ambassador had been informed to see if it was possible for him to intercede for the man, but it seems that he told the accused man that there was nothing he could do for him, and in fact

---

[1] Jack Ammonds also remarked the stork migration in a letter. On one occasion, when about to reach Jenin from a mounted patrol, he witnessed, "at high level, the wheeling of thousands of storks on stationary wings – a most impressive sight." For more natural history and Palestine Police memoirs see *Rural Thoughts from the Holy Land* by Thomas Curd.

he deserved to die. The accused man was then led into a large public square and the executioner, a huge black man, appeared carrying a scimitar. The accused was made to kneel and the scimitar was swung, almost severing the head, the task being completed on the second cut. The executioner held the severed head up for all the assembly to witness, and while they roared their approval he held high the scimitar and drank some of the victim's blood.

That was one of the most gory of his tales, but he was also able to bring information of an absconder whom I knew who was wanted for murder. The man had come to talk to him in Mecca and asked him to take back news of the meeting to his relatives and tell them that he was well and had a job as a bus driver.

Ancient Ruins and Smugglers

Just before Christmas 1944, my Station Inspector, Buck Adams, who had been my sergeant for the Hebron mounted column about six years previously, came to me with a proposition. He wanted to make a trip to see some old ruins that were reputed to date back to the time of Alexander the Great (or another Alexander?), which he had heard the Arabs talking about. They were situated in the Jordan Valley, some miles from Jiftlik. He planned to ride down to Jiftlik, stay the night at the Police Post, and then journey out to see Alexander's ruins the next day.

That part of the Jordan Valley is a most desolate wilderness called the *Ghor*, and is reputed by some to be where Jesus fasted for 40 days. For most of the year it is a barren, arid area, but for a month or two, following the winter rains, the hillsides get a little green cover – and various flowers, such as small red and white anemones, bellflowers and forget-me-not like flowers appear.

I was pleased to go with Buck, and we set off early, with three Arab colleagues, on the long ride to Jiftlik, arriving during the evening. Next morning, soon after dawn, we set off to see if we could find the old Fortress of Alexander which had been built, it was said, about 300 BC. The further we went, the rougher the ways became, until they were just stony animal tracks, either heading steeply up hill or vertically down, so that we had to lead the horses for most of the way. This hard going particularly affected my horse, Rusty, and he became very bad-tempered. While I was leading him down one particularly rough and steep hillside, he was so disgusted with the conditions that he bit me on the shoulder. I turned and struck him with my whip, and looked him in the eye, and we stared at each other. Luckily, I saw the funny side of the situation, and said to him, "Alright old chap, I know how you feel. I don't much like this bloody track myself." I gave him a pat on the neck and re-established our good relationship. That was the only time when we had not been the best of pals.

At about 11 am, we reached the ruins, and very interesting they were. Built on top of a conical hill, with only one spur leading to the summit, it was an ideally-situated defensive position. Many stones had obviously been carted away, but though the remainder were covered with mossy growths, they gave a good indication of the rooms or halls in Alexander's fort. I just wondered about the water supply in such an arid area. However, perhaps 2,300 years ago, there may have been some springs in the vicinity. The place was very remote, far from any regularly-used tracks or roads, and I felt then that I was immensely privileged to have been one of the very few Europeans to have visited those ruins.

This expedition to the ruins turned out to be a very useful patrol, for as we were returning we topped a rise and there below us was a party of about eight smugglers, resting themselves and their pack animals. They did not see us approaching, and for sure they were not expecting to be surprised by a police patrol in that remote and desolate area, just around Christmas, so we got fairly close before they were aware of us. Then, when they did spot us, they ran in all directions, trying to hide the packs of contraband – sugar mostly, and some rice. We galloped down into their camp and soon rounded up all the men and goods. It was bad luck for them that we should have been out sightseeing, and so caught them as we did, but it illustrates just how important it is for rural policemen to visit unfrequented areas.

I think it is of interest to note how the affair was dealt with. Inspector Adams instructed the smugglers to send one of their party with the animals to Nablus Police Station, while he would take the others into custody and return them under arrest. The smugglers said that one, with the contraband, would not be safe, for he might be attacked by a hyena [el dubbah] – it would be best for two to travel together. So it was agreed, and two men started off with the pack animals while the remainder came with us. I feel this shows the mutual trust there was, even between the police and the smugglers, and so we kept on good terms, while each did his duty, according to his own lights.

Arab Manners and Hospitality

Generally speaking, the Arab villagers are very well-mannered and appreciated good manners, and were also extremely hospitable towards us. There are numerous ways of saying, "Thank you," in Arabic. The most common is, "Ashkerak," [Thank you], also, "Mamnunak," [Thanks to you]. For more formal occasions one would say, "Ilhamdulillah" [Praise be/Thanks to God] or as we used to say "God bless you." I remember that Mr George Halaby, a very smart Arab who worked at the Secretariat, would always stop and talk to us in a very polite, courteous manner when I was a new constable on static duty at the Damascus Gate. It being the height of the Arab Rebellion, other Arabs criticized him for talking to us in that way, but he said to them, "I do this so that if you are in trouble with the authorities, you are more likely to be treated well." I also remember Mr Blenkinsop ("Blenks" we called him), the Assistant District Commissioner at Jenin, remarking one day what nice, courteous manners the local population had, even though the town of Jenin had suffered badly during the Uprising. (Blenks was later injured or killed when the King David Hotel was blown up.) I also remember during my Arabic oral exams the "interrogatee" very kindly trying to help me use the correct phrases!

Usually, when out on patrol, the villagers would press us to accept a meal with them and the efforts they put into entertaining us were not inconsiderable. Sometimes the hospitality was a little crude, or rough and ready, but it was always warmly dispensed. I remember on one occasion, when some hard-boiled eggs were offered as an item for lunch, a dear old Arab *fellah* sat beside me and shelled an egg, offering it with a thumb print pattern left on the white. I wiped off the print with the palm of my hand, while thinking of the old saw, "You've got to eat a peck of dirt before you die," and I suppose that, from some of this rough living, I had developed a little immunity to various germs.

Although I enjoyed the food we had out in the villages, olives were something that I did not enjoy at first. However, as the years went on and there were times when it was bread and olives or nothing, I got to like olives. Patrolling could be very difficult for those who did not like village food. Tom Slattery would not eat out in the villages when we were on the Hebron Column, and so took a haversack full of packets of biscuits when on patrol, and would not be persuaded to try village cooking.

On one of my first patrols, when I had just joined the mounted and was still at Jerusalem Rural, we were invited to a delicious feast at the Christian village of Beit Hanina (I think it was). It was a very attractive village of beautifully-built stone houses, stone-walled gardens and cypress trees, and two churches. My pal, Burglar Williams, informed the Village *Muhktar* that he was going to leave the Mounted Patrol to join the Dog Section, so the *Muhktar* said to him, "You must come and have a farewell lunch." The following week the whole patrol (six men) called in at Beit Hanina, and the *Muhktar*'s family, as well as others, had prepared a sumptuous feast. We were invited into the guesthouse and then four men brought in a huge metal tray, about 4 ft. across, surrounded by a deep rim, containing a mountain of saffron rice, flavoured with pine nuts. In the middle of the rice was a turkey. Just below the turkey was a circle of half a dozen chicken and just below the chicken were a dozen pigeons. The birds were all stuffed with spicy, savoury stuffings and accompanied by side dishes of cucumber, tomato and ladies fingers. A delicious sweet dish, made with honey and nuts, followed this. The meal was eaten with the fingers. Chapatti bread was broken into small pieces and used as a scooping utensil, and rice was eaten by forming a small ball in the palm of the hand and then pushing it into the mouth with the back of the thumb. Hands were cleaned by water being poured over them by an attendant. There was a very convivial atmosphere, as Burglar, an extremely personable young man, recalled many of the incidents he had been involved in – while on patrol in the area. A delicious cup of strong, black coffee, flavoured with cardamom, completed the meal. Of course, no women were present.

–

I was leading a patrol of six men in the Nablus area one morning, when we stopped at Madami village, and were invited to a mid-morning snack. After the villagers had brought all their offerings into the guesthouse, I counted 120 plates and dishes of various foods, including jams, cheeses, eggs, honey, yoghurt, fruit (preserved figs and quince in syrup), olives, bread, olive oil (to dunk the bread) and many other items. This village, in particular, had a wonderful reputation for its hospitality, and I think, of all the peoples I have met, the Palestinian Arab is by far the most hospitable. I feel so deeply sorry that they should have been treated the way they have, and that the British public should have been given such a wrong impression of them. They were being constantly misrepresented, and their rights being continually undermined, by the press, and more recently in other news media, which has, in so many ways, been controlled to further Jewish interests.

There is a charming fable about the importance of knowing one's limits when at a feast.

The Wise Ass – A Fable (All names are fictitious)

An invitation, in beautiful Arab script, had arrived. Hassan el Mohamed was very pleased. He smacked his lips and patted his paunch in anticipation of the good things he would eat at the peace-making feast. Four months before, his nephew had been killed by a member of the Abdul Khaldum family, though it appeared not without reason, for the ambush had been set to catch a thief. However, in the custom of the Arabian Desert, blood money must now be paid. The elders of each family had met and after lengthy discussions it had been agreed that the victim's family would receive two £P200. Sheikh Abdul Khaldum had issued the invitations for the peacemaking ceremony; Hussan el Mohamed was an honoured guest among those invited to the house of the Sheikh.

On the appointed day, at two hours before noon, Hassan el Mohamed called for his riding-ass. With much puffing and blowing he climbed onto a rock, had the ass led alongside and then, leaning over the withers, he scrambled into the saddle and set off for the sheikh's house. Arriving at the house,

Hassan waved his greeting to Sheikh Abdul Khaldum and the members of the sheikh's household. A small boy, ordered by the host, ran over to hold the ass's head while Hassan el Mohamed clumsily dismounted.

"Peace be upon you, Oh, Hassan el Mohamed," greeted Sheikh Abdul Khaldum. "I am indeed pleased and honoured to welcome you this day."

"God be with you, Oh Sheikh, great is the joy in my heart today that we should feast in peace and end this feud between yours and mine."

"It is written in the Koran, Oh Hassan, that blood money shall be paid to the family of a victim. Therefore, by Allah and the Prophet Mohamed, let peace be made between us and you will do me the great honour of eating beneath my roof."

With immense dignity and deference Sheikh Abdul Khaldum escorted Hassan into his house, sat him in the place of honour, placed cushions around him and ordered coffee to be served.

The hour for the peacemaking ceremony drew near and guest and host joined the throng on the village threshing floor. The sheikh of a neutral neighbouring clan had accepted the task of peacemaker. The two accused young men of Sheikh Abdul Khaldum's family were standing with halters about their necks – to indicate that they were at the mercy of Hassan el Mohamed's family – in the centre of the threshing floor, with the remainder of the assembly gathered in a circle. The peacemaker recalled the weeks leading to this day's ceremony and called for the blood money to be paid to the victim's family. When this had been done he tied the loose ends of the halters into knots. Each knot signified an incident that had been acknowledged, and by tying the loose ends tight it was now declared publicly that all differences had been settled between the two families. He then bade all members of the two families to shake hands and, forming into two lines, each family led past the other, each individual shaking hands with a member of the opposite family in turn.

It was now time for the feasting and Abdul el Hassan, his stomach gently shaking as he walked, was escorted back to the house by his host. As befitted a man of his rank, the sheikh had provided a splendid feast. Hassan, his mouth watering but with a great show of protestation, allowed himself to be shepherded, once more, to the place of honour. The floor was packed with delectable dishes: boiled and roast joints of mutton and small mountains of rice were surrounded by stuffed chickens; five turkeys, stuffed with rice and almonds, were, in turn, surrounded by stuffed pigeons; bowls of leben and various salads were everywhere, and in the central area of the room not one inch of the floor could be seen.

As the guest of honour, the tastiest morsels that could be found were pressed upon Hassan. Sheikh Abdul Khaldum deftly separated the breasts of the choicest chickens; the most delicious fillets from the mutton; and of course the eyes of the sheep, and unremittingly offered them to his guest. As Hassan neared saturation point, peppers and tomatoes flavoured with garlic were pressed upon him to whet his appetite anew. Then more titbits were offered until, at last, Hassan was sickened by the sight of the food.

"For me, please accept, and enjoy, this breast of pigeon," urged the Sheikh, "and for the sake of my honoured and departed father."

"For you alone will I eat it," answered Hassan as he stoutly ate the pigeon.

"Halkait, minshan el Nebi Mohamed [Now, for the Prophet Mohamed,] take the delightful piece of liver."

"Only for the prophet Mohamed could I do it," answered Hassan.

The sheikh busied himself and produced the brain from the sheep's head, *"Minshan Allah* [For God], the All Powerful, the All Merciful, eat the brain and may you become as wise as the Prophet Himself."

"For Allah, I cannot refuse," said Hassan, and with difficulty swallowed some of the brain.

Seeing the Sheikh about to force upon him some more of the food, Hassan made to move from the spread. "You have indeed honoured me today, but, not for your father, nor mine; not for your son, nor mine; not for the Prophet Mohamed, nor even for Allah, the All Powerful and All Merciful, could I eat another scrap of food!" Hassan then washed his hands, lay back upon the cushions and relaxed. He was full, too full, and needed to rest. As his hosts now began to satisfy their hunger by what had been left by their guests, Hassan lay back, closed his eyes and dozed. He dreamt of Paradise, where all the faithful can expect to reach, where all the food is of the choicest, and no one need work; where all the women are beautiful, like Sitna Mirim [Our Lady Mary], and the very scent we exuded from the pores of our skin is like the finest perfumes of the East.

While his hosts were feeding, Hassan was left in peace and dozed fitfully for an hour or so. At last he was brought back to the World of Adam and the *Shaitun* [Satan] and, on being roused, he did not feel at all well. Even the most satisfying – and in the circumstances, polite – belches he could produce failed to ease the discomfort of his rotund paunch. Realising that it was near the eleventh hour,[1] and the sun was low in the west, Hassan laboriously pulled himself up onto his feet and took leave of his host. Sheikh Abdul Khaldum, as was befitting, accompanied Hassan to his ass, untethered the beast and assisted his guest to climb once more into the saddle. He then led Hassan to the outskirts of the village where the pair took leave of each

[1]The Arab clock starts at sundown.

other.

"Go in peace, Hassan el Mohamed, my friend, and may your people and mine live in peace hereafter."

"And may peace be on you, Oh Sheikh. Thanks to Allah and thanks to you: and now I leave. Allah be with you."

So saying, Hassan with legs flapping against the ass's flanks rode down the hill towards his home.

At the bottom of the hill a lively brook bubbled its way over stones, worn smooth across the track. The ass, who had been tethered all day, was thirsty. He stopped in the middle of the stream, lowered his head and drank his fill. He stood and enjoyed the cool, refreshing water flowing over his hooves, while he waited for the prod from Hassan's stick to signal him to move on. Instead, he heard, in honeyed tone, the voice of his master, "Just for me, please, have a little more." The ass cocked an ear, then shook his head. "For the sake of Allah, The All Merciful, have another little drink." But the ass stood patiently awaiting the order to move.

Old Hassan shook his head and muttered, "Of all the animals the ass is regarded as the most stupid, but he knows when he has had sufficient to eat and drink. By the word of the Prophet, how stupid I be!"

–

By the beginning of 1945 the Middle East and the Mediterranean Areas were free of actual warlike activity, for the Axis Forces had been swept from North Africa and out of southern Italy, and the Mediterranean Sea was again open to shipping – albeit in escorted convoys, for a few hostile submarines were still active. Many of our men were long overdue for home leave, some not having been home for seven years or more, so now the Government started to send leave parties to the UK.

–

After a few months of comparative quiet the Zionists of Palestine continued their anti-British war and British soldiers and British policemen were again some of their main targets. There activities were widespread and demonstrated the large support the terrorists had from the general Jewish population. It again became necessary to take defensive precautions, so barbed wire entanglements were erected around camps and police stations, and trip flares set up. Tin cans were also hung on the wires to help sentries detect any movement of intruders. Jackals and "pi"-dogs, however, often set off the trip flares, and it was felt too expensive to keep replacing them, so we mainly relied on the tin cans! While I was busy one day working on an entanglement, I well remember a young Arab horse-dealer, from whom

I had bought a few mounts for the Force, coming by and saying, with a fair amount of scorn in his voice, "Look at this, the British Government, the greatest Government in the world, now afraid to take action against a few Jews, and having to hide behind barbed wire! What's it all coming to?" I must confess, I had no adequate reply for him, but I understood all too well. However, the people and the politicians in Britain would not listen to the truth, believing in preference the numerous articles of Zionist propaganda, and have been doing so ever since.

Robbery was one of the crimes that I had to deal with around this period, where travellers usually were stopped by armed Arab gangs and forced to hand over their possessions. This often occurred in the Ghor, where following the trail of wanted men was difficult for the area is short of water, and at times men and horses suffered greatly from thirst. I remember one day I decided the only thing to do to relieve our thirst was to ride to the Jordan River and water our mounts. When we got there, the water didn't smell too good, but the horses were so thirsty they drank their fill. I was also pretty thirsty and quite dehydrated as my water bottle had long been empty, so I also lay down and had a good drink from the river. Then, as I got up, a dead camel floated by and I thought that that was the most unholy cocktail I had ever drunk. And yet, so often when riding over this country, I used to think how lucky I was to have such an open-air life, for although it was not all ideal, the good outweighed the bad. Living as I was at that time in an Arab area, I did not get involved in the beastly outrages which the Jews were continually perpetrating against the British, even though the war with Germany was still to be won.

Then in March 1945 my name came up on the Home Leave List, and I was due to sail in April from Port Said. I greatly looked forward to this and I hoped I would get home without being torpedoed.

The Bounty Hunter

A couple of days before I left, one of my last jobs was to escort my station officer out. I was told to keep quiet about the night. Just outside Nablus, we picked up an Arab with his head well-wrapped to conceal his face. The station officer handed over a rifle and some ammunition to the Arab, and said to him, "Good luck, and may God go with you." With that the Arab disappeared into the night and I was soon to learn that he had undertaken to go bounty-hunting to kill Hamad Zawata, who was wanted for various murders, including that of two British policemen. However, I must add that he was not successful, and Hamad Zawata lived on until one night when two British detectives literally tripped over him as he slept on a threshing floor just outside a village. Then, in the absolute confusion of flying fists and wrestling, the fugitive was overpowered, and the detectives realised whom they had captured. He was eventually sentenced to three years for being in possession of a rifle, a revolver and ammunition.

Home leave at last: April-August 1945

And so in April several pals[1] and I were on our way to Port Said to embark on the Dutch ship *Ruys* [Rose], which like all Allied ships was "trooping". Our leave party numbered some few score of men who were to travel "troop deck" and were allocated the complete mess deck in one section. This was something that I had not experienced before and I didn't think much of the standard – it was certainly no luxury liner! We lived, ate and slept on the mess deck. We ate our meals on the mess tables, which seated 14 men, the meals being collected from the galley in large dixies. Each man was issued a hammock, which was slung from the ceiling over the tables, and we swung up into the hammocks to sleep. When all the hammocks were slung, the entire area was filled and, if anyone put his leg out of his hammock, it would land on the body or face of the occupant in the next hammock. The next shock was the lavatory accommodation, for all the doors had been removed, ostensibly to lighten the ship. The spectacle of rows of occupied lavatory pans, facing each other, was very embarrassing to begin with, but it soon became fully accepted, and as one entered a cubicle one might greet the sitter opposite and carry on a normal conversation throughout the performance! It is amazing how quickly one adjusts to circumstance. Although I missed the comfort of a good passenger liner berth, with the usual fine fare and entertainment, I was glad to have had the experience of travelling troopship, so that I could know just how thousands of soldiers had fared.

Queuing was part of life on these troopships. One queued for tea, cigarettes or even entertainments, and the long queues stretched around the decks, even up and down companion-ways, onto upper or lower decks. I recall one day, in the Mediterranean, while waiting my turn in the queue for the morning tea ration, an elderly gentleman standing next to me. As we shuffled forward we fell into conversation. He said to me, "It is rather incongruous to think that, a few weeks ago, I was His Majesty's Chief Justice in Swaziland, and here I am now queuing up to receive my two pennyworth of tea." He seemed to see the funny side of it and I agreed with him that the ship was at least travelling in the right direction for home leave.

We travelled through the Mediterranean in convoy, flanked by an escort of Naval Destroyers. At times the destroyers would veer off, under full steam, and drop depth charges, and we assumed that some enemy submarines

---

[1] including Dick Hook, Bryn "Taffy" Cole, Arthur "Monty" Montgomery, Bill "Burglar" Williams and E. Cameron Beattie (brother of the Lt. Cdr. Sam Beattie VC, who crashed *HMS Campbeltown* onto St. Nazaire docks in France, destroying the Normandy lock gates and thus preventing the Battleship *Tirpitz* from using the dock).

had been detected. However, one wag suggested that the reason for this activity was to "frighten, and put the wind up the passengers," and solve the constipation problem that many passengers suffer at sea! Luckily, we had an uneventful journey home, and reached Glasgow via the North Channel – the waters between Northern Ireland and Scotland – sighting the Mull of Kintyre en route. I was told by the ship's barber that the last 100 miles of the voyage was through what was then regarded as the most dangerous waters in the world, for it was here that the German U-boats hunted in packs as the ships converged from the Atlantic Ocean routes. It would have been ironic if we had been torpedoed just then, for the war in Europe was fast drawing to a close. The land on both sides of the North Channel was so clearly visible at the narrowest point, about 15 miles wide, that the shores to port and starboard appeared to be only about four miles apart.

Soon we were sailing up the Clyde and what a welcome we received from the people on the banks of the river, who waved and cheered us on. From Gourrock and Greenock to Glasgow we sailed through narrow canals and channels, and from the factories on either side women and girls poured out to greet us home again. The warmth of the welcome brought a tear to my eye. Many on the ship had been in the Western Desert and there were also a lot of Air Force chaps: I felt a bit of a cheat, for my years of the war had been very easy compared with the bombing and rationing, as well as the years of blackout, that these good ladies had endured.

On arrival at Glasgow I decided that, as the Lake District was the furthest north in Britain that I had been – on cycling holidays in my youth – I would take this opportunity to visit Edinburgh, so Taffy Cole and I took the first available train. I thought Edinburgh was a fine city and lived up to its reputation, and it appeared to have suffered very little bomb damage. Next morning, 15th May, we took the bus out to see the magnificent Forth Bridge, and while having a drink in the pub there an old Chief Petty Officer said to us, "The signal is coming through on the radio at 1.30!"
"What is coming through, Chief?" I asked.
"The German surrender!"
"That's good news. We'll have a drink on that, Chief," I replied, which we duly did before he invited us back to the Chiefs' Mess. There we continued the celebrations by cooking a pound of sausages for lunch.

Two days later I travelled home to Bearsted in Kent and gave my mother a pleasant surprise. She had known that I was en route but, it being wartime, I had been unable to tell her when or where I was sailing and she just had to await my eventual arrival. The following Sunday I went over from Bearsted to Lenham – where I had spent most of my youth – and joined the bell ringers. They were ringing the bells up when I walked into the belfry and

Fred Parks, who was the captain and had taught me how to ring 20 years previously, was pleased to see me and invited me to join them. It was the first time the bells had been rung since soon after the War began, when it was announced that the bells would only be rung in the event of invasion. The cessation of hostilities in Europe caused great excitement and rejoicing throughout the land, and everyone was highly elated. There were dances and parades everywhere, and in London a huge Victory Parade took place, with thousands of troops from all over the Empire taking part.

Kent was in "Bomb Alley", as the German bombers flew over the county on their way to London, the docks and other industrial cities: sometimes, when they were prevented from dropping their bombs over planned targets by anti-aircraft guns and intercepting aircraft, they dropped their bombs in Kent on the way back. I was shocked at the extent of the bomb damage everywhere. Living there had been very trying for my mother, for as well as the bombing, the dog fights of the Battle of Britain had gone on in the skies above Kent, so I asked her where she would like to go for a holiday and she chose Eastbourne. She had spent some years there when she was a young girl. In Eastbourne we saw large gaps in several streets where bombs had destroyed the houses. Apparently, the bombers had flown in low on terror bombing runs, with the sun behind them, so they were difficult to see, dropped their bombs and returned across the Channel.

My five months' leave passed all too quickly, and then I was back up north in Liverpool, boarding the SS *Strathmore*. The ship turned out to be infested with bedbugs, and the troops, who were going out to the Far East, were up in arms about this, so we were all paraded off the ship and taken to Huyton Camp for a week while the ship was fumigated. A mother who must have seen us or a group like us, wrote to her Palestine Policeman son, Jowett, that she had seen a group of his fellow policemen in Liverpool – some very young, new recruits, who looked like boys and also some much older, tough, hard faced looking men! We were embarked once more and that night, while waiting to sail next day, news came through that the Japanese had surrendered, so now, after six long years of war, all the world was at peace.

Chapter 13

1945 – Peace for the World but not in Palestine

Although the World War was now over, there was to be very little peace for us in Palestine. The Zionist extremists were turning all their energy to acts of terrorism in an effort to force the Government of Palestine to open their borders to unlimited Jewish immigration and the setting up of a Jewish State. The catalogue of atrocities committed by the Jewish dissidents is horrific, and hundreds of lives were lost and millions of pounds-worth of damage done. Ernest Bevin made a declaration that he was sending a Commission of Enquiry to study and report on the situation. Lord Gort, the High Commissioner, had shortly before resigned and departed for England. The railway line had been blown up in 153 places all over the country. An attack had been made on the Lydda junction and serious damage occurred to rolling stock. Other prominent railway stations had been attacked and damaged.

In Tel Aviv Government buildings were burned out, including the District Commissioner's offices and the Income Tax Office. Messrs. Spinneys Ltd. stores were broken into and much damage done. However, although the firm was English, Jews held the majority of the shares and controlling interest, so the attack may have been a mistake. After British Police had failed to break up the mobs with a series of baton charges, troops of the Airborne Divisions were called up and only succeeded in quelling riots after opening fire on the demonstrators. Unavoidably, the Jews suffered fatalities, and many British Police were injured in these disturbances. In Jaffa and Haifa, police launches were blown up and lost, and an attempt was made to sabotage the petroleum storage tanks at the oil refinery at Haifa, which was the terminal of the pipeline from Iraq.

Illegal Immigrants at Givat Hyam

Illegal immigration of Jews into Palestine was continuing at an alarming rate and boatloads of Jews were coming ashore during the hours of darkness. The Jewish population was aiding the illegal immigrants in every way possible and absorbed the new arrivals into settlements all along the coastal hinterland. Once inside the country it was practically impossible to trace the newcomers, the Government Forces meeting with violence and obstruction at every turn.

On the night of 24th November 1945 two Coastguard Stations, Givat Olga and Sidna Ali, were attacked and dynamited, causing serious damage to buildings and approximately 20 casualties among the British and Arab personnel. The following day a party of police and a few troops with police dogs followed a trail of the attackers from Givat Olga to Givat Hyam, a

Jewish colony. The inhabitants, who were all armed with cudgels, declared they would not permit the police to enter. The Superintendent i/c told the *Muhktar* he must allow the police in, but the headman replied that he was unable to do so without obtaining instruction from the Jewish authorities in Jerusalem. (Even though this was in a mandated British Territory, the Jews considered themselves to be a state living within a state.)

Many Jews from neighbouring settlements converged on Givat Hyam to reinforce the inhabitants and it was obvious that the police and military party was an insufficient force to enter the settlement. Reinforcements of troops were sent for and a military cordon was placed around the settlement. A conference of high-ranking military and government officers was held and plans made to enter Givat Hyam the next morning.

In the morning, I was one of the party of police to leave Nablus for Khibet Beit Lidd on the main coast road. By then the news of the past 36 hours was widespread throughout the country – from Biersheba to Dan – and Arabs all along the route wished us well. From Khibet Beit Lidd we continued northwards towards Givat Hyam and as we neared the settlement we met large numbers of troops, many of whom had been camped all night all along the route, caught in the seemingly endless task of brewing up tea. Eventually we reached an open space close to Givat Hyam, which was used as a military car park. A plane was continually circling the settlement, keeping a check on movements made by the inhabitants.

I gathered that the object of the operation was to bring out the men for interrogation and to check their identity, but when asked to co-operate they had flatly refused. They had barricaded themselves in, locking the gates. After some time a rumour went round that the police party was to be sent in to bring the men out for interrogation. With regulations as they stood it was necessary, first, to send the police, armed only with batons, before the armed military could be sent in to do the job. It was not expected that the police would be able to accomplish the task as the inhabitants of Givat Hyam were in an ugly mood.

At 9 am the SP went to the colony entrance and conferred with the leading members. They were told they were to bring out all the men and were given until 9.30 to comply. They would not comply, they said, until they had been in touch with "their government" – as the Jewish Agency was referred to. At 9.30 there was no sign of the instructions being complied with, and another conference between the colony committee and the SP followed. They were then given until 11 am to comply. The time our commanders allowed for discussion was a mistake for it allowed the settlers to knock down some walls and use the brick rubble as a store of missiles. At long last 11 am arrived and the police, a party of about 40, were ordered in with the SP well in the rear.

We were headed by a few ASPs and were marched up to the colony entrance, passing some troops who encouraged us on our way.

As we entered the colony and rounded a house to cross an open space, we were opposed and told we could go no further. Our officers tried once more to persuade the colonists to comply peacefully, but they were obviously determined to buck authority. We then attempted to push our way through without striking anyone; but as we advanced the whole crowd of about 150, armed with cudgels, attacked us. The situation was now far from pretty as a right royal battle commenced. The police had to defend themselves against a furious onslaught from the inhabitants, who had stark hatred written on their faces. Several police were injured and at least a dozen settlers could be seen lying prostrate, some bleeding from blows they had received to the head. Many young girls were encouraged to take part in the fight by the older women, though it was apparent that they were unwilling to do so. It was a really disgusting affair, brought on once again by the settlers themselves, determined to court controversy rather than live in peace.

One man had a huge long pole which he swung in an attempt to flatten us. It was a very heavy weapon, and I noticed that once he got it swinging it controlled him. I advanced on him with my baton, and he fell with a blow to the head. Then I found myself cut off from the rest of the party and surrounded by a screaming, hating crowd, who had managed to single me out, shouting, "Get this one." They began pelting me with bricks and stones and huge logs of wood. Luckily I was wearing a tin helmet, but even so I was badly hurt and knocked down, and I am sure I would have been killed if I had not managed to jump up and run around the building, intending to circle back. However, to my horror, I saw a 6 ft high wire fence just in front of me, and thought, "This is it! You've had it now!" But to my relief, I saw a narrow opening, close against the building, and I managed to regain the main body of the police with Inspector Dodds, my tin hat having been bent almost beyond belief.

After the initial clash, the inhabitants withdrew to one side of the open space while the police gathered under some trees on the other side in an attempt to escape the rocks and bricks that were continually being hurled at us. Only the Inspector and the Superintendent i/c had revolvers, the rest of us having batons, but it became apparent that the settlers were going to resist as a matter of policy. As the fighting had become so violent a hurried conference took place between the senior police and army officers. Insp. Dodds opened fire with one or two rounds from his revolver, and the army paratroops were called in armed with rifles. They were then to bring out all the people in the colony, men and women.

The settlers stood around taunting us with their cries of, "Bravo Gestapo," but the paratroops were battle-hardened men who had seen service in the recent War and would stand no nonsense. They had lost some of their comrades fighting the Nazi army, and more recently due to militant Zionist atrocities, and they felt little sympathy with the violent gathering. In the meantime, several hundred settlers from other settlements in the area advanced towards Givat Hyam, but were ordered to halt by the army officer commanding the various approach roads and told to withdraw. Men at the rear of one party, however, shouted, *"Kadema,"* [Onward], and the column pressed forward. Again, they were ordered to stop, but once more they responded to cries of *"Kadema,"* and started forward again. A young officer ordered his men to fire, and a machine-gun barked a short burst. At once the column scattered among the groves lining the track, but a few had been hit and killed. The complete arrogant defiance and contempt that these settlers showed towards the Government Forces of Palestine illustrates how confident they were of support from American and Pro-Zionist MPs in Britain. The ringleaders appeared to be willing to sacrifice even their own people to gain sympathy and further their own aims of displacing the Arabs and gaining political control. This was a horrible incident, and whenever such an operation took place it was certain to be incompletely reported in the press, particularly in America, and followed by the murder of some British policemen or soldiers as a reprisal.

The people from the colony were escorted to an enclosure which had been prepared previously for interrogation. When questioned as to their names and addresses, all, without exception, answered, "I am a Jew of Palestine."

Our police party was marched to our awaiting transport, accompanied by derisive cries of, "Bravo Gestapo." Later, when in the transport and headed for home, I felt an intense relief that the filthy encounter was over.

Nablus 1945 – the Whole Force is now Armed 24 hrs a Day

On my return from leave, I was fortunate enough to be posted to Nablus again, and as the only Jews living there were the ancient sect of Samarians, mentioned earlier, who lived in peace with their Arab neighbours, the Nablus area was free from Zionist terrorist outrages. This area, which was once in the Triangle of Terror, was now the safest place to be. However, some of the militant Jews decided to let the Arabs know of their military power and prowess, and on one or two occasions cars with Jewish gunmen drove through remote Arab villages bordering the Jewish areas and fired indiscriminately at the inhabitants, killing and wounding a number. So, even though we might live in a wholly Arab locality, it was still necessary to be constantly on the alert and we were armed at all times. Dining halls and messes were always cluttered up with rifles and machine guns, for experience had shown that firearms locked up in armouries are useless in an emergency.

Some Jewish terrorists had entered a police station as normal members of the public, apparently to make a legitimate complaint, and then produced some arms and rushed the police, shooting anyone in their way, while they took the armoury keys and stole arms and ammunition. A minor battle developed, and although some of the terrorists were injured and captured, many arms were stolen and not recovered. With their firearms locked in the armoury, the majority of policemen in that station were powerless to defend themselves or the station, so orders were made for all police to carry firearms at all times. For the rest of my police service in Palestine, I had a gun to hand 24 hours a day. Dining and recreation rooms were literally festooned with rifles and Bren guns, and were in everyone's way, and even in bed or in the bath a gun would be within reach. Because of this it was absolutely necessary to have first-class discipline when controlling the arms, and if a firearm was lost, this would be punished by a fine and forfeit – a sum twice the cost of the weapon.

My Divisional Commander at Nablus was Alec Campbell, under whom I had served at El Lejjun when he was in charge of the Jenin Division. He was a very fine policeman and as straight as a die. He sent for me soon after my arrival in Nablus and told me that he was unhappy with the command in Toubas Outstation where things were not as he would wish, so he was sending me there. I told him that I was hoping to serve at the District Headquarters again, but he stressed that he would be happier if I went to Toubas. So, once again, I was to serve well away from the District HQ.

Toubas

However, though not many men would have been happy to be sent there, I found the countryside around Toubas to be very interesting, with high rocky hills and steep, deep gorges. Grandeur would be a more apt description, than beauty. Toubas was roughly east of Nablus, 7 or 8 km north off the Jiftlik track. The station was in the Jordan Valley, and most of the country was bleak, hilly terrain, dropping away to the Jordan River, and for most of the year a dried up wilderness. However, just below the slope on which the police station was built lay a most lovely spring of beautiful, clear water. It was roughly circular, about 2 ft. deep and 10 to 15 ft. in diameter. The water bubbled up all over the base of the pool, between pebbles and stones of varying size, from very small pebbles to quite large boulders the size of footballs. There, surrounded by hills, both near and distant, I could well imagine Pan himself sitting beside the pool, playing his pipe. Whenever I heard the shepherd boys piping up on the hillsides, I would think of them as being descendents of Pan. I might mention here that below the slopes of Mount Hermon, in Syria, there was a similar pool known as Banias, which translated means Place of Pan. There is no "p" in Arabic, hence Banias.

The village of Toubas was about half a mile away from the station, hidden around a hillside. There was a little bit of cultivated land in the valley bottoms, but grazing for sheep, goats and cattle was the major form of land use. The other villages in that area were sparsely scattered across the hills, and it was too hot in the Jordan valley for any permanent settlement.

Reunion with Sgt. Hassan Riati

Here, at Toubas, I met up with an old Bedouin friend, Sgt. Hassan Riati, who was last with me at Givat Olga Coast Guard Station. He was such an open and honest man that I do not think he knew how to tell a lie. He was also a very brave and effective tracker. On one occasion he led a patrol which was out tracking a gang of robbers. At nightfall, realising that they had come very close to the robbers' camp, and to ensure that the wanted men would not be warned of the patrol's presence, Sgt. Hassan went forward alone to survey the situation unseen, and returned to his men with a plan of action well formed. "Do not fear," he told them, "Just do as I tell you and we will get the lot of them – dead or alive." On creeping up to where the gang were resting, they were able to surround and capture the lot very effectively, before they knew what was happening.

I was not to stay in Toubas for long, for officers in Headquarters decided to call all British police in from remote Arab areas to where they would be available for anti-terrorist patrols and road checks. And so after four months I found myself back in Nablus District HQ again.

Disillusionment led to Resignation

About this time I was very disheartened and ashamed by the way the situation was going in Palestine. Pressure from America and Zionist support in Britain took no account of Arab rights and resulted in a lack of even-handedness from the British Government in the way Arab rebels were treated in comparison with the militant Zionists. I handed in my resignation and left for home on 9th February 1946. However, while in England, I could not settle, and eventually I wrote to the Crown Agents requesting them to contact the Inspector General of Police in Palestine and ask him, on my behalf, if I could return, retaining my rank and with continuous service. The Inspector General agreed and I was on my way back in mid July 1946.

Bombing of the King David Hotel

I was two days out of Port Said, on 22nd July 1946, when the King David Hotel, which housed the Military Headquarters, was blown up – with enormous loss of over 90 lives, British, Arab and Jew. This was the work of the Irgun, led by Menachem Begin. The hotel was supplied with daily milk by a Jewish settlement, which was delivered to the kitchens in large churns. On the fatal day, churns packed with gelignite and primed were delivered. The gelignite was packed in the bottom and the top 12 or so inches were covered with milk. It was a very effective deception and shows how diabolically clever the Zionist terrorists were, which has not been appreciated by the rest of the world to this day.

Search of Tel Aviv Interrupted by Pressure from America, July 1946

Acting upon intelligence information received, the Government, with the British Army Command, planned to search the whole of Tel Aviv – at that time a city of some 200,000 inhabitants – for it was understood that many terrorists were in the city. Hundreds of police and thousands of soldiers assembled at an army camp north of Tel Aviv were secretly informed of the operation and not allowed to leave the camp. At about 2 am on the morning of the search, a large convoy of troops and police were conveyed to Tel Aviv and the city surrounded by troops. A curfew was placed upon the entire area. The city was then cordoned off into sections and barbed wire entanglements set up to isolate them. Small parties of troops, with a policeman to each group, were then sent in to search every house and office in each section, and all men and women between the ages of 18 and 40 sent to the screening centre, where CID and Army intelligence personnel checked their identities.

Steadily, we worked through the city, section by section. Arms and explosives were found in one synagogue and many wanted terrorists detained. My little party of troops did not find any arms, but we did find a very smartly dressed young woman in an elaborate "military" uniform of her own design. I often wondered what the CID made of this young lady. The whole operation took four days and was then called off. I thought the search had been completed, but many years later, while talking to a Major General who had been involved in the operation, I learnt that the search had been called off early because America had brought pressure to bear on the British Government. The American President was in fear of losing the Jewish vote in America unless he supported the Zionists against the British in the affairs of Palestine. In fact, on several significant occasions, major operations were called off before they had been completed, suggesting that there were some political levers being very firmly pulled on behalf of the Jewish community. In 1942 leading members of the Stern Gang, which even then was responsible for numerous assassinations, were arrested and Stern himself was killed, but the five members detained were later freed, "because it was felt that their release could react considerably on the die-hards of the Group (as it was requested to be called in official circles) without public security suffering in any way".[1] However, the killings and atrocities continued and accelerated in 1947. It was very unfortunate for the Arab community that they did not have equally highly-placed influential people to pull levers for them. They

---

[1] Geoffrey K. Morton, 1957, *Just The Job*, p.152

just had to trust in the good word and promises of the British Government, which appeared to be no longer able to act on its own authority, or properly support assurances that had been given to the Arab people in the past.

Return to Qalqilya

A few weeks after the Tel Aviv searches I was informed that I was to return to Qalqilya and resume my old command as Station Officer. So one bright morning I saddled my new young horse, Rustom, another grey with dappled quarters, and started out along the Azzun track. Cameron Beattie now had my old horse Rusty, and when someone had said to him, "Matey's coming back," he replied, "He's not getting his bloody horse back!" Rustom was a very good young horse, though not yet five, the age at which the vet allowed horses to join the Palestine Police. However, the new Inspector General, Col. William Nicol Gray, who knew about horseflesh, had advised us, when he visited Nablus HQ one day, to buy him while we could and keep him as a spare. It was a full day's ride to Qalqilya (35-40 km) and on reaching Azzun I knew two more hours would see me at my journey's end. I was pleased to see a few old Arab friends both at the station and in the town. Though there were some real rascals living in Qalqilya, there were many more decent citizens. When I went on patrol, one of the Arab shopkeepers remarked, "Why have you always got such a good horse?"

As mentioned previously, the station was right on the border of Arab and Jewish areas of influence: to the west was the notorious Revisionist settlement of Ramat Hakovesh, about two miles distant, from where Qalqilya Station had been attacked in 1944, so I knew what I was up against. Unlike so many British politicians, and much of the British public, I never underestimated the Zionists' plans and intentions. The nearby railway line was a frequent Zionist target for attacks, and several times the trains were derailed by explosive charges.

Terrorist Arms Caches and Revenge Murders

At times, the Government received information, from Jewish informants about arms in Jewish settlements, and searches revealed huge quantities of arms cached. At a settlement near Jalama, east of Haifa, arms and ammunition in sufficient quantity to arm a brigade of troops were found. They were carefully concealed in an armoury constructed beneath a child's playground, and the metal pipes of the swings and play equipment were the ventilation pipes of the armoury. The entrance was by way of the bullpen, and below the manger of the big Friesian bull, a press button was located. When this was pressed an electric motor moved a big concrete slab which was concealing the entrance steps to the arms store. News of this find greatly alarmed the Arab population when it was published.

Other information resulted in further searches and more Jewish arms caches were found. It was rumoured that some Jewish informers were handsomely rewarded and assisted with passages to foreign lands, but others were tracked down by Zionist leaders and shot. Certainly, several Jewish bodies were found. Some Jewish girls who were suspected of having given information to the police had their heads forcibly shaved. One girl related that she was kidnapped, gagged and taken to a room where masked men confronted her with accusations, then sentenced her to have her head shaved.

Continuous State of Readiness

As the likelihood of attacks was continuous, it was necessary to inaugurate defence schemes for all stations and billets. Up the Azzun track there was a large quantity of Dannert (coiled) barbed wire, which had been used by an army unit to practise with, before the invasion of Italy. I commandeered this, collected it up and had it transported back to the station to reinforce the perimeter. In the station, every man had to be instructed as to his precise defence position in case the alarm siren was sounded, and practice alarms were frequently instituted. Police stations were a prime target for the arms and ammunitions they contained. The men had to be in a continual readiness, which was a strain on all concerned: many men were badly affected. In April 1946 there was an attack on a strongly manned Police Tegart Fort at Ramat Gan, near Peta Tikvah, to obtain weapons. Most of the station strength had been called away to what turned out to be a fictitious land dispute between Arabs and Jews.

The gang managed to trick its way into the building by having half its members dressed as British soldiers and half as Arab prisoners. They easily disarmed the guards, took over the station and took out all the arms and ammunition, which were loaded onto a stolen army truck. The wireless operator was able to get out an "Attack" message before being overpowered. The message was received at Peta Tikvah Divisional HQ, a few miles away. Inspector John Denley[1] set out with a party, but were detained by a huge traffic jam that had been caused by two culverts having been blown up, so they had to proceed on foot. They arrived just as the lorry was turning up a side road, but two men ran out of the station with boxes of ammunition on their shoulders. One was killed and the other, Dov Grunner, was wounded and captured. He was later tried and sentenced to death. Some young Jews found guilty of terrorist activities were sentenced to corporal punishment. In reprisal, Jewish terrorists grabbed a British Army major in Tel Aviv, stripped him to the waist, tied him to a tree and whipped him in full view of passers by.

Operation Polly – January/February 1947

The Government became concerned that the British women and children

---

[1]Full account in *Palestine Police Old Comrades Association Newsletter*, Winter 2006, Number 223.

might be in danger from indiscriminate attack on buses and trains in Jewish areas. I also heard that information had been received that terrorists were plotting to blow up a bus containing British school children. So, "Operation Polly" was put into force and all married women and children were sent home to the UK for safety.

The "Palestine Question" put before the United Nations – 1947

Affairs now went from calamitous to disastrous, as pro-Zionist America continually forced the issue. In February 1947, the whole "PALESTINE QUESTION", as it was called, was brought before the United Nations. Another Commission, The United Nations Special Committee on Palestine, was appointed to report and recommend on the Palestine situation. Once again we had committee members visiting the country, taking evidence and conducting interviews. Then they retired from the Holy Land to consider the question and report to the UNO. In March 1947, the British House of Commons passed a Bill to the effect that Great Britain would definitely leave the country the following year.

Two Arab Orphan Boys

In the midst of all this political and security mayhem, normal police work continued, and a particular case deserves special mention. Two young Arab boys, brothers of about 10 and 14 years, as orphans had been adopted and taken into an Arab farmer's family. They were not badly treated but had to work hard and long hours as shepherds, and received as wages one sheep a year plus their board and lodging. It seems, however, that they were never really accepted as members of the family, but merely tolerated, spending most of their time on the hillsides tending the flocks. It came out later, in a subsequent investigation, that the two young lads unhappily visualised their bleak futures out on the hills. The elder one said, "If I could marry, you could come and live with me. We could take our few sheep and start a herd of our own. But we have no money, and without money, I can't pay the bride price for a wife." The younger boy, Mahmoud, then replied, "I know where some gold bangles are kept. If I take them and sell them, then we can have the money, so you can buy a bride." A few days later, Mahmoud was in Tulkarem market with gold bangles for sale. A shopkeeper became suspicious when the bangles were offered to him, and he called in a passing policeman. Then the story came out and poor little Mahmoud was taken into custody.

The theft of the gold had taken place in my station area, so Mahmoud was transferred to Qalqilya for the case to be fully investigated and processed. I took the little lad before the Magistrate, in his office, and wanted him to be bailed in the care of his guardian, but the guardian refused to accept any responsibility for his ward, so I was left with Mahmoud in my custody. The poor little boy was horrified by the idea that he should be locked in a cell, and my British constables agreed that he could have a bed in the barrack room with them. There he had to stay until he could again appear in court, about 10 days later. He was a nice little chap and quickly learnt some English, and tried to make himself generally useful doing odd jobs.

One day, when it was raining "cats and dogs", and it looked as though it might do so for days, Mahmoud was helping me with some carpentry. I noticed he was looking out at the weather with a whimsical smile on his face. "What do you find so amusing on a day like today?" I asked. "*Shawish*," he replied, "I was just thinking. If I had not stolen those gold bangles, I would be out on the hillside with the sheep, in all this rain, today!" There must be a moral in this story somewhere.

Mahmoud was sent to an approved school, and he wanted reassurance that it "was a school and not a prison" that he was going to. I assured him it was a school, where he would have lessons and could play football, but he would have to do as he was told.

The Baby

One day when I was standing outside the station I saw a crowd of 50 or 60 children, boys and girls from about 4 to 12 years old, coming up the street and chatting in an excited way, as if to say, "Look what we found!" Like children following the Pied Piper of Hamelin, they were following a larger boy who had an air of considerable responsibility and importance. The "Pied Piper" had a baby in his arms, which he said he had found on a doorstep, and after asking around as to what he should do, he was told to take it to the police. Luckily, one of my Arab policeman's wives took care of the baby, which was not crying but sucking the air hungrily, and gave it a bottle and settled it to rest. Cons. Abu Musa belonged to the village and knew it well, so he made enquiries and a couple of hours later he came back, exclaiming, "The mother is known!"

Mounting Zionist Terror, Non-compliance and Resistance

In 1947, the atrocities continued.[1] In May 1947 the Irgun attacked Acre prison, and many prisoners escaped. Three of the attackers were arrested and two months later they were sentenced to death in the courts. The immediate result was that two British Army sergeants were kidnapped at Nathanyia, a little Jewish seaside town, about 10 miles from Qalqilya. The Irgun Zavi Leumi let it be known that if the men were executed the two sergeants would be hanged in reprisal. One was called Martin, and when many of my friends heard that Sgt. Martin had been kidnapped, they thought it was me. I felt I

---

[1] Issa Nakhleh. *Palestine Encyclopedia* Chapter 6. For a more detailed account of Zionist Terrorist Activities in 1947. *www.palestine-encyclopedia.com/EPP/Chapter 6*

was a likely candidate for kidnap, having repelled terrorist attackers in the past, and so I always took precautions and was ever on the alert.

The execution was carried out and a few days later, 31st July 1947, the two bodies of the British Army sergeants were found hanging from trees near Kirbet Beit Lidd. The bodies were booby-trapped and as they were cut down concealed mines exploded, which injured some of the party that had gone out to recover them. People around the world were horrified when they heard this news, and many Jewish businesses in England were attacked and damaged in demonstrations against these Zionist terrorist atrocities.

Many Jews were killed as innocent bystanders in bombings and terrorist attacks, and many were appalled by the terrorist atrocities. Many also suffered violence or murder at the hands of fellow Jews if they expressed disagreement with the aims of Militant Zionism or helped the Government try to maintain law and order, but although the Jewish press continually denounced the terrorist activities, it always made excuses for them, suggesting, all along, that the way forward was to open Palestine to unlimited Jewish immigration, and there is no doubt that the overwhelming majority of Jews in Palestine, either actively or passively, supported the terrorists.

The UN Committee Recommends Partition – August 1947

We then thought that the Government was determined to stamp out the terrorism which had so disgraced the whole concept of Zionist settlement. But no, it seemed their hands were tied, for American pressure was once again brought to bear in favour of political Zionism. In August 1947, the United Nations proposals were published, which were a repetition of the 1937 Peel Commission recommendations – that Palestine should be partitioned. This small country was to be divided into Jewish and Arab land.

The British Government Prepared to Give Up the Mandate

Dear old Ernest Bevin, the Rt. Hon. Foreign Secretary, had stated that he, "would stake his political reputation," on finding a solution to the Palestine problem. He had done his damnedest, over a couple of years or so, but was dealing with a situation of British making which had become insoluble. We, the British, had by 1947 introduced into Palestine possibly 600,000 Jews legally under the quota system. Probably more than another 100,000 had entered the country illegally and they all now demanded a state and a government of their own. On the other side, 1,200,000 Arabs native to Palestine would not and could not be expected to accept such demands. And why should they? What people in the whole world would voluntarily give up sovereignty over their homeland to a crowd of interlopers? The Foreign Secretary announced that, as the parties to the Palestine problem could not agree upon proposals for a solution, the British Government had decided to give up the Mandate over Palestine and planned to withdraw by May 15th 1948.

With this announcement the fight was on and the Arabs prepared to defend their homelands. Unfortunately the hatred between Arab and Jew had grown so virulent that the Arab leaders now claimed that they would drive the Jews into the sea. They failed to realise the worldwide support the Jews would command, particularly in America: and there was much sympathy for the Jews, because of the holocaust atrocities, and apparently very little thought given to the rights of the Arabs.

About this time a loyal and faithful Arab policeman, Cons. Mahmoud Abu Elby, came to me and said he wanted to resign. I replied, "You don't want to do that Mahmoud. You have 22 years service and will receive a pension eventually." But he said that his mind was made up. "I can't stand this situation any longer – the impudent way the Jews treat us. A Jewish lorry driver lent out of his cab and shouted, 'Get out of here' – adding that they were going to take all of this, and no one does anything." I think he really meant that if an Arab behaved in this way he would have been severely dealt with, but Jews were getting away with this threatening behaviour. So, even after all those years of loyal service he would not receive a pension, because he would not have served until the end of the Mandate.

Chapter 14
More Memories of Qalqilya 1947-48
Fred Canter

In mid-1947 Insp. Martin was transferred to the north of the country, but before we follow him to his next posting we will linger a little longer in Qalqilya and see the area through eyes of a younger and newly recruited Palestine Policeman. Fred Canter was one of Matey Martin's young constables during his final posting at Qalqilya police station. Fred had been in the army in England for six months, on a pay of 17/- (17 shillings) a week, when he saw a poster depicting a smart young man in police uniform encouraging recruits to "Join the Palestine Police – £20 a month." The pay was a great deal more generous than the army pay he had been receiving, and, in addition, having been brought up in the "fear and nurture" of the Church of England, Fred had a great yearning to see the Holy Land (though he had a rude awakening concerning the sanctity of some of the places when he got there). He signed up for a three-year posting in 1946 but the Mandate ended before the three-year period was up. Coming from the austerity of wartime and post-war England, Fred, a very impressionable 19-year-old, found all his senses and sensibilities overwhelmed by the colour, scents and sounds of this fascinating, bustling and in many ways medieval society. The clothes and the formal manner of addressing people – such as the requisite prefix "Ya" [Oh] (e.g. "Ya Abu Musa" [Oh, Father of Musa]) and the elaborate, reverential manners and customs – were a constant source of fascination to Fred: for him, it was often as though the Bible had come alive.

For a townie, released from an engineering factory apprenticeship in England to undertake National Service, a posting to Qalqilya mounted section in 1947 was a great and glorious privilege. Being at an age when most new recruits in the Metropolitan Police in London would still have been cadets, it was a thrill for me to be riding out on patrol as a Mounted Constable all over Qalqilya district, the only British policeman amongst my Arab colleagues.

I arrived in Jerusalem in 1946, and following the two months basic training at Mount Scopus, I was directed to the mounted training school at Beisan, for being a very light young man – about nine stone – my wish to become a mounted man was encouraged. At Beisan they were keen to keep the new recruits in their place. We were told that it was the horses that did the real work – they only trained the riders because the horses could not write reports! We had the benefit of three equitation tutors, all 1st Sergeants. I remember the names of two of them – Sgt. "Tug" Wilson (not Cons. "Tug" Wilson at Givat Olga), whose mount, Abu Shems [Father of the Sun], was a grey like Matey's, and the legendary "Nobby" Sheed who had a beautiful Chestnut called Sandy. The third tutor's name I cannot recall but I remember his horse, Roddy! All were softly spoken but had plenty of barbed comments to make

*Khirbet Qruaish 1947: Onbashi Mustafa Samara, in hatta and agal,
and Const. Jamil, standing on a village well head.*

about our abilities to ever attain the converted "Mounted" prefix before the rank of British Constable. My progress at the school was fairly rapid but I do not attribute this to ability. Perhaps my name "Canter" helped! In equitation the term "canter" referred to the pace reserved for the very last few days of the course. However my progress is more likely to be due to the fact that a fellow recruit on the senior ride was put into hospital when his horse, a rig,[1] reared up when being led and landed on the poor chap's shoulders. Guess who got that place and the horse?

At the end of the course I was posted to Tulkarem, and after a further month I was told I was being sent to Qalqilya. Apparently they could not spare anyone to escort me, so I was given a map and told I could find my own way – which I duly did. Sgt. "Matey" Martin was the Station Sergeant in Qalqilya at the time and *Onbashi* [Corporal] Samara the Arab I/C Crime. Sgt. Martin usually stayed in the station more than the other ranks, being responsible for the organisation of the station, but he did try to ride out on patrol at least twice a week.

Most of my patrols were led by *Onbashi* Mustafa Samara, though Abu Musa, an elderly officer who had served in the Turkish Gendarmerie in pre-British days, occasionally took the lead. He was junior in rank but senior in age. He was very religious and ensured that the patrol followed all the Moslem religious rites and observances, so I was often left holding the horses while my fellow policemen prayed. Abu Musa liked to maintain a smart, youthful appearance and dyed his grey hair and moustache. There were two other mature senior constables, one of whom was Cons. Abu Deeb. The young constables were Cons. Abu Fattah, Cons. Mustapha Ali and Cons. Jamil from Jayous village. Out in the villages I saw Biblical scenes, such as the women gathering water from the well and threshing, for real, and my Arabic was improved by listening to Biblical/Koranic stories told by the Imam in the village *madafi,* while waiting for the meal to be served.

Daylong excursions in Corporal Samara's team ensured that I had at least a nodding acquaintance with most of the station's villages and surrounding countryside – the foot officers patrolled Qalqilya town. In the wealthier villages the flat-roofed, single-storey houses were made of roughly dressed stone, the roof area providing additional outdoor living space and places to dry tobacco etc., but most dwellings in the villages made extensive use of clay and earth for building materials. After a heavy rainfall the women would knead up clay to plaster the walls and replace the coating washed away in the deluge. In some houses clay and earth were used to make sleeping niches along the inside walls. This I discovered whilst posted to Tulkarem police station. On long patrols our group of new recruits from Beisan spent many

---

[1] an entire stallion with usually only one descended testicle.

nights in such rooms – while being introduced to the job by Sgt. Minnett.

I noticed the very demanding role for the village women. Water was required for most domestic activities and all the water had to be drawn from wells or cisterns quarried into the rock. This was always a task for the women, and they relied on each other's help. Two would lift a large, heavy pot onto a third woman's head. Quite young girls managed to carry large earthenware pots, containing two or three gallons of water, in this way.

Fred remembered how beautiful the countryside around Qalqilya was, and also how well the agricultural land was tilled, planted and cared for, even though the simplest of tools – such as metal-tipped wooden ploughs – were used. The most fertile land was on the plain – the Plain of Sharon – but even the stony hillsides were terraced and cultivated where possible.

Some patrols took us onto the flat, fertile Sharon Plain, where Arabs grew a wealth of vegetable crops as well as sweet melons, watermelons, exquisite sun-ripened tomatoes and bananas: but it was the fruit – oranges and grapefruits, in the neat little orchards, enclosed with sour tangerines acting as windbreaks and pollinators – that stole the show for me. When the trees were in flower the air was laden with their citrus scent and when the fruit was ripe and the orchards busy with pickers and packers, the fruity smell was delicious. Truly a wonderful land to one long denied such delights in wartime Britain! There was a large aquifer under the plain and every farmer had a little diesel pump housed in a small tin shed gently "popping" away, pumping up water. Each pump had a different note and the chorus of all the little pumps was quite musical.[1]

Our other patrols were in the rocky hills between the station and the "county town" of Nablus. Here patches of rock and boulder-strewn soil supported thin but vital crops of barley and occasionally maize, but on these hills the villagers' main staple, olive trees,[2] thrived. In the luckier villages figs and grapes were grown and always most generously offered whenever we visited.

On the barren hillsides, and in the valleys between the villages, wild flowers grew in profusion. Some, such as the irises and tulips I recognised, and their names were the same in Arabic and English, but most were new to me. In later years I came to learn what they were – different types of tiny wild *Cyclamen persicum*, wild gladiolus, irises, including the Nazareth Iris, *Michauxia campanuloides, Sternbergia* (a yellow colchicum I thought was a tulip) and the Syrian Cornflower were a few that I saw. I suppose these "lilies

---

[1] *On his return to England, Fred took his engineering skills into the workshop of a church organ-building firm – sounds were obviously an abiding interest.* (Ed.)
[2] The lovely old olive trees that grew along the Azzun track, and elsewhere I have been told, have recently been grubbed up by the Israelis.

of the field" were the source of the deliciously scented honey the bee hives in the villages produced. Goats and sheep supplied the milk – completing my dream of the Holy Land.

Cyclamen graecum

We also came across various animal species as we patrolled the countryside, including tortoises, lizards and once a snake – an asp I presumed, which I left to its own devices, remembering the Psalmist warning, "the poison of asps is in their lips" (Psalm 140:3; also Roman's 3:13). In one village they had caught a mongoose which was kept in a harness and led on a lead as a pet. Gazelles were plentiful and a pest to farmers. Once we shot one and took it to the next village where it was flensed, butchered and cooked. However it remained largely uneaten, not just because it was very tough but also because, as Mustapha explained to me, it had not been killed according to Halal requirements. He ensured that I saw the correct butchering process at the very next opportunity.

Feral dogs abounded but were best seen from the station tower at night, when the bright search-lights lit up their eyes and you were confronted with many pairs of green orbs. Once I caught a glimpse of a small and very shy fox. On another occasion, when investigating an overpowering stench, we discovered a long dead camel being devoured by a pack of hyenas. These we gave a very wide berth. Clearly the experienced Arabs were quite disturbed by the closeness of these animals.

–

During our first week in Palestine a number of new recruits and I were shown the prominent sites and Holy Places of Jerusalem by Father Eugene Hoad, the Roman Catholic chaplain of the Force. This introduction still remains very vivid in my memory. Father Hoad was a mine of information, with a lot to tell and explain about each site. Those we visited included the Ecce Homo arch; the Site of Scourging, where carved into the paving was a Crown and Anchor board that the Roman soldiers had used to pass the time; the excavations leading down to the pool at Bethesda, which clearly showed each of the several layers that had been built on the previous one;[1] and the Eye of the Needle – a very narrow arch where a man might pass but not his camel. We were also taken to the Wailing Wall, now politely called the Western Wall, which it transpired was not part of the old Hebrew Temple but a rampart, probably from Herod's time, helping to retain the Temple Mount. It was the first time I had seen Jews at prayer, and it surprised me to see them nodding and bowing frenetically as they read from their prayer book. Similarly, pushing paper messages to The Almighty into the crevices in the stonework seemed an unusual religious practice.

We were next shown the imposing Dome of the Rock[2] on the Temple Mount, completed in 691 and built on the threshing floor purchased from Araunah the Jebusite by David *(to build an altar and make a sacrificial offering: 2 Samuel 24. Solomon's temple was subsequently built on the site).* Jews believe it is where previously, Abraham, about to sacrifice his son Isaac, found a "ram caught in a thicket" which he was able to sacrifce instead of Issac. *(Moslems believe it was where Ibrahim was about to sacrifice his son Ishmael, from whom all Moslem Arabs are descended. It is also the spot from which Mohamed ascended to God.)* The mosque was clad with exquisite tiles, predominantly blue in colour, with, I presumed, motifs of religious significance in Arabic lettering. All this splendour was set off by a magnificent dome, a building form that Europeans had struggled to achieve at a much later period. This beautiful octagonal building contrasted sharply with the nearby El Aqsa Mosque, a sombre grey dome which was built 50 years later in approximately 700 AD, demonstrating the advanced state of Arabic building techniques at that time. In front of El Aqsa was a fountain and ablution pool which the intending worshippers made very great use of.

I have two strong memories of the Mount of Olives. The first was the relatively new and quite imposing Church of All Nations, and particularly the eerie mauve light which bathed the interior when we visited. This probably changes

---

[1] a perfect example of a tel – a man-made hill common throughout the Middle East.
[2] Also called the Mosque of Omar, or Umar, by European travellers.

as the sun shines through different stained-glass windows. The second was of "The Garden of the Oil Press" – Gethsemane – and the gnarled old olive trees. We were told these were saplings at the time of Christ's betrayal and arrest.

Jeremiah, I believe it was, tells of "the little brook of Kidron". I saw no rivulet, alas, probably because Spinney sold bottled Kidron water. Father Hoad made up for this disappointment by explaining that at the Day of Judgement, Arabs believe that they need to cross the Kidron along a high wire, the Faithful supported on either side by angels.

We also visited the Church of the Holy Sepulchre via the Via Dolorosa. I remember little of the latter and felt credibility stretched on learning that Golgotha, a mound inside the structure of the church, was up a long flight of steps. True, there was an appropriate hole in the rock into which a six-by-four inch post could have been fitted, but the top of the rock seemed a little unlikely for the execution site. The Tomb, made of white marble, lay at the floor level of the church. An Orthodox monk sat in the tomb's tiny, hot and claustrophobic interior, the lit candles adding to the heat. He gave me a small chipping of the tomb. The exterior of the church was festooned with scaffolding which was holding it up and together, the building having been badly damaged by an earthquake several years before.

One of the most unforgettable sights for Fred was to be found in The Street of Bad Cookery, the location of the sweet market. For a young man who was still a teenager, having recently left a country where for several years sugar was rationed and sweets non-existent, his senses were assaulted by the startling colour and wonderful fragrance of the merchandise. This included coconut ices, gob stoppers and Turkish delight – and the scents of peppermint, cloves, buttery toffee and almond were particularly memorable,

All the places the group visited with Father Hoad fascinated Fred, but, apart from the sweet market, the other place foremost in his memory is the Kishleh stables, with David's tower silhouetted against the sky above it. It was during our visit to the Kishleh that the idea of a mounted role for me first occurred. I was sorry to learn, on a fairly recent visit to Jerusalem, that archaeological excavations around and under the stables had caused their collapse!

-

Apart from the riding school, Beisan was yet another revelation. It is situated in the Jezreel Valley and quite close to the River Jordan. As there was ample ground water the nearby kibbutz had created a series of fish-rearing ponds. Bird life was also interesting as the migrating route of many bird species, from Europe to Africa and back, follows the course of the Jordan. Apart from egrets and storks, many feathered acquaintances from home could be

212

Church of Holy Sepulchre showing scaffolding erected after the earthquake in 1927. Crowds gathered for the Ceremony of the Washing of The Feet. Narrator on the right, shaded by the branch of a tree.

seen at the appropriate season. There was a big natural spring at nearby Beit Alpha and we were occasionally taken there by the horse transport vehicle, for a swim and rest and relaxation. When we were considered sufficiently competent riders we were encouraged to take our mounts out for a quite hack, so one day I took myself off to Beit Alpha for a swim. However I had underestimated the distance and, as you might suppose, it was dusk before I confidently rode into the school to find that the Inspector was far from pleased, having mounted several searches to look for me. Perhaps that incident was another reason why the school got rid of me early and posted me to Tulkarem.

Before being posted we were taken, once again by the horse transport vehicle, on an excursion to the Sea of Galilee. There was not a lot of time to do more than take a rowing boat out on the lake, then a place of tranquillity. I was also able to see the place where the Gadarine Swine behaved like lemmings (Mark Ch.5).

–

When Matey was promoted and transferred to Safed he was replaced by a 1st Foot Sergeant – I can't remember his name but his soubriquet was "Gunner". I came back from a mounted patrol one day and he asked me to go out in the car to an incident in the orange groves. Here we found that a group of itinerant Arab orange packers had been rounded up by some Jews, forced into a small, corrugated iron shed and shot dead. This was a shocking sight and one I was little prepared for. All I could do was to see if there were any survivors but there were none. I reported to the Station Sergeant, who contacted the RAF at Ras-el-ain [Head of the Spring – which flows down to Jaffa] where there were hospital and mortuary facilities, and they dealt with the bodies.

By now we were beginning to prepare for evacuation and after a while Gunner was joined by two 1st Foot Sergeants, a 1st Mounted Sergeant, a 2nd Mounted Sergeant and two 2nd Foot Sergeants. This, together with a doubling of mounted constables, more than filled the station. We were eventually decanted back into Tulkarem, where we languished with no work to do until we were packed off home.

Fred learnt later that the horses at Beisan came to a sad end. Towards the end of the Mandate some men from the 4th Parachute Battalion were invited to form a small unit of competent horsemen to complement the mounted unit at a coastguard station. They patrolled the coast for three or four months in the dying days of the Force and then returned to Beisan to help in the dispatch and burial of many of the Force's mounts.

F.C. Ex-B/M/C 4072 May 2007

We now resume Robin Martin's story.

Chapter 15

Promotion, Safed and the Northern Frontier

In about mid-1947 I was promoted to the rank of Inspector, posted to Safed in the far north and had to leave my horse Rustom. There were to be no more mounted duties. Part of my new station area included the frontier with Lebanon and Syria, and this was quite a change for me as up until now I had never served north of Nazareth.

Safed town was at that time the most northerly settlement of some size in Palestine and, at around 4,000 ft above sea level, was certainly at the highest altitude of any town. Built on a hillcrest, it was about one-third Jewish, a community that had been established there for several hundred years, I believe, and the remainder Arab. In more peaceful times it used to be referred to as "The League of Nations", as Force members who married local girls used to be posted there. When I first joined the PP, members who married local girls had to leave the Force. On our first day the Inspector General welcomed us, outlined some of the rules and regulations under which the Force was governed and concluded his talk with the instruction that, "As members of the Force, you cannot marry a Jew or an Arab girl, for that might incline you to become partial to the community you have married into. If you do marry you will have to leave the Force. Of course, such a marriage might be to your advantage. A young man wrote to me informing me that he was planning to marry and I called him to see me and asked when the event was to take place. He replied, 'Thursday, of next week, Sir.'

" 'You will be out of the Force on Wednesday next. How does that suit your arrangements?' He replied that that would suit him alright, 'For, as you know,' he went on, 'my pay is £11 a month, and if I marry Miss Bernstein, her father will give me a job of several thousand a year!'" However, there were two or three senior members who had been in the Force for some time and had married local ladies. Mr Cosgrove, a senior member of the CID, had an Arab wife and there were one or two senior officers who had Jewish wives. A few British policemen posted to Tel Aviv and other Jewish areas had Jewish girlfriends. When war came married couples could not get back to the UK so husbands were allowed to remain in the Force and were posted to Safed and the long established mixed community.

Jews and Arabs Prepare for War

However, with the situation in the country deteriorating, the community had become more divided. My police station was on one of the boundaries between the two peoples in case of trouble between the communities. Safed Divisional Police HQ was further up, on top of the hill. From now on we could expect nothing but trouble as the occupants prepared for the coming battle. Frequent skirmishes occurred as the Arabs formed into battle groups and probed the Jewish defences.

The Jews had organised themselves into defence corps, which naturally included the official Jewish Settlement Police. This was an organisation officially recruited and paid for through Government channels, and ostensibly under the control of the Inspector General of the Palestine Police Force, but in reality the JSP did pretty well what they liked. If any were disciplined, punishments by way of fines were paid by the settlement concerned. They were all likely to be members of the Haganah, the Jews secret army, an old Zionist organisation that had been in existence in Palestine since the 1920s.

While I was in charge of Safed police station, for about four months, public security steadily deteriorated on both sides, with antagonistic, warlike acts leading to local battles to take over and hold various strong positions. These battles were confined to small arms, no mortars or artillery were used, but night after night, sometimes thousands of rounds of ammunition would be blazed off. As far as we were concerned, our main task was to keep out of trouble, for with the whole population legally or illegally armed, we were not a sufficient force to control the issue. Our job was to be peacemaker if possible, holding the neutral ground, and to try to prevent these battles taking place.

My next job was to take charge of the administration of the Jewish Settlement Police in the Safed Division. This involved travelling all around the Jewish settlements, from Rosh Pina right up to Metullah in the north, on the border with Lebanon, and also across the Huleh Basin to the foothills of Mount Hermon (the mountain itself being over the Syrian border). The high ground in Syria overlooking the Huleh is today known as the Golan Heights. This was a busy job as it entailed much travelling, but was not at all interesting, for it did not involve any ordinary police duties. I mainly checked on all the settlements that had been fired on by Arab attackers, and ensured their ammunition stocks were replenished. I also arranged for the monthly wage payments of the Settlement Police.

The settlers were far from amiable. In fact I got the impression that they detested and despised the British, for they were firmly of the opinion and belief that it was our job to quell the Arabs and allow the settlers to take over the country, which they were now referring to as *Eretz Israel* [Land of Israel].

As the Arabs were then building up bands of armed men, including men from Syria and Iraq, a squadron of the 17th/21st Lancers was stationed in the area and they patrolled in armoured cars.

I was out one day visiting some settlements in the JSP vehicle on a track close to the Lebanese Frontier Post, when the Jewish Sergeant said, "It is easier and quicker to return to Safed by Metullah," but he did not tell me that we had to enter Lebanese territory to do so. Just as we neared the Frontier Post the driver said, "Here we have to do like a commando raid, and rush along the track to pick up the road," and before I could say anything, we had entered Lebanese territory. I saw the Lebanese Gendarmes rushing out, their guns at the ready. Luckily they did not open fire, but they sent a message to Inspector Dick Ridley complaining of the violation and saying that, if they had not seen my British police cap – the Arab and Jewish Palestinian police wore a *kalpak*, like a fur fez – they would have opened fire. When I reprimanded the Jewish sergeant, he replied that he had been doing it for a long time, which illustrates that the settlers had one law for themselves and another law for others. They would continually perform provocative acts and blame other people for the consequences.

As I travelled around the area, my vehicle was fired upon several times by the Arab armed gangs. My superior officer, Deputy Supt. Stacy Barham, with whom I had served in Artuf 11 years before, instructed me that, as the situation was now so dangerous, I was not to go out to the settlements other than in an armoured car. This helped to make things safer for me, but even so it was necessary to be continually on the alert for road mines or the blowing up of bridges. One day I was shot up by an organised Arab rebel band, but they did not seem very interested in pressing the attack. I imagine they were waiting for a Jewish convoy to pass. As I continued on my way, I saw two of them running between the boulders behind which they were hiding. They were dressed in breeches and battledress-type shirts, which was a popular mode of dress for Arab guerrilla fighters.

One night, about this time, a GMC (General Motors Company) armoured car disappeared from Safed District HQ. A young Arab mechanic employed by the Motor Transport Section stole it and drove it away to join the Arab Armed Force, for by now Fawzi el Kawkudji, prominent at the time of the 1936–38 Arab Rebellion, had returned to the Palestine Hills ready to command the Arab Forces. He actually sent a message to the Superintendent of the Police of the Northern District, saying that he very much regretted that he could not return the armoured car as it would be invaluable to him in the future!

The state of affairs continued to deteriorate steadily until a real war situation prevailed, with both Jews and Arabs mobilised and probing each other's defences. Neither side really wanted to antagonise us, for each needed to save their ammunition, and force, for the day that we left. Supt. Barham found himself carrying out the duties of peacemaker on a regular basis, and each week would arrange several truces. I was at HQ one day when he came back and told me of his latest efforts to stop the fighting, saying, "It is impossible to parley with some of these old religious Jews. They are absolutely insistent on 'an eye for an eye' where the Arabs are concerned. They regard them as the enemy to be eradicated, saying they would destroy them, man, woman, child and chicken – following the dictate of the Prophet Samuel, who decreed that they would destroy the Ammonites and all their cattle!" Just as he had managed to bring about a cease-fire in a local battle in Safed, an Arab attack caused the death of another Jew, and so his whole effort was nullified as fire was again opened on all sides.

Winter 1947 – Mount Hermon in all its Glory

The weather in December 1947 now turned to real winter, and being so high above sea level it was decidedly colder than in any other part of Palestine I had known. As the rain and sleet fell, a comrade who had been posted to Safed for some years told me that Mount Hermon, over the border in Syria, would now be covered in snow. And sure enough, when the weather cleared, there stood the mountain – usually only snow capped, completely white. In Arabic the mountain is named *Jebel esh Sheikh* – The Mountain of the Sheikh – as the mountain usually looks like a religious sheikh's *tarboush*, or fez, bound with a white cloth. The mountain is a beautiful sight and can be seen from Lejjun and Jenin in the cooler weather before the summer heat haze develops.

218

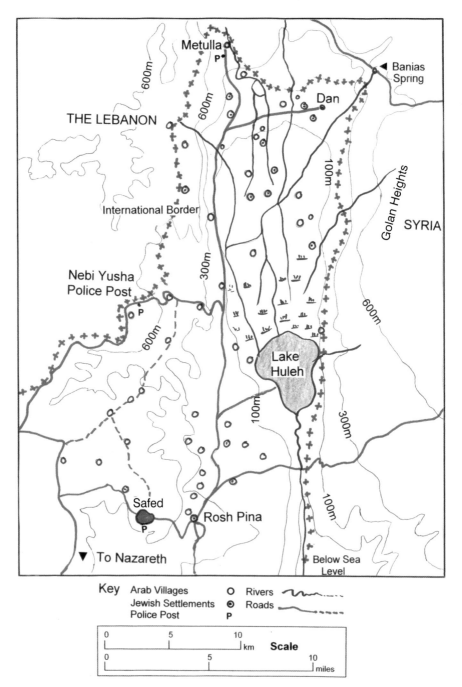

Map 5: Sketch Map of Safad District

Chapter 16
The End of the British Mandate
Metulla, turn of 1947-48

At this stage of my service change seemed to happen very quickly, and just after Christmas 1947 I was posted to Metulla to take over as Station Officer. Inspector Dick Ridley, one of the old original Palestine Gendarmerie, had been in the area a long time and was a little set in his ways. He was known as "The King of the Huleh". The Huleh[1] was a large lake and swampy region in the far north of the country. Insp. Ridley and Col. Anderson, of the 17th/ 21st Lancers, did not get on well, but as there were only four months of the mandate left to run, Dick was to remain for that time as an adviser for he had some very useful local knowledge.

Metulla was a small Jewish settlement and under normal circumstances it would have been regarded as a snip of a posting. All around were lovely views, for to the east, over the border, were the Golan Heights and the mountains of Transjordan, to the south Lake Huleh and the sea of Galilee, to the west the hills of Safed and the Northern Frontier, and to the north-east the majestic snows of Mount Hermon. But when I arrived I was only able to admire these views for a short time, for the state of public security was then so tenuous that it was impossible to appreciate the beauty as one should.

Destruction of High Explosives

One day I received a command from, probably, the Admin Officer of Divisional HQ on behalf of the Superintendent. It was rather charmingly worded, I thought, as though some honour was being bestowed upon me, telling me that I was the "officer selected to collect all the explosives in the locality, and transport them to the Royal Engineers in Haifa, who would dispose of them by explosion." What a job to be selected for at such a time! However, orders are orders, so I could only get on with it. An Irish Sergeant, a driver and I collected the stocks of gelignite and detonators from all the

---

[1] The Huleh swamp was home to a whole range of wildlife, including waterfowl, wild boar – which were common all over the Middle East in the watercourses – and water buffalo (owned by local Arabs). Inspector "Cass" F.J. Cassidy, an Irishman and one of the original Palestine Gendarmerie, and his two Syrian pointers enjoyed hunting and waterfowling all over Palestine. He and Jack Ammonds spent their local leave, just before Christmas 1939, duck shooting on the Huleh swamp. They went from Jenin to the Huleh in Cass's ramshackle old car and Jack remembers that Cass had him out before dawn, standing up to their knees in water, waiting for the birds to leave their roosts for the feeding grounds, and also at dusk waiting for them to return. The many species of waterfowl included Teal, Mallard, Pintail and Shoveler. Ian Marshall, another ex-PP also saw Northern Pochard, Red Crested Pochard, Gadwall, Tufted Duck, Ruddy Duck, Ferriginous Duck, Sandpipers, Snipe, Spotted Redshank and Common Redshank. Lake Huleh no longer exists, that area now being all cultivated land, though I learn that recently a small area has been flooded again. Cass married a Christian Arab and made his home in Palestine. He died of rabies in the War.

police stations at which they were held in the Metulla/Safed district and started on the long journey to Haifa.

Going through Acre there was a strange atmosphere of apprehension, and as we rounded a corner, armed Arabs were manning a roadblock, and it seemed that something unpleasant was imminent. However, we were let through without hindrance and given nods of recognition. We continued to Haifa, which we reached about noon. Then, just as we drove along Kingsway, a battle between Jews and Arabs broke out, and there we were, right in the middle of it – a 15 cwt. truck carrying about 5 cwt. of high explosive. I prayed that no bullets would land among our detonators, for that would have blown us right out of Kingsway to Kingdom Come. Allah was merciful, and has been many times during the course of my life. At Haifa, I made contact with the Royal Engineers, and a Sergeant reported to me and guided us out to the place where our deadly load was blown up.

Massacre in Acre

We then started our journey back to Metulla, via Acre, Nazareth and Rosh Pina. At Acre we found a horrible scene, for an armoured troop carrier, manned by guards and escorting a party of Jewish telephone engineers, had been ambushed at the roadblock and all the men wiped out. It had all happened a little while before we reached the spot, for the local police were just arriving, and the Arabs who had manned the road block had all departed. Twice that day Allah was with us, for had we been about 10 minutes earlier we should have run into the same ambush, which would have been fatal for all my small party.

Armies in the Countryside

Back in Metulla, the Jewish inhabitants were parading around the township, carrying new Czechoslovakian rifles which had just arrived from the Jewish Agency, having been recently smuggled into the country. There were two or three Arab villages in the area and they were collecting all the arms they could get to defend themselves against the Jews. By this time both Arabs and Jews knew that it was not only a case of defence, but that both would be on the attack as soon as the Mandate ended. My mind was very distraught about the whole situation and what the consequences would be.

One night in the hills at the back of Safed, a small platoon of the Irish Guards, while on a night patrol, walked into the midst of a large Arab Army carrying out night manoeuvres. It could have been a disaster, for the guards were completely surrounded. However, the Arab commander kept his head and informed the soldiers that they could pass straight through if they did not open fire. It was very diplomatic, but if a fight had started then, the whole battalion would have been called out by radio and a small war would have developed. Just then, neither the Arabs nor the British wanted a showdown, which would have served no useful purpose for either side. The job was, as far as possible, to preserve the peace for as long as possible.

The Handover Begins – Metulla and Nebi Yusha – April 1948

Now, as we moved into April, the policy was to hand over the districts and areas to the people living in them. In a wholly Jewish township, the police station and the arms therein were handed over to the Mayor and his Council. The same procedure applied in the Arab areas. After the handover in Metulla the bridge over the *wadi* at the frontier was blown up, to try to keep out Arabs from Syria and The Lebanon. On the same morning that Metulla was handed over to the Jews, a battle for Nebi Yusha Post took place about 10 miles south, overlooking the Northern Frontier Road. (Nebi Yusha Post was one of a series of little frontier fortresses. Being far in the north and 200 miles from Jerusalem, they were not very popular postings. They were initially manned by the specially enlisted Northern Frontier Force and commanded by NCOs from the main Palestine Police Force. Often NCOs were sent up to the Frontier Force as a form of discipline!) When my Superintendent came to Metulla, to hand over the station to the local inhabitants, he told me of the battle at Nebi Yusha Post. He instructed me to proceed there, with the British Sergeant and five British constables of the Metulla station personnel, take charge of the post and reinforce the Arab police under the Arab Sergeant, there. The British constables were just young boys really, who had opted for service in the Palestine Police, instead of two years National Service in the armed forces. Growing up during the war years, some appeared to have had little parental care, ran wild and paid scant attention to their educational opportunities, for they were barely able to read and write, and could hardly maintain the station diary correctly. Several were unpatriotic and I found them completely unreliable.

My Last Posting – Nebi Yusha

Trouble was brewing and most of the Jews living in the Huleh district, realising that an Arab invasion was likely, tried to leave for safer regions. The local Jewish Council, however, posted some of their people at Rosh Pina, on the only road to the south, and would not allow any of the young Jews, men or women, to leave the area, forcing them back to defend the Huleh settlements.

The Jews wanted the Nebi Yusha Post under their control so that they could have access to the Jewish settlement nearby. This settlement had held Orde Wingate in awe for helping train them during the Arab rebellion. I was posted to Nebi Yusha to prevent any Jewish take-over while we still nominally controlled the area. I anticipated an attack at any time, as I realised how important the post was as a defence point. I therefore impressed on my young British constables that, when on night duty, they must at all times be fully alert. I particularly emphasised that if they failed in their duty and we in the post were caught napping, it would probably be the end of us.

Having no faith in these youngsters, two nights later I set my alarm at 2 am and ascended the lookout tower. There, just as I had suspected, the two young guards were fast asleep, and even my noisy approach up the iron ladder had not awakened them. I was absolutely furious and roused them both with a hefty kick in the ribs. They awoke, startled and fearful, thinking they had been attacked and overpowered. I then found the prowler guard also in a deep sleep. In wartime such actions as theirs would have made them liable to the death penalty, and here I was expected to hold the post with such poor, unreliable material as this for support. Holding authority in such a dangerous situation is very worrying unless you can count on reliable and efficient staff. For the next few days I knew that I dared not sleep if we were to leave Palestine alive. The Jewish community had offered my Superintendent £30,000, to be paid into any bank in England, for 24 hrs advanced notice of when he would vacate the Safed HQ building, and it worried him greatly that they should think to go to such lengths. He said, "If they ever knew just when we were likely to leave, there would be such a battle for this place, I think few of us would ever get out alive."

Evacuation to Nazareth

About two weeks later, perhaps 8th May, two army lorries wound their way slowly up the hairpin bends and drew into the post. A young Lieutenant came in and asked for the officer i/c, and when I replied, "You are speaking to him," he then said, "We must go inside." He then said, "I have come to take you lot out. We have only half an hour – don't delay. Pack all you can of you kit into the trunks, as quickly as you can."

I then handed over the post to the Arab Sergeant, Sgt. Farris, with the arms and ammunition. I was supposed to take the two Bren-guns with me, but the Sergeant insisted, quite rightly, that he couldn't be expected to hold the post without them. So, contrary to instructions, I left one gun with him. I wished him well, for he was a friend of mine, with whom I had served years before at Givat Olga and Toubas. Our small British contingent was then evacuated to Nazareth Police HQ, where I stayed for two days. Nebi Yusha was my last command. I could not say that I had served from Dan to Beersheba, but almost, for I had done the opposite, serving from Hebron to Dan – Dan being on the Northern Frontier.

While at Nazareth, which had become a base for all the British police as they withdrew from the outstations, I heard that there had already been a fierce battle for Nebi Yusha post. The Jews had attacked in strength, but the Arab police, reinforced by many local Arab villagers, had held the post, and inflicted many casualties on the attackers. Later, however, the Jews attacked again with heavy weapons, and after a really bloody battle they managed to capture the place. Many years after, a British friend, who had been stationed there, and had returned to the area on a visit, found that it had become a Shrine of Jewish Remembrance for all the Jewish lives that had been lost in the battle for its possession. It is right on the frontier with Lebanon, and in a very commanding position, which made it such a vital strong point.

The Loss of British Army Tanks

In the early hours of the 16th May, the end of the Mandate, a regiment lost two heavy armoured tanks. I learnt many years later how this had happened when I met an ex-British officer who commanded one of King Hussein of Jordan's armoured regiments in the 1950s. In order to prevent useless and unnecessary battles with the Israeli army, he had managed to maintain contact with their commanders. On one occasion he asked the Army commander how they managed to steal those tanks. The Israeli replied, "Oh, that was easy. In the regiment there were several Jewish officers, and it was a simple matter to make contact with them. It was arranged to take three[1] tanks on exercise, and when well away from the base, they were 'handed over' to Jewish crews," – the men responsible deserted and were hidden by the Jews. The commanding officer of the regiment was so angry and ashamed because the trust he had put in these officers had been abused, that he ordered that the incident was never to be discussed. Some military authorities regarded the acquisition of these tanks as a prime factor in the defeat of the Egyptian Army in Sinai in 1948.

Final Withdrawal

Back to the last few days of the Mandate. The Nazareth Police Headquarters was now crowded to the fullest, and one was lucky to find a bed, or even a mattress, which were strewn wheresoe'er a place could be found. I was lucky enough to have had the forethought to have brought one from Nebi Yusha. After a few days, I joined a withdrawing party to the Police Station at Shafr Amr near Haifa, which was to be our embarkation depot. While at Shafr Amr I was told of some police horses, still at Jalama Police Station, that were to be shot, as there was no longer anyone to care for them. A young army NCO had been detailed to shoot them – on the grounds that he had served in the Yeomanry.[2] He did not relish the job, as he had never had to destroy a horse before, but he had been told the task was an order. Supt. Ian Proud asked me if I could do anything to help. I replied that, rather than let an inexperienced man undertake the task, I would do it myself, as I had had to shoot horses in the past. I was given an armoured car and went off to Jalama to perform this last, very sad duty. Eight lovely horses I had to shoot,

---

[1] One tank was ditched and later recovered.
[2] The Yeomanry were the Territorial Cavalry.

but I took very careful preparation to ensure that nothing went wrong, and so only eight bullets were used. However, I have often reflected on this and wondered if it would not have been better to have turned them loose and let them find a home for themselves.

What a difference was now to be seen in Haifa! Over the past week, a terrible battle had been fought for the city. Here the Jews had been so well organised that they had completely won the town, and the only Arabs remaining were dead men, women and children who had been unable to get away. Thousands of Arabs had fled to Acre, some getting away across the bay in boats, others by lorry or on foot. By now the British Administration had abrogated its duty as the governing body and had allowed the Palestine inhabitants to fight it out. The Royal Marines had held the port area, for that was vital to our evacuation plans, and now that no Arabs were left, all was quiet. The Jews had no wish to continue the battle with the British – we were leaving and they would be in control – of Haifa, anyway.

Some very old friends and comrades arrived at Shafr Amr, up from Jerusalem – my dear old pal Oscar Simpson being among them. (He was the storekeeper in the Kishleh to begin with, but feeling this a dead end job, he asked to be transferred and was put in charge of a station in a little place called Enab [Grapes]. He was a weekend drinking pal at the Vienna Café.) Oscar was in the last convoy to leave Jerusalem. It comprised Civil Servants, police and army personnel. He told me that, as the convoy left travelling up St. Paul's Road towards Ramallah, all hell was let loose in the city as the battle for control of it began. The Arab Legion, Transjordan's army, was there in force and was at that time a match for the Jewish Armed Forces. Jerusalem was split into two zones, the Jewish zone being New Jerusalem and the western area. The Old City and the east remained in Arab control.

Finally, on the 12th May 1948, three days before the Palestine Mandate officially ended, I boarded the SS Samaria and sailed for England. I left sad at heart and ashamed of the British Government and the politicians concerned in the whole sorry affair over the past 30 years, since the time that we had helped the Arabs drive out the Turks – with a promise that we would help them gain their independence – only to cause half a million of them to become refugees from the Jews in their own country.

July 1983 (Revised July 2007)

The view of Haifa harbour from Mount Carmel – site of the first German colony.

Fellow Members of my Recruit Squad

Listed below are the fellow members of my squad, who travelled out to Palestine on the *SS Rajputana* in March 1936. All except one boarded at Woolwich; Walker boarded at Southampton.

(The force numbers were issued second time around. The gaps in continuity resulted because the first holders of the numbers were still serving.)

344　Ronnie Armstrong. He was the tallest and oldest member of the squad, being 6ft 4ins tall and 25 years old. Ex-Winchester School, and bank employee, at Bexley Heath I think. He was a fine batsman and a member of the Police Force Team. A real suave gent, completely unflappable, his cricketing abilities and accounting skills resulted in his being employed in MeaShearim Police Station and then at HQ in the Quartermaster's Depot, so he could easily attend cricket matches. We were on very friendly terms all my service. After the Mandate terminated, he took up a post with the Groundnut Scheme in Tanganyika.

345　Geoffrey Binstead. A handsome man with a winning smile, quite a gymnast and very keen on PT. He was selected to be i/c of the Fire Service in Haifa, having, I think, been a volunteer or auxiliary fireman in the London suburbs. He was later transferred to Hong Kong where he became chief of the Fire Brigade, I believe. A close friend of mine during the training period, I lost touch when we were posted.

346　Len Board. He was my cabin mate on the voyage out to Palestine. He was a genial fellow, from a southern borough of the Metropolis, and we remained on good terms throughout the training period. He eventually reached the rank of British Inspector and was posted to a station on the coastal plain near Ramleh. There, he was murdered by Jewish terrorists, who lay in wait for him, when he was out for a recreational ride in the district.

348　Sam Culverhouse. He was a Westcountryman, from near Bath. A keen sportsman, he played football for Bath City. In our early days he was always a quiet and unassuming character, but later, when in drink, he felt he could fight the world. He laughingly told me of how he came off very much the worst when challenging an Australian Army Captain in a Jordanian Restaurant – after he had removed his stripes and challenged the Australian Captain to remove his! He took over Givat Olga Coast Guard Station from me. Being higher up the list he had been promoted two weeks before me.

352　Les Harding. Les had been an apprentice Merchant Navy Officer, but as there were no vacancies in the Merchant Navy[1] he had done the Short Service Commission training for the RAF. However having failed to obtain a commission, he then applied for, and was accepted into the PP. He was a very nice chap, but unfortunately I lost touch with him after our training period.

353   Tom Hookey. As mentioned earlier, Tom was a farmer's son from the Isle of Wight. His main complaint was the food at Mount Scopus when we first arrived, but I felt I played no small part in persuading him to stay in the Force. I lost touch after training but eventually he stayed until the end of the Mandate.

354   James. A very smart chap and formerly of the Honourable Artillery Company, famous and exclusive – the aristocrats of the Territorials. After a few years he gained a P1 promotion[2] to Nyasaland and then went on to Malaya.

356   Peter Jelasics. Peter claimed to be of Albanian or Yugoslav descent, and from his name and handsome, swarthy appearance, this must be accepted as true. He was full of fun and the joy of living, and added to his good looks he had a very melodious voice. I lost touch with him after training but he stayed on to be promoted to British Inspector.

357   Jenner. He came from Tunbridge Wells, ex-Tonbridge School, and was quite a linguist, speaking German, French and Spanish. He was advised that his linguistic skills would be very useful in CID, but he appears not to have been very contented in Palestine and did not stay long.

358   Jack Lay. Jack came from the Southampton area. He was a very smart man-about-town, and claimed to play centre forward for the Southampton Football Club. Certainly he was very good when on form and played for the Force Football Team on several occasions. He left the Force during the War and was commissioned in the Occupied Territory Administration, when he served in North Africa. He eventually settled in Breamore near Fordingbridge.

359   Laindsay. He was another tall, pleasant and amiable character. He was very young, under 20, but also very keen, and sure to have got on well, but I lost contact with him after the training period.

---

[1] Because of the worldwide economic recession many ships were laid up. I remember, while on a cycling holiday in Cornwall in 1935, seeing that many estuaries and ports down there were full of ships that had been laid up.
2 The Palestine Police and the British South Africa Police in Rhodesia were considered the main training centres for the Colonial Police throughout the Empire. The Indian Imperial Police operated separately.

362   Aubrey Nye. Aubrey was a tall, very slim, pleasant young man who cultivated his film star looks. He was posted to Beisan, but left the Force before the War and later joined the Army.

365   Owen "The Colonel" – so named by us on account of his deep, bass voice and his slow deliberate speech. He planned to become a writer and said, "You must travel if you want to write." He remained in Palestine until the end of the Mandate, and we lost touch, but I did not hear of any books he had written.

367   Dixie Pike. He was a dark, swarthy Cornishman, who told me that Cornishmen regarded the rest of England as a foreign land. He had completed a Merchant Navy Apprenticeship and held a First Mate's Ticket, but had been unable to obtain an officer's berth at sea with so many boats laid up, and had completed several voyages as an AB. When the RAF had introduced the Short Service Commission he was accepted for, and completed, the training, but was put into the Reserve. He then applied for and was accepted into the Palestine Police. He was a useful boxer and could take good care of himself. He was posted to Haifa and went onto the Port and Marine Section.

370   Robb. He was always looking to pick a fight (though he was not very good at it) and appeared to have something to prove. A few days into training I was just able to prevent him from picking a fight with a Military Policeman. He and several others were involved in a reprisal killing, after "Tiny" Stevens, a very nice man, had been shot and killed near Tireh, in 1937/8, and all were discharged from the Force and sent home to the UK.

371   Walker. He came from Dorset. He was clean cut, tall and handsome, and with his public school education and impeccable manners, he would have gone to the top in a Colonial Police Career, I am sure. Tragically it was not to be, for he was killed in a road accident near Nazareth. He was in the back of a Ford Pick-up and it probably overturned.

372   Watkins H.J.W. I lost touch with him after training but he was another very pleasant member of the squad, easy to get along with and always eager to do his best.

373   Willows. He was a nice, bubbly, if rather impetuous young fellow, who inadvertently started the Arab Police Revolt in Tulkarem, when he used a rifle, loaded with a round in the breech, to knock on a door, and the Arab policeman who was behind him was shot dead when the rifle discharged the bullet. If he had had the proper training, it would not have happened. After the incident I lost touch

– he probably went home.

374   John Wren hailed from Northamptonshire. I was told that he was a member of the Wren's Shoe Polish family, but I never confirmed this with John. He was another tall, nice, young man, easy to get along with, who had had the benefit of a good education. But he had a tragic end. Within weeks of being transferred from the Depot to Nablus, he was killed at a road block near Khan Lubhan, when the police vehicle he was driving was stopped and attacked by Arab rebels.

Left:
John Wren's last ride.

Right:
Armoured car in Bethlehem.

230

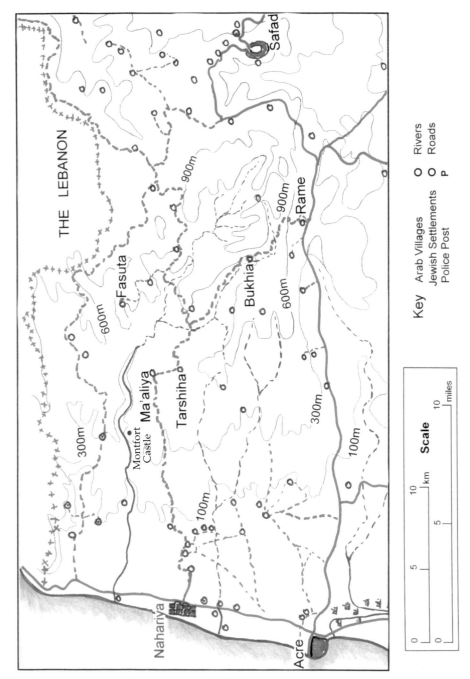

Sketch Map 6 : Sketch Map of the East Acre District.

Key

Arab Villages   O   Rivers
Jewish Settlements   O   Roads
Police Post   P

THE LEBANON

Safad

Rame

Fasuta

Bukhia

Ma'aliya

Tarshiha

Montfort
Castle

Nahariya

Acre

900m

900m

600m

600m

600m

300m

300m

100m

100m

100m

Scale

km

miles

The Tescol Mounted Columns in the North of Palestine

Jack Ammonds

Letter from ex-British Sergeant Jack Ammonds to Sharon Wallace, daughter of Joseph Kirby-Turner – who enlisted at the same time as Jack, but died in the early 1960s – giving information of her father at that time, the kind of life they lived and the conditions they served in.

Jack and ex-British Sergeant Joseph "Bill" Kirby-Turner 434 served on mounted columns in the north of Palestine during the 1936-39 Arab revolts. Jack was a farmer's son and had learnt to ride on the farm. He had also been in the Army Cadet Corps at school and had learnt to handle guns, as well as to use shotguns on the farm. Joseph was an excellent rider and had been a riding instructor. He had attended one of the well-known London schools. At the outbreak of war Jack volunteered to join the forces and was eventually posted to Iraq. Bill left Palestine in 1940 to join the Sarawak Police.

Written in about 2002, the following is an extract from the letter.

Dear Sharon

I was surprised to receive your letter on 2nd May, so quickly, as had only just been 'phoned the day previously, by Robin (Matey) Martin, asking agreement for my name to be mentioned as a possible source of information about your father. Yes, indeed, we served together on the mounted section of the Palestine Police Force – for a while, between 1937 and '39 – but our association began much earlier; however, I had best start at the beginning.

We attended together at the Crown Agents for the Colonies for the interview, about the middle of May 1936, and were afterwards dispatched to Harley Street, for the attention of Dr Manson-Barr[1], who must have made a fortune from examining candidates for the P.P. After the 'medical' your father asked me where I was headed for. I replied that I was about to proceed to Bow, where my elder sister was serving with the Church Army. "I'll take you there," he said, and off we went in, I think, a red and white sports banger. I was dumped off at a hostel for wayward girls, and, as you may imagine, got a variety of glances from the inmates!

In due course, our band of twenty hopefuls sailed for Port Said from Marseilles – having travelled to Marseilles

---

[1] Well-known expert on tropical diseases. Dr Manson-Bar, later Sir Philip, advised the medical authorities in Palestine during the First World War on the development of Malaria Diagnosis Stations and ways of minimising the incidence of malaria by draining and oiling marshes.

by train to save time – in the SS Maloja, and after crossing The Canal at Kantara, endured the unpleasant journey by rail to Jerusalem, arriving there in the early morning of 11th June. Normally parties of recruits sailed from Tilbury, but as the Emergency was in full swing reinforcements to the Police were urgently required, and by crossing France a week's time was gained on the journey. Following our overland trip, further batches of recruits, numbering respectively 30 and 40 followed the same route.

That same morning of our arrival we were individually interviewed by RHB Spicer, the Inspector General of Police, and afterwards issued with our uniforms. Basically our uniforms consisted of two suits of blue serge for winter use, two of khaki drill for the summer, and including tin hats, .303 rifles S.M.L.E. of World War NO 1 pattern and 50 rounds of ammunition. Normally the initial training course lasted three months, but as the Jerusalem area was short-handed, after a few sessions on the 'Square' we were called upon, in pairs, for night duty at various strategic points in the city. I felt sorry for those who had hardly seen a rifle before, and never handled one. After some three weeks our group was split up and members scattered throughout the country. I, and a chap called Anderson, from Bukie in northern Scotland, were posted to Nazareth District, and eventually found our way to Beisan, an Arab town on the edge of the Jordan Valley, and at the mouth of an East/West plain area. I think your father was posted to the Lydda District and the Ramleh area, where the Inspector General kept a small pack of Foxhounds – the object of chase being jackals. Ramleh was considered a favoured spot for the more socially inclined!

I well understand your concerns to gain information of your father's interests and activities in Palestine, and that his experiences there remained familiar in mind throughout the remainder of his life. Perhaps that is not unusual – that is, or was, the case with pretty well 100% of those who served in the Holy Land.

The Arab uprising – or revolt, call it what you will – which took place in 1936, and its resurgence from 1938 to 1939, was but a revolt against Jewish immigration, both lawful and unlawful, into a country which they considered as belonging to themselves, and which they had occupied over many centuries. And it was the expression of that belief, in the form of a guerrilla movement, which the police, and the masses of Army personnel, were obliged to contend.

To provide personnel for the mounted columns, individuals, both British and Arab, and additional temporary enlisted personnel, with previous Police experience or service in the Transjordan Frontier Force, were recruited to swell numbers. This brought the total complement of men to an average of 40/50 per column.

Excluding the southern desert areas, Palestine is a very mountainous country, it was therefore by the very nature of things that, for their existence and difficulty in ferreting them out, the insurgents sought refuge, and chiefly operated from, such mountainous areas. It would seem that the mounted columns were designed as a form of punishment for the villages which were over sympathetic towards the guerrilla movement and harboured the gangs; and generally to disrupt their activities. The chances of bringing the rebels to 'action' were pretty slim, as they had the advantage of choosing time and place, and a quick getaway if required. In all honesty, one must admit that the rebels seldom used the advantage they held over the Police columns – and looked upon the military as priority targets[1]. During these operations, we lived entirely on the villages and also fed the horses on them. Those who before hand had no liking for Arab food soon learnt to appreciate it, or go hungry. As throughout most of the year the weather was fine, we slept outside on village-provided bedding, but otherwise commandeered whatever housing was available.

I have always contended that I was a member of the very first column which operated amongst the northern mountains and villages, inland and between Acre and Safad. It lasted for a fortnight, from the end of March 1937 and into April. I well remember that year, for my birthday fell on Easter Sunday, 28th March, and I wrote a letter home, sitting alongside my horse, beneath an olive tree, on the outskirts of Rame village, on the Acre/Safad road.

---

[1] Jack further comments that, although it was ideal ambush country, with numerous rocks and gullies from which to stage an attack, apart from the evacuation from Bukhia village related below, no shot was ever fired at them. A sort of gentleman's agreement appears to have prevailed as far as the Police and Arab rebels were concerned, the rebels reserving their fire for the Army mainly.

*1937/38 East Acre District Tescol B mounted patrol members,
during a mid-day break and "feed up".*

Mid-day refreshments in an Arab village Sgt. McGill on left.

Tescol B pack W/T (wireless telegraphy) operator, Operator Willis.
He was later taken off an Arab bus by an armed gang and shot.

Offshoot of an Arab gang.

I was then posted to the Police Post at Yavneel, a Jewish settlement in the Tiberius Division, on the edge of the Ard el Hima valley, southwest of Lake Tiberius (Sea of Galilee), to help patrol that area. There were three personnel at the post, B Cons. "Jamidar" (means groom in India) Parker was constable in-charge, and as well as myself there was an Arab Constable, Cons. Ali Saleem, later replaced by Cons. Jerius Said, a Christian Arab from Nablus.

My next column, and from which I never returned to base – except to collect kit, commenced from early December 1937 and extended in various forms into the greater part of the following year. On this occasion two columns, designated Tescol A and Trescol B,[1] operated in conjunction, keeping in touch by W/T (wireless transmitter) – sets and batteries being carried by mules. Also, mules carried Lewis Guns and ammunition. This time the area of operation was but an enlargement of that of the first column. I served on Tescol B, which assembled at Safad; and it was there that I met up with your father. I'd arrived from the Tiberius Division, and he from that of Lydda, having come part way by rail. As with Tescol A, Tescol B moved amongst the villages well into the New Year (1938), but spent a couple of days over Christmas, semi-stationary, in the Christian Arab village of Fasuta, not all that far from the Lebanese frontier. You can imagine the grumbling that went on, but then there was the consolation of a plentiful supply of good Arak (Pernod), smuggled across the border!

In the New Year, personnel from the two columns were joined, and volunteers elected to remain on in a semi-settled state in Tarshiha village, whilst the remainder were returned to their parent units – your father and I being amongst the former. Four or five respectable houses, overlooking the large village pond, were occupied, and a mess established. Whilst on the columns we drew ration allowance in lieu of actual rations, supplied by the contraction company headed by Mr Spinney – a leftover in Palestine from World War No1. We continued to draw the allowance, and by living to a great extent on local produce, did very well, especially as we were able to use the NAAFI with the

---

[1] The senior officer of the columns was ASP Tessyman, who personally commanded Column A. B/1 Mathews commanded Tescol B.

Army Detachment in the neighbouring Christian village of Ma'aliya – a bottle of whisky costing but 5/-!

From Tarshiha – a hotbed of rebel activity – we carried out patrols mainly eastwards, but on one occasion went to the north west of Ma'aliya. I well remember riding over a ridge and viewing a familiar feature, across a shallow valley. On the crest of the ridge a perfect type medieval castle was located. It seemed so incongruous in that hard setting. From maps, I later identified it as Montfort, of Crusader origin.

During excursions amongst the villages, we were frequently accompanied by military personnel from Ma'aliya village, and occasionally by an aeroplane – once there were two – from the RAF.

A mid-day meal was always eaten at a selected village, which took quite a while to prepare, almost always involving the preparation of chicken. I was amused at the universal method of capturing the selected birds, which was by chasing them until they gave in! After arriving at Sumata one day and ordering a meal, we were greatly surprised by the speed at which the meal was served up. It was later reported that at the time of our arrival a meal was already being prepared for insurgents, and we had consumed it in their place! To indicate their annoyance we heard that they had laid in ambush on our route into the village. If this was so, then it was fortunate that we took a shortcut back to Tarshiha, via the Wadi Kharn – Valley of the Horns – and a terribly difficult track amongst rocks and boulders and dwarf oak trees.

A further incident during the occupation of Tarshiha, in which K.T. prominently figured, concerned the evacuation of a handful of Jews from Bukhia village, where they and their ancestors had been living amongst, and as Arabs, from probably Biblical times. The Jewish Agency, or some such organisation, suddenly decided that they should be removed on safety grounds. For this a great big open lorry arrived in Tarshiha, and we were instructed to provide an escort and see the operation through. As we had no transport, assistance was requested from the military at Ma'laiya. The Jewish lorry driver was stayed in Tarshiha, and your father took over the vehicle. Arriving at Bukhia and stating

238

Yavneel 1936: Cons. Jerius Said, a Christian Arab from Nazareth.

Bukhia village scene at the time of the evacuation of the ancient Jewish community there.

Jenin 1940: 1st Mounted Sgt. Jack Ammonds No 427, on Oscar.

Jenin 1940: Oscar, above the army camp, enjoying the lush spring vegetation.

the object of the mission, the Jews were unwilling to be transported away. The Mukhtar – headman – stated that as long as the Jews remained he was responsible for their safety, but he could not be held responsible for what might happen if they were forcibly removed. However, orders being orders, we set about collecting the individuals concerned, and with what household chattels they could gather, loaded them onto the lorry and set off back. I might mention here that in Douglas V Duff's book "Galilee Galloper" p92, the Jews of Bukhia are mentioned as living "in an inaccessible spot amongst the mountains". In fact the village lies at the base of a mountain range, and as I remember its chief characteristic is a wonderful spring of ice-cold water.

Duff served in the PP early on and wrote several books. One other, which I have, is entitled "Bailing with – a Teaspoon". Apparently, one of his claims is that he was the sole survivor of a ship sunk off the French coast in the early days of the 1914-18 War, and that as a thanksgiving he would enter the Priesthood, but found himself in Palestine instead!

But to return to The Evacuation – we proceeded but a couple of kilos from the village, where stone roadblocks were encountered – built from adjacent, stone, field-dividing walls. The track was, of course, earthen and essentially 'one-way' – so all the vehicles came to a halt. A desultory rifle fire was opened from the mountainside on the right. We piled from the vehicles into the alongside ditch, returning the fire. While this was in progress, I heard the roar of an engine to the rear, left track. Glancing over my shoulder, I was to see your father, at the evacuee lorry driving wheel, grim faced and driving across the wall-divided fields, parallel to the track, bucking like a bronco over the obstructions. He finally regained the track ahead of the other vehicles and well ahead. When things had quietened down, and the roadblocks removed, with readiness to proceed, the lorry refused to start! Its passengers, and some few items of personal possessions, were transferred to the army vehicles, and off we set, abandoning the lorry. We passed that way a few days later with the horses and found as expected, a burnt-out vehicle.

Soon after the above related incident, our horses were withdrawn to Acre, it being considered that patrolling from Tarshiha was too hazardous. We were, therefore, left without any form of transport, and after a short while were moved to an ex-army, tented camp near Jish Village. We remained at Jish for three or four months, before finally being disbanded. Some of the lads were returned to previous locations, while six or seven were posted to Acre, including both your father and myself.

During the stay at Tarshiha and at Jish camp, there were three sergeants in charge, to wit – McGill, "Bulletproof" Fullbrook and Tommy Hook. I later had cause to dislike McGill intensely[1], Bulletproof I never saw again, and it was some thirty years before I again met up with Tommy Hook, when he telephoned me, at home in Harrogate. With our wives, we afterwards saw a good deal of each other. Tommy has passed on now but as a memento of him I still have, the Old Police Station clock from Tiberius. Most of the Acre stay was again in an ex-army camp, known as Caesar's Camp, and located on the shoreline, north of the town.

From my recollections, your father was either posted away from Acre, or proceeded on Home Leave about March 1939, whilst I remained on until July 1939. After leave, I returned to Palestine, but whether your father also did, I do not know, but I never saw him again.

A multitude of books have been published on Palestine, but mostly expositions of Jewish claims; however the best I have come across, putting forth the Arab point of view, is by George Antonius and entitled "The Arab Awakening".

I wonder if, from your father, you've inherited a love of horses? I remember on Tescol B he had a well set-up, light grey, named Sultan, which had previously belonged to the ex-Inspector General. The horses assigned to British personnel were Government-owned, but those of the Arabs were personal property, for which allowances were drawn.

If you think I can be of further help on specific points please let me know, and I will endeavour to oblige. But just now, I'm happy to feel that to some degree I'm making repayment for that journey to Bow, so many years ago!

Sincerely

Jack K. Ammonds

---

[1] When at Jenin Station, Jack discovered some "unofficial" dealings of McGill's. This knowledge had a detrimental affect on Jack's subsequent PP career.

Further Memories of The Jordan Valley and The Sea Of Galilee

Jack Ammonds

I have many memories of Palestine days to recall, but some, particularly of my early days there, stand out with indelible clarity and I recount them below.

The Bowl of Soup

During the 1936 "Disturbances" in Palestine – a periodic protest by the Arab Community against the British Government's policy of allowing an annual influx of Jewish immigrants – one of the favourite tricks of the Arab dissidents, or "ouselbats" as they were generally known by the Military, was to sabotage the Iraq Petroleum Company's oil pipe line, conveying the oil from Kirkuk in Iraq to the Refineries at Haifa. The metal pipe would be exposed, a fire lit over it and then rifle shots fired into the softened metal.

At the height of the "Disturbances" we in Beisan (Biblical Beth Shean) were directed to quit, overnight, our sleeping quarters, a house in the town, and doss down on the flat roof of the Police Station, an old Turkish fort. At night, when the pipeline had been set on fire, an extensive glow was to be seen far away to the north. At the crack of dawn, a party would leave to escort a repair gang, returning about mid afternoon to the billet. Then breakfast, lunch and dinner were eaten within a few hours and it was back to the Police Station before nightfall. On one particular occasion, when I was a member of the escort party, we arrived at the Arab village of Kawkab el Hawa, a short distance south of the damaged pipeline, where the village Muktar was ordered to prepare lunch for the whole party – perhaps some twenty persons. Kawkab el Hawa was built amongst ancient ruins, which I took to be Roman, but in this I was mistaken, later learning that they were of Crusader origin. In those far-away days the castle site was called Belvoir, and was perched in a strategic position, high on a wild rocky escarpment overlooking the northern part of the Jordan Valley.[1] In fact it was from Kawkab el Hawa that I first caught a glimpse of the southern tip of the Sea of Galilee. We proceeded to the pipeline and on completion of the repairs to the line we returned to the village where lunch had been prepared. Unusually, the meal was set out on lengths of table and we sat on chairs, altogether contrary to the usual custom of squatting crossed-legged on the floor, and with the food on floor mats. As per-usual, rice was piled high on circular platters and topped with whole roast lambs, surrounded by roast chicken and pigeons. Along the table's edges were dishes of salads and soups. It was my first experience of eating in an Arab village and I soon saw it was a free-for-all, everyone reaching out by

---

[1] Smail, R.C. *The Crusaders.*

hand or spoon for that fancied within reach. Directly before me was a dish of soup, and, to myself I thought, "If I get stuck into this, with luck I'll have it to myself." I set about the soup with gusto, when suddenly, and to my dismay, a spoon from my right dipped into it! I was so overcome with repulsion that I had great difficulty in keeping the food, I had eaten, down!

However, necessity being akin to invention, it can equally be said that compromise is a necessity of existence! It did not take me long before I was eating from communal bowls, and drinking from communal cups, with the best of them!

The "Invaders"

On a lovely springtime morning in 1937, Robin Salter (ex 17th/21st Lancers) and I decided to take our horses out for exercise, and proceeded to follow an earthen track which led from Beisan, directly across the Jordan valley, to a river bridge at Jisr Sheikh Hussein [Bridge of Sheikh Hussein]. As it was early in the year the effects of the winter rains were all around us, the whole valley floor being covered with greenery and wild flowers, most prominent among the latter being anemones – the Biblical lilies of the field. These were growing in extensive patches, each of a distinctive colour ranging from deep purple to red and white. The reason for this was a complete mystery to me, but the overall picture was a true delight.

After progressing a fair distance, we saw coming towards us what appeared to be a long procession. As we rode we speculated a good deal about this, and as we and the procession drew together the individuals took on the shape of horsemen. Robin and I then agreed it must be a detachment of the Trans-Jordan Frontier Force, but closer still, the horsemen became Bedouin, being dressed as such. When we were about 100 to 150 yds apart from the horsemen, the procession turned off the track to the left, rode for some 50 yds into an open space, turned about, halted and faced the roadway.

We saw they were all carrying rifles across the saddle pommels and though we were unarmed we kept on down the track, wondering at the fix we had got ourselves into! On coming right opposite the group, a party of some 12 or 15 detached itself and galloped towards us waving their rifles. They came within about 30 yards, wheeled about and rejoined the main party. A second, similar bunch galloped at us and this time I thought we'd be bowled over as they came within 20 yards before turning about. At this juncture we felt we had had enough and took the "warning"! We turned the horses round and began to walk them back up the track. After gaining some distance, the horses were put into a trot, then a canter and finally a gallop!

On arriving back at Beisan a turn-out party was organised. It boarded a standard 30 cwt Morris lorry and set off to investigate. When we arrived at the spot we found no trace of the "invaders", but later learnt that it had been a party of Bedouin from Transjordan, on a visit to friends on the Palestine side of the river, who had forgotten to leave their rifles behind. Or, perhaps thinking that it being Sunday, there would not be any one around?

The Jewish Doctor and a Police Tracker Dog

A little before my time in Beisan, prior to the "Disturbances" in 1936, a Jewish Doctor had practised there. I had heard that his ministrations were largely charitable but with the occurrence of the trouble he had been deported from the area as he was considered a security risk. When things had cooled off he unadvisedly returned, only to be promptly murdered one night. The Doctor had in fact been shot through a door, apparently as he was about to open it.

It was decided that the Police Tracker Dogs, kennelled at Jerusalem, would be needed to help investigate this crime. They arrived the following day in the charge of Sgt. "Jock" Adams. It was too late that day to begin work, so an attempt at trailing was deferred until the following morning. This left the trail at least 36 hrs. old!

Investigations indicated that the murder or murderers had used bedding in a downstairs room whilst awaiting their opportunity and the dog took the scent from this pile of bedding. The Doberman Pincer trailing dogs were worked on a length of light rope and this dog led off up the street at an easy walking pace – head held in the normal position, slowly moving from side to side. I was a member of the escort party that followed Jock Adams. Hundreds of people must have used that street during the intervening period since the incident, to say nothing of donkeys, sheep and goats, and motor vehicles, yet the dog moved along with purpose.

The trail led to the outskirts of the town, then swung to the left: we had completed a 5/8th circuit when the dog checked at a heap of banana prunings in the pathway. It scratched at the pile, pushed in its nose, picked up something and brought it to the dog master. It was an expended rifle cartridge casing. The Doberman Pincher continuing the trail, completed three quarters of the circuit of the town before re-entering it. At an ancient section of a marble pillar lying by the roadside, the dog again checked and bayed. Jock explained that the person, whose scent was being followed, had rested on the pillar. Continuing the trail, the dog led to the threshold stone beneath a doorway to a courtyard. As is usual, there was a surface drainage hole beneath and, again as is usual, it had become blocked in the dry weather. From this cavity two full bandoliers of rifle ammunition were extracted.

It was not a certainty that the person whose scent had been followed had anything to do with the house, or had been harboured there; but, if that person had remained at the house for any length of time before leaving, the dog would not follow his fresher scent, requiring a new scent from the same person to continue.

For my part, being a young and inexperienced policeman, there was rather disconcerting sequel to the affair. The doctor had to be taken up the Emek Plain to Affule and I was detailed as one of the dual escort. The body, covered with a sheet, was loaded onto the back of the standard open 30 cwt truck and I, being the junior, had to ride in the back with the body. All went well to begin with but when the going became rough the feet of the corpse escaped the sheet! Then as the track improved and the driver picked up speed, the wind got under the sheet and blew it off the body and I only just managed to grab the sheet before it was about to disappear over the tailboard!

Mosquitoes and Frogs

Some 10 or 12 miles south-east of Beisan, the Agricultural Department owned a large banana experimental plot. Information was received that Arab dissidents planned to sabotage the plants during a certain night. A tall, thin chap of the name of Allan and I were detailed to spend the night there. We were transported well before dusk in the usual vehicle, complete with rifles and a Lewis gun, which, after depositing us, returned to base.

There was a mud and wattle flat-roofed shack in the centre of the plantations, and gaining the roof, by means of a rickety ladder which we pulled up after us, we contemplated a not too pleasant night! During our stay no attempt was made to chop down the banana plants, but as soon as dusk descended, mosquitoes, in their thousands emerged – from water ducts, pools and channels – and set about us. Simultaneously, from these same channels, frogs began their nightly chorus. There seemed to be thousands of them, all croaking at once! The din was unbelievable, so much so, that to hear each other speak we had to shout! To avoid the mosquitoes, and despite the heat, we spent the night completely covered up with blankets: but, there was no escape from the frog chorus! Daybreak came at last, and I must say that seldom has it been more welcome!

Rifle Carelessness

On one occasion, during that summer of 1936, I was alone in the billet when I received a note to report to the Police Station for escort duty. Such duties usually meant riding in the back of the assistant superintendent's car with one other chap when he went on a visit. Some time before an edict had been issued to the effect that personnel had to be in twos when moving about the town, or travelling between the billet and police station. However, as I was alone I had, perforce, to proceed alone. To guard against being caught unawares I placed a cartridge into the firing-chamber of my rifle, and left the safety catch off. Arriving at the Police Station, some one said, "….they are waiting for you," and I clambered into the back of the ASP's car.

We were well on our way to the destination, when I suppose for lack of something better to do, I found myself fingering the rifle bolt mechanism in the region of the cocking-piece. One cannot imagine the shock I received on realising that the cocking-piece was in the cocked position, with the catch on. Instead of playing with the bolt mechanism I might just as well have been playing with the trigger, with possible horrendous results! During the hurry to get away from the Police Station I had forgotten all about the loaded rifle, and, although fortunately without disastrous result, the incident taught me an important lesson!

The Ancient City (of Beisan)

In ancient times Beisan was on the highway between the civilisations of Egypt and those of Mesopotamia (Assyria and Babylon) and there are many significant archaeological remains of those civilisations in that vicinity. They include remains of Canaanite, Egyptian, Greek, Roman and Byzantine times.

One Sunday morning, Robin Slater and I decided on an exploration. Most of the ruins are located on a large mound, which undoubtedly was formed by many succeeding cities, being built on top of one another. At least one of the gateways was stone built, and there were large sections of marble pillars lying about, but most of the buildings appeared to have been of mud brick.

There were two features that stand out in my memory. The first was an amphitheatre without the mound where the usual facilitates – terraced seating and the wild beast accommodation – were still discernible: the other was the extensive mosaic flooring, of beautiful colouring and at different levels. The central mosaic we took to be a calendar of individual months, represented by human figures with feet towards the central circle and an inscription at each head. On other sections of the flooring different animals and fruits were depicted, making one realize that many animals and fruits were in common use more than 2,000 years ago.

The site had obviously been partially excavated. It was covered by a corrugated iron roof and surrounded by perimeter walls. The latter were about six feet high above which was a gap of some 18 inches to the lower roof level. The door to the enclosure being locked we climbed inside through the afore-mentioned gap, and had a look around. We returned the same afternoon with a couple of other chaps, when the guard was on duty. Before being allowed in we had to remove our shoes!

On the second visit I bought two signet ring stones from the guard, perhaps of bloodstone – one of a centaur, beautifully inscribed with a horizontally held spear. The other, more badly worn, was of two figures engaged in combat.

Mist over the Valley

During the winter period of 1936-37 I was instructed to saddle up my horse,

Sharban, and accompany a large party of the Transjordan Frontier Force – perhaps a couple of troops – which was to lay an overnight ambush on one of the main fords across the Jordan River well to the southeast of Beisan. The senior ranks of the T.J.F.F. were officers seconded from the British Cavalry regiments and the other ranks locally enlisted. On the occasion in question the Hon. John Hooper commanded the troops.

Information had been received that a large quantity of arms and ammunition was to be smuggled overnight into Palestine from Transjordan, and the object of the operation was to intercept this activity. We set off from Beisan in the early afternoon and towards evening reached a substantial hill about a mile distant from the ford, on top of which the horses were picketed. At dusk the early ambush party, of which I was one, proceeded to the ford, and at midnight the second party took over while we returned to the picket lines. I strapped myself into blanket and groundsheet and lay down to sleep by Sharban.

With the glimmerings of dawn over and beyond the Trans Jordan Mountains, the camp was aroused. In the faint first light I saw that, although the top of the hill was in the clear, the whole of the valley floor was shrouded in a thick white mist. Bedouin encampments, scattered over the whole of the valley, were coming to life. They were hidden by the mists but their activity was indicted by the tinkling of hundreds of bells as the animals – mainly goats and sheep – began to stir. As the light increased so did the sound of the bells. With the approach of sun-up, and for a little while afterwards, the combination of the shiny-white, fleecy, sunlit mist, and the music of the unseen bell chorus, coming to me from the many different directions of the various small encampments, was a never to be forgotten experience. The effect was similar to flying over the Alps and looking down on cloud cover: but then the music is missing!

The bulk of the Jordan Valley is more that 600 ft below sea level, so in summer, as soon as the rising sun tops the Trans Jordan Mountains, away to the east, it becomes unbearably hot.

Moonrise over the Valley

In late January or early February 1937 I was transferred from Beisan to Yavneel. I arrived three days after three Jews had been murdered by Arabs on the road between the colonies of Yavneel and Beit Gan, which were only a short distance apart. Yavneel was one of the older Jewish Colonies, established, I believe, before the First World War – initially by individual settlers. It is reached by a winding, hairpin road that rises from the southern shore of the Sea of Galilee (Lake Tiberius). One reaches a high crest and the road then dips down into a wide saucer before leading to the colony at the far side, sheltering under another hill range. A local bus owner ran a thrice daily, return trip from the colony to Tiberius.

Yavneel Police Post was attached to Samakh Police Station and was, undoubtedly, the smallest Police Establishment in the whole of Palestine, the total strength being three – two British Constables and one Arab Constable. I joined with "Jamidar" Parker – an ex-Hussar and one of the best, and Ali Saleem, the Arab. Unfortunately, Cons. Saleem died of appendicitis and was replaced by Julius Said, a Christian Arab from Nazareth and a first class chap. We had no transport other than horses. I would ride into Tiberius about every six weeks, leading a second horse, so that their shoes could be replace or refitted. Otherwise we used the local bus, on which travel for us was free.

Late one evening, the bus owner/driver came to the Post and asked if I would go with him in a taxi to Tiberius to collect his bus as he had left it there for repairs. It was dark by the time we set off towards the town. As we began the descent from the escarpment rim a full moon was rising above the Trans Jordan Mountains and shining across the lake. From the innumerable ripples on the lake, millions of dancing diamonds were reflected to us. I fail to find words to adequately describe the beauty of those "dancing diamonds". The experience was all too short and its recounting, perhaps, briefer still, yet the memory has lasted all my days.

The Sheep Count

A few years ago (1999) I came indoors, from whittling down a split length of wild cherry wood to form a hammer handle and on turning on the television I came across a scene of flocks of sheep being driven to pasture. It took my mind back to 1940 and my days in Jenin, when I was instructed to proceed with a mounted patrol to a Bedouin camp. There I was to carry out a sheep count. An offence of some sort had been committed, the nature of which I have long since forgotten, and it had been decided that a punishment of a communal fine was to be levied. To some extent the fine was to be based on the ability to pay – hence the sheep count.

The encampment of the usual black hair tents was located on the rounded, upper slopes of a range of high hills overlooking the Jordan valley, to the south-west of Beisan. After explaining the object of the visit I instructed the notable to send word to the shepherds to bring in the flocks, and I accompanied one of the groups of messengers. Having travelled a mile or more we arrived at the edge of a deep valley, the opposite side of which the flock of sheep was to be seen, scattered over a wide area, grazing. Those with us hallooed to their carers to return their charges to the encampment. Immediately the shepherds began to comply with the order and the sheep did also, forming themselves into single files on the numerous hillside paths. Where a subsidiary pathway led to a major one, or where two major paths came together, the break in the file of sheep at that point allowed the other file to proceed. The second file then continued to pass until a break occurred, when the first line of animals began to move again. Nowhere did the animals attempt to bunch or dispute the "right of way". It was therefore a slow business to collect the various flocks to the encampment, though the count was simplified when the sheep, of their own accord, divided into their respective owners' enclosures.

The shepherds playing their pipes in the age-old traditional manner and unheard by us, was of course the cause of my original wonderment. The sight of the sheep's responses to the shepherd's music has lived with me for over 50 years. I likened it to a tree, less its leaves in wintertime, yet without any thickening of the stem towards the ground.

Jack Ammonds 2007

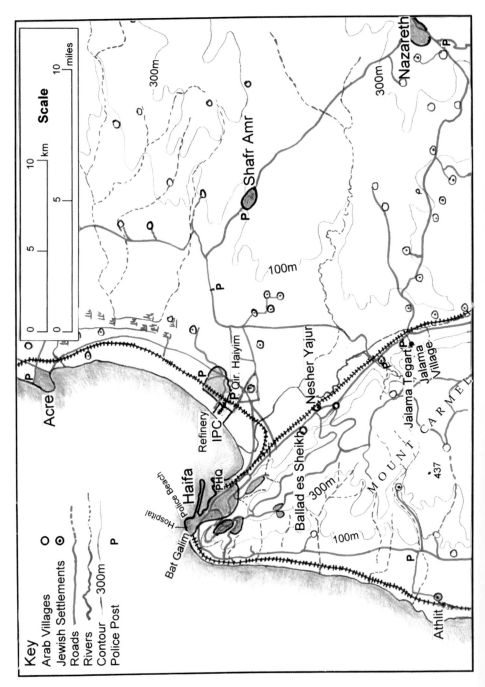

Sketch Map of the Haifa Area

Haifa District 1947-48

The Ballad-es-Sheik Petroleum Enterprise

Martin Duchesne

In the 1930s Ballad-es-Sheik [Village/Town of the Sheik] was a small, traditional Arab village of stone buildings, about five miles east of Haifa on the Nazereth/Tiberias road. Even by 1947 those old buildings were still at the heart of the *ballad*, but were outnumbered by a collection of concrete and breezeblock additions, mainly shops but they also included one or two moderately substantial houses, in one of which lived the *Mukhtar*. He was well educated in the British mode – a product of the secondary school system we had introduced – and by then a mature, middle-aged man of considerable presence and dignity and had the almost impossible task of controlling the village, which had grown beyond recognition with the industrialisation of the Haifa area during the War.

By 1947, Ballad-es-Sheik was a shantytown-metropolis, sprawling for three miles or so along the Nazereth/Tiberias road and spreading back into the foothills of Mount Carmel which rose behind the town. Wooden huts; corrugated iron sheds; huts made of sacking, salvaged military packing cases, cardboard and/or scavenged plywood; the odd bare stone dwelling standing next to the occasional small, surprisingly neat, concrete villa – with a little roof garden of potted geraniums, were all mixed in with dwellings made from beaten-out petrol tins and oil drums – plus of course the occasional small shop, butchery and baker. Chickens, dogs, donkeys and children were everywhere. There was a limited electricity supply, piped water was supplied to communal standpipes in most parts and there was a basic drainage system, but by no means was it universal. When the rains came an odorous overflow poured down the *jebel* [mountain] to the roadside drainage ditches! The *ballad,* a picture so often repeated in urban Palestine, provided many thousands of assorted Arab peoples with somewhere to live and access to work in nearby, prosperous Haifa. During the day it was fairly quiet, with much of the male population off to work in and around the city and port, where they swept the streets, worked the docks, drove the taxis and manned the railway; the petroleum storage depot; the refinery; and the myriad small industrial works which had sprouted upon the plane during the war. Come the evening, most of the population seemed to take to the paths and alleyways of the *ballad,* going about their business and pleasure as in every other Arab township. There were, of course, the usual coffee shops and hashish joints, even an eating-house or two! The place teemed with life once darkness fell.

Surprisingly, except for the odd affray and the occasional minor riot, it was

1947/48 Ballad-es-Sheik: Morris Scout Car and Crew.
B/C Jones – Driver (l) and B/C Stout – Gunner (r).

1947/48 Jalama Village: B/C Jones on Scout Car;
B/Sgt. Duchesne standing.

a reasonably orderly place, given that most of the inhabitants were from the more humble ranks of the social scale and poor by any standard. The Mukhtar was a powerful personality and kept order effectively, albeit in the old-fashioned Turkish way.

Formal policing was the responsibility of Jalama Tegart. We mounted regular foot patrols, usually in the daytime, with British and Arab officers at least in pairs, for even with the *Mukhtar* and the *ballad's* apparent orderliness, it was potentially a difficult sort of town. Additionally, the Mounted Section covered the higher, hilly areas, on their way to more rural parts, so that, overall, our presence was regularly felt. The township was kept under routine surveillance, if not policed in depth – there was not sufficient manpower for that! There was no outward sign of major crime but it is fair to say that the Contravention Officer in Jalama, and the Haifa Magistrate's Court, were kept fairly busy with our input.

Against this backdrop there were a number of Army storage depots, supply dumps and installations peacefully secure along the main road. Apart from minor incidents, petty thefts and suchlike, problems were seldom reported, except for one puzzling one, involving one of the major installations. The principal fuel depot and filling station for Army vehicles in the northern half of Palestine was sited on the main road, on the *ballad* side, and provided huge quantities of petrol and diesel to the many Army units in this militarily active area. There were batteries of pumps, jerry cans by the thousand and 50-gallon drums stacked high: even bowsers were filled there, all supplied direct by pipeline from the Haifa IPC (Iraq Petroleum Company) Refinery, five or so miles away to the west towards the sea. This installation was strategically and operationally important and kept the military wheels rolling through the troubles. It even, on occasions, helped our garage foreman with a gallon or two when we needed to balance the books.

There was though, in that hot and sunny autumn of 1947, something of a mystery with which our I (Investigation) Branch was involved. The depot had an evaporation allowance of some 5,000 gallons a week (which indicates the scale of operation) but gradually over the preceding months this "evaporation" had crept up to nearly 25,000 gallons! The SIB (Special Investigations Branch – Political; CID was concerned with criminal investigations) were called in and they asked for our help with an extremely thorough investigation and ongoing check, but no major irregularities were found. It was a very well run and documented operation. Then came the United Nations Declaration that Palestine was to be partitioned and problems like this were lost in the major unrest which quickly developed.

Once the troubles began again one of Jalama Police Station's duties was to keep the section of road, between the Acre turn-off just to the north-east of

Haifa, Jalama and beyond, open to traffic. This was not as easy as it may sound, because adjoining Ballad-es-Sheik on the east was a long-established Jewish settlement, Nesher Yajur. It was not only a conventional agricultural settlement, but also the site of the largest cement works in the Middle East. This works ran night and day, baking the Carmel limestone into high quality cement, an absolutely vital resource for Palestine given the huge amount of civil engineering projects then taking off, following the end of the War. But it was also a significant economic asset, as a vibrant export trade was developing. Because the works drew much of its labour and technical support from the Jewish population of Hafia the problems with the road were greatly increased, for twice a day, every day, back and forth, a convoy of buses ran the gauntlet between the dormitories of Hadar and the Nesher works, with an ambush always threatening.

To preserve the peace, the Jalama Morris Scout Car kept a continuous British Police presence on that section of the road (we manned the buses too but that is another story). Every couple of hours or so we parked the armoured car by the road in the main square of Ballad-es-Sheik to act as a deterrent and to give the crew a break. We did this for many months becoming, I suppose, an unnoticed feature of the landscape around which the life of the ballad swarmed, while a continuous stream of traffic passed to and fro between the northeast of the country and Haifa.

On one such break, Paddy Kilmartin, the Police Station garage foreman who was driving the armoured vehicle, parked in a different position which gave a wider view of the square and its surrounds. He idly remarked, "I wonder why so many vehicles are driving up to that shack and filling cans from the standpipe? Must be a water shortage somewhere." The standpipe he pointed to was some 100 yards from the road, on the edge of the square. We were puzzled, so in ensuing breaks successive car crews watched, more curious than suspicious, as at all hours dozens of cars, taxis and vans, drove up to this tap, even donkeys with panniers, and all filled jerry cans and assorted containers before driving off again. It was a hive of activity, with a constant stream of customers for the water.

A day or so later B/C Pat Devlin, the turret Bren gunner, thought he'd take a closer look. Perhaps he was thirsty. It was hot in the square. Maybe he was just prompted by Irish curiosity. Whatever the motivation, he strolled over, got close, turned round and came tearing back. "*Shaweesh!*" he blurted out, "It's b***dy PETROL coming out of that water tap!" Kilmartin went over discreetly, ran back and confirmed that it was indeed petrol, "and the silly b*****s are smoking too. Lets get out of here fast!" Seldom has 6' 2" of well-built, long-legged Irishman folded himself into a Morris Scout Car driving seat so quickly!

Later that day a quickly assembled investigation team, headed by our Arab Inspector "I" and supported by the SIB with a mine detector, traced the "water" pipe – right back to the main road – alongside which the pipeline from the refinery was buried. They gingerly excavated a three-foot deep hole and found that the water pipe was actually plumbed in to the main pipeline, which had been drilled, the water pipe inserted and then sealed with large amounts of clay, which made a surprisingly good petrol-proof seal – although it must be said that there was an increasingly strong smell of petroleum fuel as the excavation deepened! However the three feet of covering earth had prevented any trace of petrol on the surface when the main pipe had been scanned for leaks during the earlier investigation. Thus an unlimited supply of high-grade petrol was provided to the "Ballad-es-Sheik Petroleum Enterprise Company" – all by way of a kitchen tap!

With closure of the facility, "evaporation" at the fuel depot immediately returned to normal, but the next time I saw my friend the *Mukhtar* he seemed rather less friendly than he usually was, and the general population turned distinctly cold. I wonder why!

M.D Ex-B/Sgt. 3401 (First printed in the P.P.O.C.A Newsletter)

Policing at Haifa HQ

Ron Bourne

As very young men Ron, and his younger brother Richard, enlisted into the Palestine Police for the last year-and-a-half of the British Mandate and had very little idea what they were letting themselves in for. To begin with they thought the job was fun, but soon realised it could easily prove fatal.

It was late 1946, I was 19 ½ years old. The war had finished the year before and I had been working on the railway for past three years when a large placard, showing a smart young fellow in a neat khaki uniform and the words "JOIN THE PALESTINE POLICE – £20 AND ALL FOUND," attracted my attention. The invitation to be in uniform and visit the Holy Land appealed to me. I talked it over with my 18-year-old brother, Richard, and we both decided to join.

We awaited the outcome of interviews at the Crown Agents for the Colonies and medicals in Harley Street and were notified in January 1947 that our applications had been accepted. After making our way to Liverpool we boarded the *SS Empress Australia*, bound for Port Said, stopping en route at Gibraltar and Malta. At Port Said we boarded a train bound southwards to El Kantara and then crossed to the east side of the Suez Canal and El Kantara railway station. After spending a very cold night huddled together in a single brick building that was the station, we boarded a train travelling north to Gaza. There we transferred to 3-ton lorries and were driven to Jenin Police Training Camp. After a long day we were glad to bed down in Hut 13.

Following two months of law, weapons training, Arabic and drill, the members of our group were posted to various stations in Palestine – Richard was sent to Jerusalem and I to Haifa Headquarters, together with a colleague, Ray Hughes from Runcorn. Ray and I arrived at Haifa HQ in early April 1947 and became members of the Haifa Operation Patrols (HOP). In the following weeks Ray and I became familiar with the town and our various duties – including telephone duty in the wireless room (situated on the roof of HQ); static guard duty at the Police Beach at Bat Galim;[1] bank escort duty; and escort duty on the mail run to Jenin.

A Fatal Evening Out and Danger from Small Arms

Everything was going fine until Saturday, 19th July 1947, when Ray, being off duty, asked me to go with him to the open-air cinema in the Jewish quarter

---

[1] This was a small beach near Haifa General Hospital where off duty policemen, their families and friends could bathe. It was semi-enclosed, with armed policemen on sentry duty outside the main gate, when it was open. I was not aware of any trouble at the beach but, towards the end of the Mandate it was no longer used owing to the increasing violence in the country.

of Hadar Hacarmel. As I was down for telephone duty in the wireless room that evenin he asked the chap in the next room, B/C 2196 Dixie Dean, to go with him instead – and that was the last time I saw Ray. Apparently he and Dixie went to a bar for a drink after going to the cinema and as they made their way back from the bar terrorists came up behind them and shot them in the back. I received the telephone call reporting the incident at 8 pm, informing me that two men, believed to be policemen in civy clothes, had been shot in Hadar Harcarmel. The wireless operator radioed the patrol car to investigate. Don Atkinson was the radio operator in the car that was first on the scene and I can remember him ringing from the hospital to say that the dead policeman had been identified as Ray. Unfortunately Dixie died 10 days later. It was only then that I realised that life in the Palestine Police was not all duty and fun. These terrorists were for real.

Shortly after this incident Richard applied for, and successfully obtained, a transfer from Jerusalem to HOP. He took the place of Ray and shared the room with me. We were then allocated to the armoured car patrols, my brother as car commander and I as wireless operator, very often in the same car: the other member of the three-man-crew was, of course, the driver. The commander stood in the turret, which could swing around. The car was armed with two Bren guns, one in the turret for the commander and the other between the wireless operator and driver in the cab.

Towards the end of night patrols we would often park on the top of Mount Carmel and enjoy a smoke while watching the dawn breaking over the sea. One morning our driver noticed a man who, when about 70 yds away, was identified as an Arab, walking across the scrubland carrying something on his head. I got out of the car to investigate and shouted to him, whereupon he dropped the object, which turned out to be a table, and ran. I gave chase but had only gone a few yards when my revolver was jerked out of my holster and landed on the rocky ground with the result that it fired. I do not know where the bullet went, but from that day on I only loaded my gun with five rounds, and left the top chamber empty. I picked up my gun and made my way to where I had last seen the man and found him shivering under a small shrub. He obviously thought that I had fired at him as he shouted, "Don't shoot," as I approached. I arrested him and we took him and the table to the Carmel Police Station and handed him over to the Arab Inspector on duty there. It appeared that he had stolen the table from outside one of the cafes in the area.

Jewish Terrorist Attack on the Haifa Police Station

On 29th September 1947 Jewish terrorists blew up Haifa Police HQ. That day our car had been delegated to escort duty to Jerusalem, so we had placed a 5.30 am call to be ready at 7. The call was late and we were not roused until

5.55 am so Richard and I rushed to dress and get ready. I was sitting on my bed putting on my boots at 6 am when there was an enormous explosion. The building shook, windows blew in and I was blown off the bed. After a minute or so I got up and saw that Richard had suffered the same fate, though, fortunately, neither of us were injured. It transpired that a barrel bomb had been rolled off the top of a lorry fitted with a ramp so that the bomb could clear the perimeter fence, and had landed on the wall of the ground floor door of the HQ. Police whistles were blown by personnel in the vicinity, but within minutes the bomb had exploded, killing four British policemen, injuring scores of others and badly damaging the first three floors of the building. Of course we never got to do our duty, as escort to Jerusalem, that day but patrolled the area around the HQ, looking for the terrorists who had driven away before the bomb exploded. After that attack the height of the security fence was increased to 18 ft.

Stuck in the Bog

On a nice sunny day, early in 1948, while we were quietly patrolling Haifa town on the afternoon shift (2-10 pm), we received a call to go to the aid of another armoured car that had become bogged down about 12 miles east of Haifa on the Nazareth road. Apparently the car had been travelling to Nazareth and on approaching a Jewish Kibbutz the crew found that part of the road had been blown up and the colony was being attacked by a group of Arabs. The armoured car, unable to continue, turned off the road and proceeded across the fields, but after it had gone several hundred yards it became bogged down in a marshy section of the field. Unable to move, assistance was called for, and that's where we came in. We made our way to the scene and across the fields to the stranded car, hoping to tow it out of the marsh. However, when we got within about 10 yards of the car we also became bogged down. Try as we might we could not move either car, both having sunk to their axles – so we also had to call for help. The shooting between the Jews and Arabs continued and the occasional bullet would whine in our direction, but there was nothing to be done but batten down and wait for assistance. Hours went by, darkness fell and dressed only in our khaki gear we began to feel cold and hungry. Then about midnight we heard the loud rumbling of a large vehicle coming along the road, while searchlights flashed across the ground. Suddenly it came across the fields towards us and as it got nearer we could see it was an Army 70-ton Sherman Recovery Tank – and weren't we pleased to see it! We shouted to the tank personnel to beware of the marshy ground – but to no avail. It too became bogged down, only yards from us! Together with the tank crew, we tried to dig out all the vehicles but failed. So yet another call went out for assistance! In the meantime, the tank crew were able to brew up some tea and we were very thankful for a nice hot drink.

Help eventually arrived about 4 am – in the form of six half-track Army vehicles. They approached from a different route and didn't venture too near our marshy ground. They proceeded to fix long wire cables, first to the tank and then to the armoured cars, and all vehicles were finally pulled out from the bog. It was nearing 6 am when we started to drive back to Haifa, only to receive a wireless message that the road had been mined. I informed my driver but he said, "Bugger it! I want my breakfast!" He put his foot down and drove like mad to HQ. There we ate a hearty meal before going to bed.

A Friend from Home.

One day we were detailed with two other armoured cars to escort 20 buses of Jewish immigrants from Haifa Docks to the clearance camp at Athlit on the coast road. The convoy consisted of the lead car (us), 10 buses and another car, followed by the remaining buses and a third car. British constables were also posted on each bus. We set off from Haifa down the coast road, going merrily along when my driver asked, "What's that?" Overtaking us in the middle of the road was a complete large wheel and tyre! We watched it roll down the road into the roadside ditch and then a message came through on the intercom, "Stop the convoy. One of the buses has lost a wheel." While the occupants of the broken-down-bus were being transferred to other buses I helped control the traffic, stopping the oncoming traffic so the rear car officer could let the following traffic through. He then stopped the traffic while I let oncoming traffic proceed. During this procedure I waved an Army Dispatch Motorcyclist through. He went down the road, turned around, came back to me and asked if I was from Cardiff, South Wales. When I replied in the affirmative, he asked me if I was Ron Bourne. "Yes," I replied, "but who are you?" On removing his goggles and helmet I recognised the boy I used to sit next to in school – Ray Llewellyn. It's a small world!

The Last Days

On 15th May 1948 the British Mandate ended, by which time many British Police and their families had been shipped home, my brother included. We, who were still in Haifa, were confined to Police HQ, our policing days over: it was just a matter of waiting for orders and a ship for home to the UK. For three days after the 15th May there was fighting between the Jews and the Arabs for control of Haifa town. The Jews eventually won and scores of dead Arabs were left in the streets. Things quietened down after the battle and we remained in HQ until the latter part of May when I sailed home in the *SS Cheshire*, arriving back in the UK in June 1948.

R.B. Ex-B/P 2519 (2007)

Peace on Earth, Good Will to all Men, but not in 1948 Palestine

Martin Duchesne

It was January 1st 1948 in the Holy Land. The great Christian festival of Christmas had passed comparatively quietly in Haifa District, but the three tribes, Arabs, Jews and British, all looked a little apprehensively towards what the New Year would bring. The old order was changing; the British had finally declared their intention to withdraw from Palestine, sick of the strife as Jews and Arabs sniped for possession and predominance. The United Nations had decreed the previous November that the Holy Land was to be divided into two separate states: Arab Palestine and Israel, the latter an independent state for the Jewish people who had suffered so grievously in Europe at the hands of the Germans and had, so it was claimed, been "promised" a homeland some 30 years previously by the Balfour Declaration.

Understandably, the Arab world reacted with outrage. It had been bad enough for the Palestinians to have been governed by the British in the 30 years following the First World War, in which the Ottoman empire had been driven from the Middle East by the British, Anzac and French forces, with the full scale aid of the Arab peoples. But now to have foreign Jews granted much of the coastal strip, as well as the very best land in the country, as their own to govern – including the significant acreage still owned and occupied by the Arab majority – in an independent state centred in, and largely in control of, the Holy City of Jerusalem, was quite unacceptable to the Arab nations. Similarly unacceptable to the Arab was that much of the rest of the territory designated as Israel by the United Nations, although patchily settled by immigrant Jews during the previous 50 or so years of Zionism, was traditionally Arab and largely Arab owned. The huge majority of its population were Arabs who worked and farmed the land as they had done since time immemorial!

Throughout Palestine the new Jewish settlements had been, it would seem, carefully planned to intermingle with the centuries-old Arab villages and towns. In granting the new Jewish state territorial continuity, by definition, many Palestinians became subjugated to the new state and were no longer part of Arab Palestine. The old order changeth, not democratically but by dictate of the United Nations, an utterly foreign body to the Middle Eastern peoples. Their resentment was understandable even to Western observers.

On the other side of the coin, it was convenient to forget – and remains so to this day – that the prosperous lands held by the Jews had been bought by the Zionists and inter-war immigrants, often for gold, which was secreted away by the Arab landowners and elders – not shared with the peasant population who lived on and worked the land. These purchased, and now coveted, and fertile lands, which formed the core of the proposed new state of Israel, had been developed in 50 hard years by the Jewish immigrant settlers. To the foundation holdings had been added many, originally, less attractive areas – desert, swamp and scrub – metamorphosed by massive capital investment, dedicated hard labour and skills of a sort quite different from the Arab way of doing things. The Jews had accomplished an incredible transformation in these poor areas and were greatly admired for this by the outside world, particularly Europe and especially the USA. President Truman was a staunch protagonist of the Zionist cause.

All this, combined with knowledge of the horrors inflicted upon the Jews in Europe during the war years, created much sympathy for the Jewish population both in the Government and Administration of Palestine and in the rest of the world – despite the terrorist campaign which had been conducted with such ferocity by extremist Jews since 1944. It was a desperately complex and volatile situation, just waiting to erupt, which it did most spectacularly. We know; we were there.

The British Police and the other Crown forces were, most certainly, in the middle of it. Progressively, since the UN Resolution on Partition had been announced in November 1947, with the British withdrawal being declared for June 1948, the hard-won law and order established during our 30 years of control of the Holy Land, started to break down. This was quite different from the previous Arab insurrection and the insidious post-war Jewish terrorism. The country erupted into chaos. The whole structure of law and order which we British had so painstakingly established, already severely undermined by the introduction of Jewish urban terrorism, began slowly to dissolve. In line with these developments, the emphasis of our policing changed from primarily preventing and dealing with crime and disorder in a troubled but generally orderly land, to a much more gendarmerie-like activity, striving to keep some semblance of law and order, some protection for the general population, in a country disintegrating in every way.

The new "troubles" which so quickly developed were of a different kind. The Arabs throughout Palestine took up arms, not so much in open rebellion to begin with, but in a slowly rising tide of incidents against the Jews: raids on settlements, ambushes, roadside killings, abductions, murders and night-time skirmishes. It was astonishing where all the weapons and ammunition came from. I saw German, Italian and American, even Japanese, Second World War equipment in plenty, including Mauser rifles and machine pistols and even heavy Machine Guns from the 1914-18 conflict, not to mention weapons of earlier vintage, such as antique Turkish and Eastern European weapons, probably of more danger to the user than to his opponent.

In retaliation, and concurrently, with the clear object of gaining as much control and land as possible before Partition, the Jews struck back. Attacks on Arab villages, shootings, bombings and abductions grew in number. Jewish-extremist-terrorist attacks on Arabs villages escalated, those in the more southerly, Jewish allocated areas, being particularly prominent. This, in turn, resulted in the Arab nations surrounding Palestine starting to infiltrate the still Mandated territory, including not only men with small arms, but also with mortars, artillery and armoured units. The initial object being to cause panic amongst the Jewish settlements, especially in the north of the country, was quickly achieved. Trouble was also spreading rapidly to the bigger towns, particularly those like Jerusalem, Haifa and Hebron, with mixed populations. Waddi Rushmir, for example, dividing Haifa with Arabs on one side of the waddi and Jews entrenched on Mount Carmel on the other, became a no-man's land. We British were still in the middle, as usual.

It was against that backdrop that this story, one of many, occurred. On that New Years Day, 1948, three British police from Jalama Tegart were parked in their little Morris Scout Car (no radios fitted) on the edge of the Station's area, at the junction of the Haifa Nazereth/Tiberias main route south and east, and the Haifa/Acre road to the north and west. This was a key position on the borders of the Jewish/Arab interface, in the central north of the country. The task was to monitor, and hopefully control, the Jewish and Arab traffic and pedestrian movements to and from Haifa, and perhaps, by the Scout Car's very presence, deter troublemakers from entering or leaving the city-port and also help prevent the trickle of armament traffic flow from becoming a flood. On keeping a watchful eye on all that went past, and indeed actively stopping and searching suspicious vehicles and unruly-looking pedestrians for weapons and explosives, the object was to try to dampen down the antics of both sides, at least during the daylight hours.

It was a bright, sunny winter day and traffic was light. At about 0900 hours we thought that it was going to be a quiet one – suspiciously quiet in hindsight, as there had been few Arabs about since our patrol started at 0715 hours, which, in itself, was most unusual. Then out of the blue, speeding from Haifa, came a GMC Armoured Car of HOP (Haifa Operations Patrol) which drew up a few yards away. As HOP Car Commanders were wont to do, an order to, "Come over," was shouted. I asked B/C Devlin, on the Bren in the turret, to keep me covered just in case it was an Irgun ruse, as we had never seen a HOP car this far out before. Cautiously I went over to the GMC with my hand on my pistol. Fortunately I was greeted by three excited B/Cs saying that there was a riot at the Iranian Petroleum Company refinery, three or four miles up the Acre Road. The GMC had been radioed to come as far as this to set up a roadblock, but couldn't go further as the crossroads was the limit of the Haifa City area, in which this car had discretionary movement.

Other authorised HOP cars were on their way, but we were to go straight to the refinery to see what we could do to quieten things down.

We arrived at the main gates of the refinery, one of which was swinging open and with no guard, to be greeted by an apparently dazed, agitated, capless Inspector. I don't know whether he was British or Jewish, but he gabbled that everyone was dead. The Arab workforce was on the rampage. He suggested that we should go into the refinery straightaway to prevent a cataclysmic disaster. This we did, making a clockwise circuit of the plant following a paved road. Arabs were scurrying everywhere, but as Devlin swivelled the Bren in the turret, Paddy Kilmartin blew the horn and I pointed my Sten from the other hatch the rioters just melted away. We chased some of them through a hole in the perimeter fence but they just disappeared in that enviable way that Arabs do.

We then circled the site, which was by now virtually empty except for a stray Arab climbing one of the cracking towers with a rifle on his back. Devlin suggested he bring him down with a burst from the Bren, to which I agreed, when Paddy Kilmartin called out, "For ***** sake don't fire – the whole ******** place will go up!" He was so right and Devlin's trigger finger relaxed spontaneously! The Arab saw us, rapidly slithered down the ladder and disappeared like all the rest.

Our refinery tour completed, the Arab workforce dispersed and the threat of spectacular property damage averted, the Jalama Tegart Morris Scout Car returned to the main gate and office building, where we found the first of the HOP cars, with the Bourne Brothers and Driver Dennis Naughton, in control. A rather white faced B/C Ron Bourne came over and said that they had been into the Refinery too. All was now calm and under control and further Police units were on their way from Haifa. They could not raise Qiryat Haiyim, whose area the refinery was in, either by radio or telephone. Ron then said that it was a horrible mess, an absolute massacre – dozens dead, not a single survivor. The Arab clerical and admin staff had attacked their Jewish colleagues, with whom they had worked peaceably for many years, with bricks and stones and had killed them all. It was carnage. (The body count afterwards was 73). Ron said that HOP Car 8 had corralled a number of Arabs in a small compound inside the Refinery, but the majority had disappeared and there was not an Arab anywhere to be seen let alone apprehended and charged – they had all gone to ground!

Then the Station Inspector from Qiryat Haiyim arrived in their Morris Scout car to take control of the situation, the Refinery being in that station's area. I reported to the Inspector. With the telephone lines still down and the only radio contact being indirect, through the HOP Control Room, which was separate from the station network, it was agreed that our car should go to

Shafr Amr to report the incident to DSP Ian Proud i/c Haifa Rural. There was always the possibility that this incident was the precursor of a countrywide uprising and those in charge needed to know, first hand, and fast.

So, with the supporting HOP units from Haifa beginning to arrive and the Qiryat Haiyim Inspector in charge, we left the Car 8 crew, with the stricken Refinery Inspector, to straighten things out. There was nothing further we three could do. We were, moreover, trespassing on another Station Area, without direct orders to be there.

On arrival at Shafr Amr we found that Ian Proud, our greatly respected DSP, and his equally respected 2 i/c, ASP Coles, were holding a New Year's *huffli* for the local *Muhktars* and Jewish settlement elders. The Jews were devastated by the news and rushed off, but their Arab neighbours seemed not overly surprised and continued to enjoy British hospitality and the exceptionally strong lemonade and tonic water provided! Mr Coles gave each of us from Jalama a large glass of lemonade, the very same that the Arab dignitaries were drinking, and sent us back to the Tegart. I have no memory of the journey and I don't think the driver, Paddy Kilmartin, had either, but ever since I have not enjoyed a tumbler full of gin!! Even with a dash of lemonade!

Ron Bourne's Addition to the Account

On New Years Day 1948, our car No. 8, received a call from the Radio Room to go to Haifa Oil Refinery where a riot had taken place. I believe our car was the first Armoured Car to enter the refinery, where we found a number of Arabs running in all directions. We eventually rounded some 50 of them in a small compound in the refinery and waited for back-up cars to arrive. I remember going into one of the offices to find some eight or nine Jews lying in pools of blood with their heads smashed in, some still groaning but beyond our powers to help. As I left the office, Martin Duchesne's Morris Recce car drove up and I informed him that the office staff had been massacred.

We then searched the other offices and found dead and dying everywhere. Sometime after, a second Morris Recce Car arrived with a British Inspector and I remember him reading the Riot Act to the Arabs we had secured in the compound. We remained there for some hours until the Army eventually arrived with 3-ton trucks and I assisted in loading the Jewish dead onto the lorries. There were no survivors. It was late in the afternoon when we returned to Haifa HQ and I discovered my blue winter uniform was covered in blood. I hadn't realised this until then with all that was going on.

-

This was just one of the many horrors that marked that period in Palestine, leading up the end of the Mandate. Such was the life for us, as young Palestine Policemen, in those last few confused months, and such was the shape of things to come. It got worse and worse and has, as we all know, continued this way for nearly 60 years.

M.D. & R.B. (2007)

Glossary

AB	able seaman
ANZAC/Anzac	Australian and New Zealand Army Corps
ASP	Assistant Superintendent
B/C	British constable
BP	British police
B/Sgt	British sergeant
butts	a depression underneath the targets where the markers stand and indicate with marker flags where the bullets have landed.
CID	Criminal Investigation Bureau
cwt	hundredweight
DSP	District Superintendent
H Com	High Commissioner
HE	His Excellency
HQ	Headquarters
I/C i/c	in charge
JSP	Jewish Settlement Police
MT	motor transport
NAAFI/Naafi	Navy, Army and Air Force Institutes
NCO	non-commissioned officer – corporal, sergeant, sergeant major
P.P.O.C.A.	Palestine Police Old Comrades Association
PHQ	police head quarters
SIB	Special Investigations Branch
SP	superintendent
SAA	small arms ammunition
TAC	temporary additional constables
TJFF	Transjordan Frontier Force
UNO	United Nations Organization
W/T	Wireless/ Telegraphy
agal	rope for the head-cloth

ballad	town/village
fellaheen	farmers
haj	One who has made the pilgrimage to Mecca.
hamile	village clans
hatta	head-cloth (also *kafiah*)
hufflie	party
jebel	mountain
khirbet	hamlet
madafi	guesthouse. Every village has a guesthouse where visitors and strangers are entertained. In large villages there are several clans and each clan has their own guesthouse.
Muhktar	Jewish or Arab headman of the village
Shawish/Shaweesh	Sergeant
wadi	valley
Yishuv	The Jewish People